LUV And Other Plays

Murray Schisgal

DODD, MEAD & COMPANY · NEW YORK

Library of Congress Cataloging in Publication Data

Schisgal, Murray, 1926-
  Luv and other plays.

  I. Title.
PS3569.C5L84 1983   812'.54   83-9072
ISBN 0-396-08214-9 (pbk.)

To my children,
Jane and Zachary,
and my godchildren,
Jacob and Rebecca Hoffman

Contents

Introduction

I couldn't fall asleep without telling myself a story. I needed another reality, another set of circumstances that had nothing to do with my conscious life. From the bits and pieces of the day's events, I scrounged about for the thread of a story: once I had one, my imagination took over and wove a facsimile of myself into an elaborate melodramatic narrative at the conclusion of which I inevitably triumphed and was loudly applauded by my relatives and neighbors.

When I was older I began to rely on comics and radio programs for my story ideas; years later, movies and library books.

But always the pattern was the same: I intruded myself into the story and carried it off in a direction that would permit me the hero's role.

Words came next. A passion for words: how they looked on the printed page; how they sounded when they were spoken; the power inherent in them.

I wrote poetry.

I worked part-time as a pin-boy in a bowling alley, an usher at a movie house, a truck driver's assistant, a helper in a bakery, etcetera, etcetera.

I told myself stories, at all hours of the day and night, for the fun of it.

At sixteen I quit high school and volunteered for the Navy. I was inducted shortly after my seventeenth birthday.

I spent a couple of years at sea, reading everything I could lay my hands on, writing words and their meanings and committing them to memory.

A letter I sent to my best boyhood friend, David Kugelman, who was with the Army in Italy, was returned to me with the word "Deceased" stamped on the envelope.

I knew how to play the clarinet and saxophone, so when I got out of the Navy I joined several small bands and worked around the city. I also went to night school to get my high school diploma. In my spare time I wrote short stories.

It didn't take me long to realize that I wasn't much of a musician. I sold my clarinet and saxophone and I took a train to Miami where I found a job as a dishwasher in a cafeteria. In a few weeks I was promoted to busboy. I listened to people tell each other stories.

After a while I hitchhiked to New Orleans where I met an artist who smiled hello to everyone he passed on the street. We made a deal: the first one to get a job would support the other one until he got a job. My friend found a job the next day, behind a drugstore food counter. I took my three meals a day there and with no job in sight, I started writing a novel which I eventually abandoned.

I hitchhiked to Houston, and was thrown in jail for vagrancy. I wired home for money and as soon as I hit New York I hitchhiked to Canada. Not long after I wired home for money again.

I worked pushing a hand truck in the garment industry, as a clerk in several department stores, in the post office during the Christmas holidays, as a waiter in the Catskills during the summer holidays, etcetera, etcetera.

At night I went to Long Island University.

I started mailing my short stories to literary publications. I kept a scrupulous record of when I mailed something out and when something was returned to me.

In those days you could enter law school after two years of college. I did so, on the G.I. Bill of Rights, thinking that if I could practice law I'd be able to earn a decent living and still have time to continue writing.

I engaged in a fierce correspondence with my friend and mentor, George Bailin. We wrote to one another almost nightly, although we lived only a few blocks apart. In our lengthy letters we detailed our plans and ambitions, our opinions and observations. Somehow we got into a theological argument about God's presence on earth. We stopped writing abruptly. It's now over thirty years since we've spoken to each other.

I opened a law office on Delancey Street. My partner used it to get laid. I used it to write. Whenever anyone came in and asked us to take on a legal problem we were both in a state of total panic.

I decided I couldn't write and practice law at the same time so I quit law.

I worked as an order clerk, as a biographical researcher, as a typist, as a teacher of English in a Chassidic Yeshiva, etcetera, etcetera. I also went to the New School at night to get a bachelor's degree.

And I wrote. It all added up to about sixty-five short stories and three novels. Nothing was published. But I kept a scrupulous record of when I mailed something out and when something was returned to me.

I fell in love with Reene Schapiro. Before giving my body to her in holy matrimony, I asked her to sign a contract which stated that I was a writer and consequently not required to provide her with the necessities of life. She refused to sign. I married her anyway.

I taught at a high school in Harlem.

Out of frustration, without training and without any particular interest in the theater, I wrote five one-act plays, each taking about a month to write.

The plays I wrote were *At Mrs. Zimboff's*; *Little Johnny*; *The Typists*; *A Simple Kind of Love Story*; and *The Postman* (later the title was changed to *The Tiger*).

People who read my plays said nice things about them. I had never gotten a similar response for my short stories and novels. I started to write more plays.

My wife and I saved two or three thousand dollars. We planned to spend a week in London and then go on to Spain where we could live cheaply and I could write full time until our money was gone.

Bill Fox (a New School classmate who became a successful novelist) introduced me to Jerry Tallmer (in those days a critic for *The Village Voice*). After reading a

2

couple of my plays, Jerry suggested I look up a Charles Marowitz when I arrived in London.

I did. Charles read the one-act plays and said he would like to go into rehearsal at once with three of them: *The Typists*; *The Postman*; and *A Simple Kind of Love Story*. He would produce and direct them.

I said okay.

They were presented in a theater of about fifty seats. My wife sold coffee in the lobby at intermission, and at the end of the evening a hat was passed from hand to hand.

The following morning I read on the front page of the *London Times:*

VARIATIONS OF A THEME

MR. SCHISGAL'S TRIPLE BILL

The three plays which make up Mr. Murray Schisgal's triple bill Schrecks, *presented last night by the In-Stage group at the theatre of the British Drama League, Fitzroy Square, are all, in a sense, variations on one theme: the hysteria which lies beneath the surface of city life and may at any time, disconcertingly, break out.*

Two full-length plays of mine were produced at the Arts Theatre in London shortly thereafter: *Ducks and Lovers* and *Luv*.

The first play I had produced at home was *The Typists*. It starred James Coco and Sylvia Gassel and was directed by David Brooks at Lucille Lortel's White Barn Theatre in Connecticut.

Anne Jackson and Eli Wallach starred in a production of *The Typists* and *The Tiger* at the Orpheum Theatre in 1963. The producer was Claire Nichtern; the director, Arthur Storch.

In 1964, *Luv*, starring Anne Jackson, Eli Wallach, and Alan Arkin, opened at the Booth Theatre. It was directed by Mike Nichols.

At the age of thirty-seven I began to earn a living as a writer.

I learned a little about the theater.

I didn't love the theater.

But I was enjoying myself.

I wrote plays because I seemed to have a knack for it, and they paid me for my work.

I went to the bank each week with my royalty check of approximately five thousand dollars and deposited it. The bank teller was disgusted by my naiveté.

Everybody liked me.

Try as I might, I couldn't pay for my own dinner.

Strangers asked me to go to bed with them.

I flew to the capitals of Europe and ate frogs' legs with the better class.

I was in constant communication with Hollywood and the major television studios.

I held to one note: I want to write what I feel I want to write.

In 1966 I did three one-act plays at the Berkshire Playhouse in Stockbridge, Massachusetts. They were: *The Old Jew*; *Reverberations* (later the title was changed to *The Basement*); and *Fragments*. The cast was Dustin Hoffman, Gene Hackman, Estelle Parsons and Graham Jarvis; the director, Martin Fried.

Two of the plays were subsequently produced at the Cherry Lane Theatre: *The Basement* and *Fragments*. Gene Hackman starred and the cast included James Coco,

3

Sylvia Gassel, Tresa Hughes, and Humbert Astredo; the director was Larry Arrick and the producers, Edgar Lansbury and Marc Merson.

The reviews were decidedly mixed.

I was dispatched to the swollen ranks of Promising Young American Playwright Who It's Time We Punched in the Mouth.

I was not encouraged to go in a new direction.

I was reprimanded by the ticket sellers.

And I was suddenly made aware of the obvious fact that theater is Serious Business.

People's lives and careers were at stake.

Lots of moola was at stake.

You want to write what you feel you want to write, go work in churches!

You want to earn a livelihood in the theater, deliver the cookies!

Hollywood stopped calling.

My agent stopped calling.

One could easily be intimidated, made self-conscious, start hearing the audience shuffling and coughing under the typewriter keys.

One could easily wish he had gone into another line of work, some other profession that wasn't always a matter of life or death, like accounting.

But I was a writer by choice, and a playwright by temperament, and damn if I didn't find, at times, the theater an exciting place to work in.

I started to learn my trade in earnest.

I made more mistakes than most.

I did plays on Broadway, off-Broadway, off-off-Broadway, regional theater, repertory theater, college theater, etcetera, etcetera.

When I couldn't make a buck at it I worked in films and television, usually writing what I was told to write.

But for the stage, in spite of the realities of "the business," I continued to write what I felt I wanted to write.

(Under the Dramatist's Guild contract no one can change a line of the playwright's without his permission. In film and television the writer is lucky if he is told who's rewriting his lines.)

All Over Town was produced on Broadway by Adela Holzer. Let me quote from an article written by Helen Dudar that appeared in the *New York Times* on October 31, 1982, to explain that play's importance to me:

> *Mr. Schisgal's disillusionment with critics and with Broadway is rooted in his shock over the failure in early 1975 of "All Over Town," a Feydeauesque comedy which had 11 doors and a really complicated plot. Directed by Dustin Hoffman who a few years earlier had starred in Mr. Schisgal's "Jimmy Shine," the play opened to notices that were not enthusiastic enough to support a run. Mr. Schisgal is still so incensed at the memory—"It was work that I admired and felt had a real theatrical excitement"— that he is pounding the table to emphasize before he is finished.*
>
> *"Frequently I can see what I do is bad. When the critics say so, I accept it—I made a mistake. But when I see a work which I like and admire, the work of Dustin's direction, the work of Cleavon Little and Polly Holliday and Barnard Hughes, and it's treated cavalierly, I say, 'Tootsie, I will not accept that relationship that gives them [the critics] the right to make those judgments.' Don't you understand? A playwright is compelled by circumstances to write his play for critics, not for an audience."*

That was it. My goodbye to Broadway. In 1975. If I had had the will power, I would have said goodbye to writing for the theater as well, just as many of my fellow playwrights had done over the years, and pursued a more sensible career in film or television.

But I couldn't kick the habit. The high of writing what I felt I wanted to write was too much of a turn-on for me. I did try to control my weakness for the theater.

I worked on the film *Agatha* and coauthored the film *Tootsie*.

I did several television pilots.

I wrote a novel, *Days and Nights of a French Horn Player,* which was published by Little, Brown & Co.

I did a full-length play, *Popkins,* at the Margo Jones Theatre in Dallas, *The Downstairs Boys* (formerly titled *A Way of Life*) at the Cincinnati Playhouse, and a musical of *Jimmy Shine* at U.C.L.A., and other plays in other places.

In New York I worked off-off-Broadway, doing *The Pushcart Peddlers* at Curt Dempster's Ensemble Studio Theatre and *Walter* and *The Flatulist* at Rip Torn's Sanctuary Theatre.

I stayed away from Broadway.

In 1981 I was commissioned by the John Drew Theatre in East Hampton to write a one-act play for Anne Jackson and Eli Wallach. I wrote *A Need for Brussels Sprouts,* and Arthur Storch directed it during the summer of that year.

Arthur, who ran Syracuse Stage at the University of Syracuse, then asked me to write a companion piece for Anne and Eli. I wrote *A Need for Less Expertise* and under the generic title of *Twice Around the Park* both one-acters were presented at the university's theater in the spring of 1982.

Peter Witt optioned the plays and arranged for a ten-week tour leading to, of all places, Broadway!

I argued against it, urging that we tour indefinitely and never come in.

But when I was shown how much money I could make, from subsidiary rights, foreign rights, cable rights, further tour rights, etcetera, etcetera, I shut up.

Quoting once again from the *New York Times* article of October 31, 1982 (I was interviewed while we were playing the Mechanic Theatre in Baltimore, a week before opening at the Cort in New York):

> *"I tell you how I feel—I feel I don't stand a chance," he [Schisgal] said. "I feel everyone is anxious for the thing to fail. Because oddly enough, I don't feel anyone in the theater or any critics or any theater owners would walk two steps to go out of their way to genuinely wish me well. Yeah, me, personally. No, not me personally. I think there's no one who presents a work who ever, who ever is given sympathetic attention unless there is a relationship of some kind developed. I have no relationships, in spite of being in the theater 25 years. I'm a newborn babe and I'm comin' in innocent and naive."*

Not quite. Now that I'm a bit removed from the heat of battle, perhaps I can express myself coolly and dispassionately.

The theater is no place for a career.

It's okay when you're young and trying to make a name for yourself, or when you have a few extra bucks and want to shoot craps, but otherwise it's best to work elsewhere.

(It's also okay if the Pulitzer Prize is more important to you than a bowl of hot soup.)

There are more critics earning a living from the theater today than there are playwrights.

There are more critics building careers for themselves on the broken bones of playwrights than there are playwrights who are not suffering from chronic migraine headaches.

There are very few knowledgeable producers left and those that are left are crazy.

I don't know very many theater owners but those I know scare the shit out of me.

Smart talented actors and smart talented directors always talk about doing a play on Broadway but never do so; that's why they're smart and talented.

Success isn't destructive to the playwright; self-consciousness is. I hate talking or writing about anything I write. I hate seeing a play of mine after its initial production. For me it's over, done with, an experience as unsatisfying and unfilling as last week's dinner. The rewards of writing occur, for me, while the writing is taking place. It's a scary and exhilarating (but more often tedious and plodding) adventure. To play in the fields of my imagination is, as I've already written, essential to my well-being. That's why I write. The rest is public relations.

The only reason to spend a lifetime writing is a medical one: it's difficult to breathe when not doing so.

Of course the more intelligent reason is to make money.

In either case self-consciousness is the killer.

I never met Walter Kerr but I respect and I am grateful to him: he has a genuine love for the theater and for the people who work in the theater.

I have over the years made friends and enemies in equal number and I am proud of each and every one of them.

I have no intention of ever writing a play again.

I want only to work in film and television.

Yet I have to say that if I ever want to write what I feel I want to write, I may be forced to change my mind.

The truth is I can't think of any professional life more challenging, more exciting and more emotionally fulfilling than a life in the theater.

The Typists

I once worked for an employment agency that sent out typists to companies that needed typing done for either a few hours or a few days. At the end of that time, the typists returned to the agency and were sent out to another company for another few hours or few days.

The advantage of this kind of job was that you didn't have to work every day. You could stay home and write or paint or practice a musical instrument for as long as you liked, without pay, of course.

I was usually sent out with a fellow named John Bageris (today a teacher and painter of wonderful abstractions). We'd sit beside each other, typing names and addresses on endless sheets of paper. When the supervisor wasn't in the room we stopped typing and talked about everything under the sun. But as soon as the supervisor walked in, we'd start typing furiously again.

When I wrote the play I heard the clacking sound of the typewriters, I saw Sylvia and Paul age in front of my eyes, and I prayed with all my heart that I could live another life.

—M.S.
March 9, 1983

7

THE TYPISTS, *on a double bill with* THE TIGER, *opened in New York on February 4, 1963, at the Orpheum Theatre. The plays were presented by Claire Nichtern.*

SYLVIA PAYTON   *Anne Jackson*

PAUL CUNNINGHAM   *Eli Wallach*

Directed by ARTHUR STORCH

Set Design by WOLFGANG ROTH

At twenty-odd years of age.

An office: forward, center, a pair of simple metal typewriter tables, with leaves extended, on which there are two old standard typewriters, stacks of postcards, and a bulky telephone directory on each; rear, a large window, two tall green steel file cabinets, a desk between them on which there are a great many telephone directories and a telephone, a door to the restroom; at the right wall, forward, a water cooler, a wooden coat hanger, the entrance door; in the left wall, the door to the employer's office.

The sun streams through the window; as the play progresses it fades imperceptibly until, at the end, the room is almost in complete darkness.

The same clothes are worn throughout by the actors, although altered to suit the physical changes—subtle, almost unnoticed when they occur— that take place during the course of the play.

SYLVIA PAYTON enters from right. She is late for work. She throws her coat on the hanger, rushes across the room, deposits her lunch bag in the top drawer of a cabinet, removes cover from her typewriter and begins typing rapidly, glancing anxiously at the employer's door. In a moment she relaxes; she types slowly and hums to herself; she takes her comb and mirror from her pocketbook and fixes her hair. The front door opens. She puts everything away and without turning to see who has entered she starts to type rapidly again. PAUL CUNNINGHAM approaches, passing his lunch bag from hand to hand.

PAUL

Good morning. I'm Paul Cunningham. I was hired yesterday by . . .
(Laughing uneasily)
That's funny. I forgot his name. You'll have to excuse me. First day on the job . . . I'm a little nervous. It was the boss who hired me, though; at least that's what he said.

SYLVIA

I know. He told me.
(Rising, shaking his hand)
Sylvia. Miss Sylvia Payton. Glad to meet you, Mr. Cunningham. If you'll hang up your coat I'll show you what you have to do.

PAUL

I'm sorry I'm late, Miss Payton. I got on the wrong train by mistake. Generally you'll find that I'm a pretty prompt person.

SYLVIA

Oh, that's all right. Just make sure it doesn't happen too often. He's very strict when it comes to being here on time. And now that he's made me responsible for this whole department . . . Of course I won't say anything to him about this morning.

9

PAUL

I'd appreciate that a lot.

SYLVIA

Don't even mention it. Believe me, I didn't ask him to be made a supervisor. I don't like telling anyone what to do; that's part of my nature, I guess. You give me your lunch bag, Mr. Cunningham. I'll put it in the file cabinet; that's where I keep mine.

PAUL

Thanks. I was sure lucky to get this job. I go to school at night and a lot of firms don't hire you if they know that.

SYLVIA

You must be a very ambitious person. What are you studying?

PAUL
(Proudly)

Law. Another three years and I should get my degree. Boy, that's one day I'm looking forward to.

SYLVIA

It must be extremely difficult to have a job and go to school at the same time.

PAUL

It's been real rough so far. But it has its advantages. When I get out, I'm going to have the satisfaction of knowing I did it myself, with my own sweat and my own money; that's more than most fellows my age can say.

SYLVIA

How true that is.

PAUL

Listen, I have an uncle who's a lawyer, a pretty darn famous lawyer, too. Francis T. Cunningham. You ask anybody in the legal field about Francis T. Cunningham and they'll tell you how much he's worth. Well, if I wanted to, I just have to pick up that phone, give him a ring and my worrying days would be over. But that's not for me; no, sir. I'll do it alone or I'm not doing it at all.

SYLVIA
(Uncovers PAUL's *typewriter, opens directory for him)*

I think you're a hundred percent right. You know, I once went with a boy—it was nothing serious, it could have been, but ... I won't go into that now. Anyway, his father was helping him through medical school. He didn't have to earn a penny of his own. Do you think he finished? What happened was that his father remarried and stopped giving him money. He fell completely apart; you never saw anything like it.

PAUL

There's no substitute for character.

10

That's exactly the point. Well, we'd better get to work before he starts screaming. We're on a promotion campaign now and it's a very important job. I suppose that's why you were hired. What we do is type out the names and addresses of prospective customers on these postcards. The advertisement is printed on the back. We get the information we want straight from the telephone book. Don't leave out any names; go right down the line. He checks everything and he can be awfully mean if he wants to. I've just started on the A's, so you'll start with the . . .

PAUL

B's.

SYLVIA

Right. That way we'll be sure to get everyone.

PAUL

It sounds easy enough.

SYLVIA

It is. And after awhile you can do it without even thinking.
(They are both seated, typing)

PAUL

Ooops! My first card and my first mistake. I'm afraid I'm a little rusty. I haven't been doing much typing lately.
(He is about to throw card into basket)

SYLVIA

No, don't throw it away. If he sees it, he'll raise the roof. At the beginning you ought to type more slowly. Lean back in your chair. Posture's very important. And strike each key with the same steady rhythm.

PAUL

Like this?

SYLVIA

Better, much better; don't move your head; keep your eyes on the material you're typing.

PAUL
(Sitting rigidly, uncomfortably)
It's really nice of you to help me this way.

SYLVIA

I'm only too glad to, Mr. Cunningham.

PAUL

Paul.

11

SYLVIA
(Staring at him, warmly)

Paul.

(The buzzer rings once)

That's for me.

(Quickly tidying herself)

He doesn't usually call me in this early. You go on with your work, Paul. He gets furious when he doesn't hear these typewriters going. He probably wants to know why it took us so long to get started this morning. Don't worry. I'll cover up for you.

PAUL
(Holding her arm)

Thanks for everything, Sylvia.

SYLVIA

You're welcome . . . Paul.

(PAUL watches her as she swings her hips self-consciously and exits to employer's office. He then starts to type, makes an error, crumples card and is about to throw it into basket; on second thought he slips the card into his pocket. Again he types and makes an error, looks guiltily toward the employer's office and slips card into his pocket. All the while he whistles to the tune of "Way Down Upon the Swanee River . . .")

SYLVIA
(Entering, angrily)

He's got some goddamn nerve! What does he think I am, a child? I see it doesn't pay to be nice to people. Well, he can just go and look for someone else to do his dirty work. I'm leaving!

(Gathers her things together)

PAUL

What happened?

SYLVIA

Bawling me out for being five minutes late; that's nerve, believe me.

PAUL
(Laughing)

So you were late this morning, too?

SYLVIA

There's nothing funny about it, Paul. When you've devoted as much time and energy as I have to this firm, giving them the best you're capable of, then maybe you'll see things differently. Where are my gloves?

PAUL
(Rising, gives them to her)

Here they are. Listen, Sylvia; you're excited. Why don't you think about it, huh?

SYLVIA

There's nothing to think about. When he asks you where I went, you just tell him for me that I don't care to associate with a firm that has no feelings for its employees.
(She struggles with coat; he helps her put it on)

PAUL

It's not easy finding a job now, I can tell you that.

SYLVIA

With my experience? You must be joking. I've been made many many offers in the past that I've refused out of a sense of loyalty to that . . . to that sex maniac in there. This is my reward.

PAUL

I wouldn't give him the satisfaction; no, sir.

SYLVIA

What satisfaction?

PAUL

Well, it stands to reason that he wanted you to quit, doesn't it? He knows you're a sensitive girl. By leaving you're doing just what he wants.

SYLVIA

You think he deliberately . . .

PAUL

Why else would he have bawled you out?

SYLVIA
(Slight pause; takes off coat, puts it on hanger)
I'd die before I gave him the satisfaction. If that's what he has in mind, he's got another guess coming. I'm leaving at my convenience, not his.

PAUL

Now you're talking.

SYLVIA

Believe me, there'll come a day when he'll really need me. "Miss Payton, won't you please help me get this job through in time?" Then it'll be my turn. I'll just laugh right in his stupid face and walk out.

PAUL

Boy, I'd like to be here to see it. Is he married?

SYLVIA

Who would marry him? Ugly as sin, that's what he is.
(They type, laugh over the noise of their typing, then suddenly stop)

SYLVIA

We had a girl working here once; she was a riot. She used to draw these caricatures and mail them to him; anonymously, of course. But you should have seen them; they were the funniest thing.

(They type, laugh, stop suddenly)

PAUL

The last job I had was for this woman, Mrs. Jameson. She was as blind as a bat without her glasses. You know what we used to do? Whenever we got the chance we hid her glasses somewhere in the office. For two or three days until she'd find them, we didn't have to do anything, not a single piece of work. We just sat around talking all day.

SYLVIA

I was with an insurance company when I graduated from high school. There was this man in charge there, Mr. Williams, his name was, and he used to have loose hands, if you know what I mean.

PAUL

I know.

SYLVIA

Well, one day he was telling me how to type a policy and he let his hands fall—very, very casually—on my shoulder. So I turned around and looked up at him and spat right in his face.

PAUL

You were fired, I bet.

SYLVIA

As a matter of fact we got along very well after that.

(They type; stop suddenly; turn to one another)

PAUL

Have you read any good books lately?

SYLVIA

I read a very good detective novel last week. It was called *Murder in Bombay*.

PAUL

I'm a science fiction man myself.

(They type; stop suddenly; turn to one another)

SYLVIA

Can I ask you something?

PAUL

Sure. What is it?

14

SYLVIA

If you had to choose between getting a million dollars or losing a leg which would you take?

PAUL

Right leg or left leg?

SYLVIA

Any leg.

PAUL
(Pause)

I'd take the million dollars.

SYLVIA

I wouldn't. I'd keep my legs.
(They type; stop suddenly. They both stare at the audience, PAUL leaning forward, SYLVIA back in her chair, her face expressionless, her hands in her lap)

PAUL

I was born in a poor section of Brooklyn. My parents were at each other's throat most of the time. It was a miserable childhood. I had no brothers or sisters; there was only the three of us living in this old run-down house, with cats crying and screaming all night in the alley. Why my parents ever got married, I don't know, and why they stayed together for as long as they did I don't know that either. They're separated now. But it doesn't much matter anymore. They were as unlike as any two people could be. All my father wanted was to be left alone to smoke his pipe and listen to the radio. My mother—she was a pretty woman, she knew how to dress, all right— she liked to go out and enjoy herself. I was stuck between the two of them and they pulled on both sides. I couldn't talk to one without the other accusing me of being ungrateful; I couldn't touch or kiss one of them without being afraid that the other one would see me and there would be a fight. I had to keep my thoughts to myself. I had to grow up wishing for some kind of miracle. I remember coming home from school one afternoon. I must have been twelve or thirteen. There was this man in the living room with my mother. They weren't doing anything; they were just sitting and talking. But I felt that something was going on. I seemed to stop breathing and I ran out of the house and threw up on the curbstone. Later on I swore to myself that I would make a miracle happen; that I wouldn't ever have to be where I didn't want to be and I wouldn't have to do what I didn't want to do; that I could be myself, without being afraid. But it's rough. With a background like mine you're always trying to catch up; it's as if you were born two steps behind the next fellow.
(They type; stop suddenly. They both stare at the audience, SYLVIA leaning forward, PAUL back in his chair, etc.)

SYLVIA

My family never had money problems. In that respect we were very fortunate. My father made a good living, while he was alive, that is. He passed away when I was seventeen. You could say he and my mother had a fairly happy marriage. At least we never knew when they were angry with one another, and that's a good thing for children. I have a sister. Charlotte. She's older than I am. She's married now and we don't bother much with each other. But when we were younger you wouldn't believe what went on. Every time we quarreled, according to my parents she was right; I was always wrong. She got everything she wanted, no matter what, and I had to be content with the leftovers. It was just unbearable. Anyway, my father was sick for a long time before he passed away. He had this ring, it was a beautiful ring, with a large onyx stone in it, and when I was a girl I used to play with it. I'd close one eye and I'd look inside of it and I'd see hundreds and hundreds of beautiful red and blue stars. My father had always promised me that ring; he always said it belonged to me. I thought for certain he'd give it to me before he passed away, but he didn't say anything about it; not a word. Well, afterward, I saw it. You know where I saw it? On my sister's finger. He had given it to her. Now I don't think that's a background that leaves many possibilities for development. I don't forgive my father; definitely not. And I don't forgive my sister. My mother, whom I now support with my hard work, still says I'm wrong.

(They type; stop suddenly; turn to one another)

PAUL

Do you go to the movies?

SYLVIA

Not too often.

PAUL

Me neither.

SYLVIA

Do you like to watch television?

PAUL

I never get the chance. Don't forget I go to school five nights a week. But my wife watches it a lot; that's all she does.

SYLVIA
(Surprised)

I didn't know you were married.

PAUL
(Types)
This machine's full of errors. I'm getting nowhere fast.
(He is about to crumple card)

SYLVIA
(Rising)

Let me see that, please.
(Examines card, incommensurate anger)
Now this could be erased. We don't approve of wasting material when it can be saved. That isn't the policy of this office.

16

PAUL

Okay. You don't have to be mad. I'll do it.

SYLVIA

I'm not mad. But I am responsible for what goes on in this department. I'm sick and tired of covering up for your mistakes. Everyone must think I'm a piece of rag to be stepped on. First him and now you.

PAUL

Do you mind telling me what you're talking about!

SYLVIA

You know very well what I'm talking about. This is my thanks; this is what I get for trying to be helpful and nice to people. I'm wrong, I know. I'm always wrong. Everything I do is wrong. Well, Mr. Cunningham, I've had enough, quite enough, and I won't take any more from you or anyone else. I won't! I won't!
(She flees to the restroom. P A U L *slaps the typewriter, goes to telephone, dials)*

PAUL
(Loudly)

Let me speak to Mr. Francis T. Cunningham, please. Who's calling? Paul Cunningham!
(Softly)

Hello, Uncle Frank. It's me again. Paul. How . . . how are you? Everything all right? That's good. Oh, everything's fine with me; still plugging away. I got a new job; yeah, typing, office work; just enough for bread. Uhuh. Uncle, can't you give me a hand? It's too rough for me. I can't hold down a job and go to school five nights a week; it's killing me. I know, I know. But I thought if you could give me a part-time job in your office, or maybe one of your friends, if you spoke to them . . . Yeah, sure. I understand. It's okay. Yeah. Send my regards.
(P A U L returns to typewriter. S Y L V I A enters, exchanges her directory. Her appearance is that of a woman in her thirties)

SYLVIA

I'm sorry for losing my temper, Paul. It won't happen again.

PAUL

Forget it.
(He types)

SYLVIA

You've become an expert at that machine.

PAUL
(Glumly)

At least I'm an expert at something.

SYLVIA

Is anything the matter?

17

PAUL

No, but I was just thinking. What am I knocking myself out for? School almost every night, weekends I'm home studying, I can't remember the last time I took a decent vacation. What for? You're young only once; this is the time to enjoy yourself.

SYLVIA
(At typewriter)

I don't know how true that is. You probably could enjoy yourself a great deal more if you were a lawyer; that's why some sacrifices have to be made now.

PAUL

That's the kind of logic that leads nowhere. By your reasoning all lawyers should be happy men. No, sir; that isn't the way life is. You could be a ditch-digger and be happy if you know how to live. I tell you, I've had it. A fellow in my position has to take advantage of what's offered to him. He's got to be practical and look the facts right in the eye.

(Tapping table)

This here is what's offered to me. This is my chance and from now on I start concentrating on this job. I'll show him I'm on the ball and maybe he'll find something else for me, give me a promotion, a better salary. Why not? An outfit this big always needs men who aren't afraid to work. Listen, I've got two kids at home. I've got to start thinking of them, too.

SYLVIA
(Stiffly)

You have two children?

PAUL

Sure. I don't waste any time. Look, I've got their pictures here. We took these last summer.

(He shows her photographs inside wallet)

Well, what do you think?

SYLVIA
(Coldly)

They're beautiful, Paul. What's their names?

PAUL

Frank and Sally. But we call the boy Buddy; he hates it when we call him Frank; funny rascal. They're not bad for a character like me, are they? You know what I'm going to do, Syl? I'm going right in to him and ask him what my chances for advancement are. I might as well get all this settled now. Frankly I can use a little more money, too. The expenses are killing me. If we had a union in this place, we'd get some action. I may do something about that yet.

(He heads for employer's office, turns)

What . . . what would you say is the best way to approach him?

I honestly don't know, Paul. He changes from one minute to the next. But if he isn't wearing his glasses, that's a bad sign; I know that much.

PAUL

Glasses . . . I got it. Wish me luck?

SYLVIA

I hope you get something good.
(After PAUL *exits, she goes to phone, dials)*
Ma? Sylvia. No, I'm all right. Did the lamp come? Well, just make sure when it comes that it isn't damaged; you'll have to sign for it and that means you inspected it. Look at it carefully; if there isn't any damage you can sign, but if there's anything wrong with it, the smallest thing, refuse to sign and tell the man to take it back. Do you understand? I hope so. Did I . . . get any calls? I didn't say I was expecting any, don't put words in my mouth, I merely asked you if I got any. Never mind. It's not important. Did Charlotte call? How is she?
*(*PAUL *enters. He has the appearance of a man in his thirties.* SYLVIA *carries on the remainder of her call as though talking to a boyfriend)*

SYLVIA

Oh, stop being silly. I really couldn't. I have something this Saturday. I mean it.
(Laughing)
No, no. Well, perhaps Sunday. Call me at home. All right. Bye.

PAUL
(At typewriter)
It looks good, real good. He's considering it. He says they may need someone on the sales staff. I'm first on the list.

SYLVIA

That does sound good. What about the raise?

PAUL

I'll have to wait awhile, he said. But I'll get it. He was impressed, especially when I told him I had some legal experience. You should have seen his eyes open up. It's only a question of time, and once I start moving, you watch, it's going to take a pretty fast man to keep up with me.

SYLVIA

You certainly have ambition, Paul.

PAUL
(Rises to exchange directory)
Listen, I don't intend to spend the rest of my life working here or anyplace else. I'll make my bundle and that's it. There's a world outside that window, a world with a thousand different things to see and do, and I'm going to see and do every last one of them; you watch.

SYLVIA

There's a million different things to do in the world.

PAUL

Lie in the sun ...

SYLVIA

Dance ...

PAUL

Travel ...

SYLVIA

Wear pretty clothes ...

PAUL

Visit places ...

SYLVIA

Meet interesting people ...

PAUL

Mountains. A place with mountains ...

SYLVIA
(Grabs PAUL'S lapels, her emotions soaring)
Oh, Paul, I'm so filled with the desire to live, to experience things, to laugh ... Oh, I want to laugh, Paul!
(Silence. PAUL stares dumbly at her, clears his throat. Stiffly they return to their chairs, type energetically)

PAUL
(In a moment, calmly)
When do we have lunch?

SYLVIA

We can have it any time we want. But I usually have it at one. The later you have it the shorter the afternoon is.

PAUL

How about waiting until one-thirty?

SYLVIA

That isn't easy.

PAUL

I know, but then we'd only have a couple of more hours to go. The afternoon would fly. What do you say?

SYLVIA

I'm willing, if you are.

PAUL

It's a deal, then. One-thirty lunch.
(They shake hands)

SYLVIA

One-thirty.

PAUL

Right.

(They both type)

SYLVIA

You know, I'm getting hungry already.

PAUL

So am I. I didn't have any breakfast.

SYLVIA

I had a cup of coffee, that's all.

PAUL

What have you got for lunch?

SYLVIA

A tuna-fish sandwich with tomatoes and mayonnaise, an orange and a piece of layer
cake. What did you bring?

PAUL

Two turkey sandwiches and an apple, I think.

SYLVIA

One-thirty.

(They shake hands)

PAUL

That's the deal.

(They both type)

PAUL

We went down to Chinatown last weekend. What a meal we had.

SYLVIA

I'm crazy about Chinese food. I once went with a fellow who knew how to speak
Chinese and you should have seen the things he ordered; the most fantastic dishes,
with chicken livers and mushrooms and almonds . . .

PAUL

The Chinese people can cook, all right, but when it comes to *real* cooking you can't beat the Italians. There's a place we go to on the West Side; you should taste their veal parmesan or their chicken cacciatore. And they make a spaghetti sauce, you could . . .

SYLVIA
(Goes to file cabinet)

I think I'll eat now.

PAUL
(Rising, furiously)

We made a deal, didn't we?

SYLVIA

Don't be childish. If I want to eat now, I'll eat now, and that's all there is to it.

PAUL

You women are all alike. No backbone. No self-discipline. Go ahead and eat, I'm not going to stop you. But I'm sticking to my word.

SYLVIA

I didn't say I was going to eat, Mr. Cunningham. I merely said I was thinking of eating; listen before you speak.
(She waves at him blank postcards which she has taken from cabinet)
And if you want to know something else, I could probably wait longer than you; I could probably go without lunch, which is more than some people can say.

PAUL
(At typewriter)

Is that so?

SYLVIA
(At typewriter)

That's so exactly.

PAUL

We'll see, Miss Supervisor.

SYLVIA

You're jealous. It's coming out all over you. I am supervisor . . .

PAUL
(Waving his arm)

Of this whole department. Boy, I'll never forget that as long as I live.
(Mimicking her in a small voice)
"Believe me, Mr. Cunningham, I didn't ask him to be made supervisor. I don't like telling anyone what to do; that's part of my nature . . ."
(He falls on typewriter in a fit of laughter)

22

SYLVIA

You just keep that up and you won't be working here much longer, I assure you of that, Mr. Cunningham.

PAUL

Tell him. Go ahead and tell him. You'd be doing me a favor!

SYLVIA

What? You mean a man with your legal experience, with your plans and ambitions, requires a favor from me?

PAUL

Miss Payton, I loathe you!

SYLVIA

That, Mr. Cunningham, would be a gross understatement to describe my feelings for you. You make me sick!

PAUL

Why don't you quit, then?

SYLVIA

Why don't you?

PAUL

I wouldn't give you the satisfaction.

SYLVIA

And I wouldn't give you the satisfaction!
(They both type, loudly, rapidly)

PAUL
(Slaps keys)

What the hell am I doing? This isn't what I want. No, goddamn it!

SYLVIA
(Without looking at him)

I wonder if the man knows what he wants.

PAUL
(Almost ominously)

You bet I do. And do you know what it is? You know what I'd really like to do? Now, right here in this office?
(Rises, moves around SYLVIA'S chair)

I'd like to rip the clothes right off your back, piece by piece. I'd like to dig my fingers into your flesh and feel your body break and sweat under mine. Do you understand me, Miss Payton?

23

SYLVIA
(Rises; softly)

Paul.

PAUL

It's been eating me up, ever since I first saw you. I want you, Miss Payton. Now! Now! This minute! Here, on the floor, screaming your lungs out and with your legs kicking up in the air. That's all I've been thinking of at that stupid typewriter; that's all that's been on my mind.
(Pause)

Now you know.

SYLVIA

And what do you think I've been thinking of? My body aches with wanting you, Paul.
(Turning, pointing to his typewriter)

How many times have I closed my eyes, just hoping you'd do something instead of sitting there like a stone statue!
(She falls back into him; he embraces her around the waist, standing behind her)

PAUL

Sylvia.

SYLVIA

I'll have to tell my mother, Paul. And you should tell your wife. Oh, I'll be good to the children. I promise you that.

PAUL
(Stunned)

Tell my wife?

SYLVIA

We will get married, won't we?

PAUL

Sylvia, listen . . .

SYLVIA
(Turning to face him)

We will get married, won't we?

PAUL

Aw, the hell with it! I'm going to eat.
(Gets lunch bag, throws coat over arm)

SYLVIA
(At typewriter)

It's my fault, I know; you don't have to tell me.

PAUL

It's nobody's fault. It's . . . the way things are.
(At door)
Can I get you anything?

SYLVIA

I'm not eating.

PAUL

Suit yourself.
(PAUL exits. SYLVIA runs to cabinet, takes out lunch bag; she eats her sandwich ravenously. The door is suddenly thrown open. Quickly SYLVIA turns, clutching the sandwich to her chest, hiding it)

PAUL

Are you sure you don't want anything?

SYLVIA
(With a mouthful of food)
Positive.

PAUL

All right.
(PAUL exits. SYLVIA goes to the phone, slowly, lethargically, dials)

SYLVIA

Ma? Sylvia. Nothing's wrong. I'm having my lunch now. The sandwich is fine. Did the table come? How is it? Are you sure? Sometimes they get damaged in shipping. Did you look carefully? Well, I hope so. Yes. Did I get any calls? No, I wasn't expecting any; I just asked.
(Pause)
What did Charlotte say? That's just like her. She could come at least once a week to see how you are. All right, have it your own way. I'm too tired to argue with you. How are the children? That's nice.
(Pause)
An eighty-five average doesn't mean he's a genius; no, not by any stretch of the imagination. I'm not saying she has stupid children; that isn't what I said, but I can't stand it when you raise them to the sky. I repeat, an eighty-five average is not in the genius class, and if you want proof ask anyone in the educational field. Oh, all right, all right; let's just drop it. I'll see you later. Of course I'm coming home. Where do you think I'd go? Fine. Good-bye.
(SYLVIA throws the remainder of her sandwich into basket, reluctantly sits down at typewriter. As she types and swings the carriage across—for want of something to do—she sings the material she is typing with the lilting intonation of a small girl bouncing a ball on the sidewalk while reciting doggerel)

SYLVIA
(Typing)
Mrs. Anna Robinson, of 4 East 32nd Street, in the city and state of New York.

25

(Taking card out, putting new card in; forlornly)
How are you today, Mrs. Anna Robinson? It has been so nice talking to you. Who
have we here? Oh, it's
(Typing)
Mr. Arnold Robinson, of 1032 Lexington Avenue, in the city and state of New York.
(Taking card out, putting new card in)
It was so pleasant talking to you, Mr. Robinson. Send my regards to the family. Why,
if it isn't
(Typing)
Mrs. Beatrice Robinson, who lives no less on Park Avenue, in the city and state of
New York.
(Taking card out, putting new card in)
Must you leave so soon, Mrs. Robinson?
*(S Y L V I A takes a gumdrop from a bag of candy, continues typing. P A U L enters.
He is now in his forties. He carries a container of coffee)*

PAUL
(Referring to her candy)
Up to your old tricks again, Sylvia? You'll never keep your figure that way.

SYLVIA
Don't worry about my figure; just worry about your own.

PAUL
(Pulling his stomach in)
You've got a point there. Here, I brought you some coffee.

SYLVIA
Thanks.
(Gets newspaper)
How is it outside?

PAUL
A little chilly, but the sun's strong; nice. I took a walk up to the park. You never saw
so many characters sitting on the benches and sunning themselves. I sure would like
to know how they do it.

SYLVIA
Half of them are probably on relief.

PAUL
We work and they sun themselves.

SYLVIA
You should see the cars some of them have.

PAUL
You don't have to tell me. I know.

SYLVIA

I read in the newspapers that by the year 2000 people will work only three hours a day and have a three-day week.

PAUL

That's not going to help me.

SYLVIA
(At typewriter; opens newspaper)

We could try to get into a union.

PAUL

Do you know one that isn't crooked?

SYLVIA

How I wish this day was over.

PAUL

It'll feel good getting these shoes off.

SYLVIA

I'll wash my hair and do a little ironing.

PAUL

No date tonight?

SYLVIA

Don't be funny.

PAUL
(At typewriter)

You know, I was thinking, Syl. Ever since I was a kid I always thought I would like to be independent, to live my own life, without getting involved with responsibilities and families. Inside of me I suppose I always was afraid of that. But, you know, everything I've done in my life has taken me away from what I thought I'd like to be when I was a kid. I got married as soon as I could; I had children right away; I made it so tough for myself I couldn't get through law school. I couldn't live the kind of life I thought I wanted. I've been asking myself lately, what is it I really wanted? You know what the answer to that is, Syl? You know what it has to be? What I got. What I am. Maybe all I really wanted was to be sorry for myself.

SYLVIA

Does anyone know what they want, Paul?

PAUL

Don't you?

Not any more. I thought I knew, just as you did. But if that's what I wanted, why am I where I am today?

PAUL

It doesn't make sense, does it?

SYLVIA

I swore that at the first opportunity I'd break away from my mother and my sister; I'd have nothing more to do with them and that would be happiness for me. But here I am still living with my mother and every day I ask how my sister is, what she's doing, how her husband is, the children ... And I don't give a damn. Not a damn.

PAUL

The things I don't give a damn about ... Syl, let's look into it. This is important.

SYLVIA

I've always said there's nothing more important than getting to know yourself. When you realize that people can live their whole lives without knowing themselves, without really getting to understand themselves, it ... it reaches the ridiculous.

PAUL
(Rising)

You're absolutely right.

SYLVIA
(Rising)

Let's see what's behind it all. Let's study it a moment.

PAUL

All right, let's get to it. Why?

SYLVIA

Why?

PAUL

Why do you say that leaving your family would make you happy? If that's all there was to it, you could have left them years ago. No, there's something you're hiding.

SYLVIA

You're not telling the truth. If all you wanted was to feel sorry for yourself, all you'd have to do is sit in a corner and feel sorry for yourself; that's all there is to it. But, no; that isn't it.

PAUL

Then what is it?

SYLVIA

What are you hiding?

(As one speaks, wagging a finger, the other paces back and forth, nodding without listening, following a separate train of thought)

PAUL

The fact remains that you do care what happens to your family, you care a lot, an awful lot; that's why you phone every day, that's why you're always asking about your sister. You have to keep them together; you need them more than they need you because you never developed emotionally enough to forget the past and start a new life for yourself.

SYLVIA

You deliberately put yourself in situations in which you had to fail. Why is it I never heard you say you loved your wife? What was behind your marriage at such an early age? Why didn't you wait until you finished school so that you'd have a fair chance of getting ahead?

PAUL

Simply because you wanted something from them. It had nothing to do with your father's ring; you use that for a smoke screen.

SYLVIA

Now we're coming closer to the truth. You had to rush into marriage, have children and become burdened with impossible responsibilities, the very things you were afraid of; you had to fail because it wasn't that you wanted to feel sorry for yourself, but you wanted other people to feel sorry for you.

PAUL

That's it! They alone could give you what you wanted; no one else, not even a husband; that's why you never got married. Now we're coming closer to it . . .

SYLVIA

So that they would pity and pamper you like a child; you mistook that for love, which was what you really wanted from them, the love which you couldn't get from your parents.

(They suddenly stand face to face)

PAUL

There it is! You wanted love!

SYLVIA

You wanted love, of course!

PAUL

Don't you see it now, Syl?

SYLVIA

It's all so clear.

PAUL

When you know something about yourself, then you can start doing something about it.

(They march back to their typewriters)

SYLVIA

This has been one of the most pleasant conversations I've ever had, Paul.

PAUL

I enjoyed it myself.
(Glancing at wristwatch)
And the afternoon's going pretty fast.

SYLVIA

Thank God for that.
(They both type)

PAUL

You know, thinking about it. I'm sure a lot better off than you are.

SYLVIA

Why's that?

PAUL

Well, I've got a place of my own; I did marry, have children. You could say I fulfilled a pretty important part of my life.

SYLVIA

That's nonsense. Do you think it requires any special ability to get married and have children?

PAUL

All I'm saying is that there are some people who would be awfully glad if they could have gotten married.

SYLVIA

Are you referring to me, Mr. Cunningham?

PAUL

I didn't mention any names, did I? But if the shoe fits, wear it, Miss Payton!

SYLVIA
(Grimly)

Don't make me laugh. If I had to make the choice—and I assure you I don't—I would much prefer being single than being forced to continue an unhappy marriage.

PAUL

An unhappy marriage? Where do you get that from? Did you ever hear me say that?

SYLVIA

I can put one and one together, Mr. Cunningham. We both know that if you had your way about it you would have left her long ago.

PAUL

Is that right?

SYLVIA

That's exactly right.

PAUL

Well, for your information, Miss Payton, my wife is the finest *(Rising)*, do you hear me? The finest, the most decent woman I ever had the good fortune to meet.

SYLVIA

Please, Mr. Cunningham.

PAUL

And for your further information, I wouldn't trade her for a dozen like you.

SYLVIA

You couldn't possibly.
(The buzzer rings; she fixes her hair, etc.)
Thank God, at last I'll have a moment away from you.

PAUL

I bet you think I don't know what goes on in there?

SYLVIA

What is he raving about now?

PAUL

Go ahead in. I can hear your boyfriend panting behind the door.

SYLVIA

Jealous?

PAUL

Of you?

SYLVIA

It's happened before.

PAUL
(Turning away from her, loud undertone)

You bitch!

SYLVIA
(Turning, flaring)

31

What did you say?

(No answer)

You'd better be quiet.

(She exits. PAUL *goes to hanger and without unwrapping or removing the whiskey bottle from his coat pocket pours a drink into a water cup, swallows it, then fills the cup again. He dials the phone)*

PAUL

Barbara. Paul. How're the kids? That's good. Oh, pretty much the same. Listen, Barb, I'm ... I'm sorry about last night. I had a little too much to drink. No, no, don't go excusing it. I just want you to know I didn't mean any of it. I think an awful ... an awful lot of you, you know that, and I respect you, I always have. It's when I'm drinking, it's the whiskey that does the talking. I'm going to stop, I promise you. Barb, you forgive me, don't you? Well, say it; I want to hear you say it; please.

(Pause)

Thank you. I'll try to get home early and we'll do something, we'll do something different, something ... different, I promise you. All right. Don't forget. So long.

(He finishes his drink, crumples cup and slips it into his pocket. Sylvia enters, carrying several sheets of paper, which she places on Paul's typewriter. She is now in her forties)

SYLVIA

He wants you to type copies of these. He's waiting for them.

PAUL

What's that?

SYLVIA
(At typewriter)

You heard me.

PAUL

Well, you hear me now. You can go right in there and tell him to go to hell. I'm not his secretary.

SYLVIA

Why don't you tell him yourself?

PAUL

That's a good idea!

(Moves to employer's office, grabbing papers from typewriter, turns)

That's a damn good idea!

(Exits)

SYLVIA
(Typing, singsong, as before)

Mr. Thomas Weaver, of 424 Harley Street, in the Bronx, New York.

(Taking card out, putting card in)

I hope that you're having a pleasant day, Mr. Thomas Weaver. Now who is this coming along? Oh, it's
(Typing)
Miss Tina Lee Weaver, of number 78 Monroe Avenue, in the Bronx, New York. How are you . . .
(P A U L enters. He shouts at employer's door as he rips papers in half and throws them in the air)

PAUL

There, there, that's what I think of you and your job, you old bastard!

SYLVIA

Paul!

PAUL

Why don't you go in and see your boyfriend now? You'll see him hiding behind the desk. If he stayed on his feet like a man I would have punched him right in the nose.

SYLVIA

Did you . . . quit?

PAUL

What the hell do you think I did? Trying to pull that stuff on me. I'm not his secretary and I never was.
(Shouting at employer's door)
Do you hear me, you old bastard! I'm not your secretary and I never was!

SYLVIA
(Rising, with concern)
Please, Paul, be quiet; you're in enough trouble.

PAUL

Trouble? Me? Ha! That's the funniest thing I heard yet. You're looking at a free man, Miss Payton; a free and independent man. Yes, sir. I haven't felt this good in years.

SYLVIA
(Following him to coat hanger)
But what will you do?

PAUL
(Removing whiskey bottle from coat, throwing wrapper away)
Start living for one thing; start being myself; start being a man again. You know what it means to be a man, Miss Payton? You don't meet men any more; they're all afraid of losing their jobs, afraid of spending a dollar, afraid of their own shadows. But not this man. No, sir. I don't lick anybody's boots. What are you staring at? This? It's an old custom of mine. Care to join me? No, I didn't think so.
(He drinks from bottle)

SYLVIA

Paul, don't; this isn't like you.

PAUL

How do you know what I'm like? How does anybody know? We all live alone, Miss
Payton; we all live alone in a cruel and lonely world.
(He drinks)

SYLVIA

How true that is.

PAUL

You know what I'm going to do? Yes, sir. The hell with it. I'm dropping everything,
leaving everything. The first bus heading west tomorrow, you know who's going to
be on it? I am. You bet.
(He raises bottle to mouth)

SYLVIA
(Tries to take bottle from him)
Paul, you've had enough of that.

PAUL
(Pulls bottle away from her)
Listen, this is no spur-of-the-minute thing with me, and it's not the whiskey doing
the talking either. I've been thinking of it for a long long time. This city stinks for
my money; there's nothing here but a lot of smoke, noise and corruption. I don't know
where that bus is going to take me, but I'm not getting off until I find a place where
there's plenty of fresh air, lots of room, that's what I want, lots of room, and mountains, mountains as high as you can see. Yes, sir. When I find that place I'm getting
off and that's where I'm staying.

SYLVIA

I always dreamt of going somewhere like that, ever since I was a girl; someplace
away from everyone and everything I know.

PAUL

Do you mean that?

SYLVIA

I'd give anything.

PAUL
(Puts bottle on typewriter table)
Syl.

SYLVIA

Yes, Paul?

PAUL

Listen, we . . . we get along pretty well, don't wc?

SYLVIA

We get along extremely well.

PAUL
(Standing behind her)
The times I thought of taking you in my arms and holding you . . .

SYLVIA

Oh, if you only had, Paul.

PAUL

It's not too late, is it?

SYLVIA

No, no, it's not.

PAUL

The two of us, together.
(He holds her about the waist; she clasps his hands)

SYLVIA

Oh, Paul. I'm so happy. I'll call my mother. And you call your wife. I don't want
there to be any hard feelings. Let's make it as pleasant as possible for everyone.

PAUL
(Stunned)
You want me to call my wife?

SYLVIA

Of course, silly; we're getting married, aren't we?

PAUL

But you don't understand . . .

SYLVIA

We are getting married, aren't we?

PAUL

Aw, what's the use.

SYLVIA

I know; it's my fault; no matter what I do or say it's my fault.

PAUL

No, my fault; it's my fault. I'm no good, Sylvia. I never was. I never had the guts to
do anything but feel sorry for myself. I've been a lazy, selfish son-of-a-bitch all my
life. I never did a damn thing that amounted to a bag of beans. And now . . . Oh, my
God!
(Leaning on typewriter, he sobs loudly)

35

SYLVIA

Paul, stop it; what are you doing? What's wrong?

PAUL

I don't care for myself; it's not for me. My life's over. My wife ...
(Shouting)
That bitch can go to hell! But the kids, Sylvia. I love those kids. Now what's going
to happen to them? I don't have a job; there's no money put away, nothing. What
did I do? What was I trying to prove?

SYLVIA

Why don't you go in and speak to him? Apologize, tell him anything. You're one of
the best typists he's ever had; don't forget that.

PAUL

Do you think there's a chance? I can type; no one can say I can't. That's one thing
I can do. Look, Sylvia. Look.
(He stands with his back to the typewriter and with his hands behind him types)
Check that. Go ahead. You'll find there isn't a single mistake. And this, look at this.
*(He stands between both typewriters, spreads his arms out and types on both
machines simultaneously)*

SYLVIA

I know, Paul; you're very good.

PAUL

There. Perfect. Check it. Check it. And this, Sylvia, look at this.

SYLVIA

That's enough, Paul. I believe you. I know you can ...
(He stands on the chair at his typewriter, removes one shoe, gives it to SYLVIA,
*and types with his stockinged foot, swings carriage across with his large toe, then
slumps down in chair)*
Come down from there. You are good, you're very good.

PAUL

They deserve everything I can give them, Syl. I love those kids.
(He lifts up his foot; SYLVIA *puts on his shoe)*

SYLVIA

I know. Now let's get you fixed up so you'll look presentable when you see him.
(Straightens his tie, brushes his jacket, etc.)
Stand still. Stop moving around.

PAUL

He'll never give me another chance, not after what I said to him.

SYLVIA

You just walk in and speak to him. There. Now you look fine. I'll fix things up out here. And we'd better get rid of this bottle.
(She takes it away from him as he raises it to his mouth)

PAUL

No more of that for me. I learned my lesson.

SYLVIA

I hope so. Well, go ahead in.

PAUL

Syl, I just want you to know this: if I get my job back, you're going to see some changes. Paul Cunningham has grown up at last.

SYLVIA

Go ahead in.

PAUL

No, not until I thank you for . . . for everything you've done.

SYLVIA

I didn't do a thing.

PAUL

Yes you did; more than I can thank you for. Did you ever think, Syl, what would have happened if the two of us had met before I married Barbara?

SYLVIA
(Wistfully)

Yes, I thought of it, many times.

PAUL
(Moving toward her)

Syl, listen to me . . .

SYLVIA
(Raising her hands, moving away from him)

Not that again. Please. Go in. Go on in.
(PAUL exists to employer's office. SYLVIA empties whiskey bottle in drain of water cooler, then drops bottle into basket; she picks papers from floor; sits at typewriter, puts eyeglasses on, and types. PAUL enters. He is now in his fifties)

PAUL

It's all right; it's all right. He's taken me back.

SYLVIA

I'm so glad for you.

PAUL

He was darn nice about it, too. He just listened to me and then he said, "It's understandable, Mr. Cunningham. We all have our problems."

SYLVIA

He can be nice when he wants to.

PAUL

"We all have our problems." He's not a stupid man.

SYLVIA

On the contrary, he understands a great many things.

PAUL

You know, we should buy him something; a little gift from the staff, something to show our appreciation.
(Rubbing hands, sits at typewriter)
Well, let's get to it. There's not much left to the day now.

SYLVIA

Yes, soon it'll be over.
(They type in silence. Suddenly PAUL *breaks out in forced laughter)*

SYLVIA

What's so amusing?

PAUL

Miss Supervisor . . . I'll never forget that as long as I live. "Believe me, Mr. Cunningham, I didn't ask him to be made a supervisor. I don't like telling anyone what to do."

SYLVIA

We all have our pretensions, Paul.

PAUL
(Clearing his throat)

That's very true.
(They type. SYLVIA *starts to laugh)*

PAUL

What is it? What . . . what is it? What?

SYLVIA

I was just thinking of a boy I once went with.

PAUL

. The Chinese fellow?

38

No, no. I don't know any Chinese fellow. This boy was an entertainer. He could make you laugh by just looking at you.

PAUL

Did I ever tell you, Sylvia, that I used to take singing lessons?

SYLVIA

No?

PAUL

I did. When I was eight, nine . . .

SYLVIA
(Rises, collects typed cards)

I didn't know that.

PAUL
(Sings)

Way down upon the Swanee River . . . Far, far from home . . .

SYLVIA

You do have a voice.

PAUL
(Sings monosyllabically)

Da, *da,* da, da, da, *da, da* . . .

SYLVIA
(At employer's door)

Shh, not too loudly.
(SYLVIA exits, without tidying herself, to employer's office. PAUL types and sings monosyllabically, using his typewriter as if it were a musical instrument. On the card he has just typed he notices an error, crumples it and slips it into his pocket; he continues singing. SYLVIA enters. They are now in their middle-sixties, aged, slow-moving, but not gray-wigged, not senile)

PAUL
(Looking at his watch)

Sylvia, it's twelve minutes to five.

SYLVIA

We don't generally stop until ten minutes to, Paul.

PAUL

I know. But I thought . . .

SYLVIA

That wouldn't be fair.

PAUL
You're right, as always.
(They type)

PAUL
Now, Sylvia?
(Without looking at timepiece)

SYLVIA
There's still . . . I would say a minute.
(They type)

PAUL
Now, Sylvia?

SYLVIA
Yes . . . Now.

PAUL
Thank God.

SYLVIA
I am tired. A good hot bath and then to bed with me.
(Rising he inadvertently brushes a card off the table; he picks it up, reads)

PAUL
"All wool knickers. From factory to you. At a tremendous saving." Knickers. We've been selling knickers.

SYLVIA
(Covering typewriters)
Come, come, let's put everything away.

PAUL
(Going to coat hanger)
Not many people wear knickers nowadays, do they? Knickers. They're warm, though; and practical, they're very practical.

SYLVIA
(As PAUL struggles with his coat)
Here, let me help you with that. Isn't it too early yet?

PAUL
Just getting ready.
(He helps her put on her coat)

SYLVIA
What time is it, Paul? It doesn't feel like five.

PAUL
(Looking at wristwatch)

Another . . . two minutes.
(They sit down at typewriters, in their coats, immobile, expressionless, waiting for the two minutes to pass. Then PAUL looks at his watch)

PAUL
(Rising)

It's time.

SYLVIA
(As they move toward the employer's office)

I have such a bad recollection. What is this new man's name, Paul?

PAUL

Smith or Stone or . . . I never could remember names.

SYLVIA

We'll give him a friendly good-bye just the same.
(They stand on the threshold of the office, wave and cry shrilly)

PAUL

Good night. Good night in there.

SYLVIA

Have a pleasant evening. Good night.

PAUL

I'll walk you to the subway, Sylvia.

SYLVIA

That would be very nice.
(SYLVIA stands by the door, buttoning her coat. PAUL removes some crumpled cards from his pocket, he looks at them, forlornly, lets them fall from his hands to the floor. He starts toward SYLVIA but changes his mind, returns, gets down on his haunches and picks up some crumpled cards; he looks around the office for a place to put them; finding none he slips them back into his pockets and exits with SYLVIA)

CURTAIN

The Tiger

I knew a fellow in the sixties who was the quintessential pseudointellectual/revolutionary. He worked at some soft featherbedding job and spent his evenings ranting against the system and for a world of orgastic and cultural plenty. He was always planning a huge literary work, but never got beyond explaining its significance to a small band of his admirers. He spoke with such enthusiasm and conviction that one could almost taste his accomplishments.

Among his admirers was a young lady who not only agreed with every crackpot scheme our hero advocated, but went so far as to proclaim his genius.

They were married and the last I heard he was made an officer of his union and she had written and published an original study on the nature of the overachiever.

As for the theme of the play: for every boy there's a girl and it doesn't much matter what circumstances bring them together.

—M.S.
March 14, 1983

THE TIGER, *on a double bill with* THE TYPISTS, *opened in New York on February 4, 1963, at the Orpheum Theatre. The plays were presented by Claire Nichtern.*

GLORIA   *Anne Jackson*

BEN   *Eli Wallach*

Directed by ARTHUR STORCH

Set design by WOLFGANG ROTH

A basement room, dingy, cluttered, stacks of books lying about. On the left a short flight of steps and a door leading into the street. Next to the steps is a bureau on which there is a plant and more books. In the rear a cot, a lamp, a phonograph on a small table; running over the cot is a string of laundry. Against the right wall, at an angle, is a door to the kitchen, on the door is a blackboard—the words: TODAY'S WORD, SYM-BIOSIS *are written on the blackboard. Forward, left, a wooden chair; right, a frayed bulky upholstered chair. Red water pipes cross the ceiling and come down at both sides of the room.*

Flashes of lightning break the darkness. Thunder, the sound of heavy rain.

The door is suddenly thrown open. BEN *enters, carrying* GLORIA *over his shoulder, like a sack; his raincoat is tied around the upper part of her body.*

GLORIA
(Muffled voice; kicking her legs)
For your own sake . . . put me down. Put me down . . .

BEN
(Carries her across to bed)
Stop it! Stop it! Do you think I'm playing games with you? Is that what you think? Ha! That's a laugh. This is strength you're feeling on your bones, lady, primitive, animal strength. There's no arguing with that. Oh, no.
(GLORIA is seated on edge of bed; BEN *turns on lamp)*
Now you stay there. Don't move. Don't budge an inch. I'll be right with you. In a minute . . . In a minute . . .
(He runs to door, closes it, pulls curtains over small window above bureau. GLORIA *rises, moves blindly about the room.* BEN *grabs her, drags her to the wooden chair)*
Come back. Come back here.
(He ties her wrists behind the chair with the belt of his raincoat)

GLORIA
(Muffled voice)
What are you doing? Take this off. Please. I can't breathe under here, I can't . . .

BEN
Scream; scream all you want. You have my permission. It's not going to help you, though. Not here, it won't. We're quite alone. Quite, quite alone. No conditions. I insist on that. I don't accept conditions of any kind. That's a point for you to keep in mind.
(She is tied to chair; he moves around to face her)
There. That's it. Each of us in his proper place.
(Removes raincoat from her)
You like flirting, don't you, lady? Do anything for a good time. I had those propositions before. Don't make any mistake about that.
(He takes towel from line, wipes his face)

GLORIA

But I never flirted with you. I didn't. I swear, that's the truth. This is silly. Please let me go.

BEN

Go? Let you go? After all that trouble of dragging you through those back alleys? After getting my new pants wet? Oh, no. Not a chance. Not tonight, lady. I've got something else in mind for you.

GLORIA

I don't know what you want; really, I don't. But I won't tell anyone anything. I promise. So far as I'm concerned none of this ever happened. I didn't see you. I kept my eyes closed. Look. They're still closed. I have no idea what you look like. Just let me go. Please, let me go . . .
(She sobs)

BEN

(Sits on steps, removes shoes, wet socks, takes pair of socks from bureau, puts them on; shoes remain off)
Cry. Yes. Cry. Your tears are beautiful. I can watch you all night. It's as natural for you to cry as it is for the tiger to stalk its prey and gorge itself. Cry. Go ahead. Human history is filled with countless relevant examples.

GLORIA

Why did you take me? Why out of everybody did you have to take me?

BEN

Things are what they have to be, that's why they are. You don't get it, do you? I stood in the doorway of that decrepit stationery store for three hours, for more than three hours, who knows how many. I let six, seven, eight of you go by, and then you came click-clacking along in those high-heeled shoes of yours, and I knew you were the one, it was you. At first I had a . . . a almost uncontrollable impulse to finish you off right there. Finish you off and be done with it. But when I touched you, when my fingers grabbed hold of you, a voice deep inside of me said, "No. Don't. Wait. Take her. Let it be something special and . . . and sacred even. A ritual, a ritual of . . ."

GLORIA

You're not that inhuman.

BEN

That human! That human!
(Hangs wet socks on line; in despair)
Nobody understands. Not even Schopenhauer or . . . or Nietzsche. They always have that carrot dangling in front of your nose. Be more than you are, be more than human, transcend, go above, beyond, up, up, up . . .
(At blackboard)
But no! That isn't it. I say, be less than you are. To be what you are.
(Draws a descending line)

46

Be less! less! less! than you are.
(Erases blackboard)

GLORIA

I can't talk to you. You're . . .

BEN

I'm what?

GLORIA

Nothing. Nothing.

BEN

Insane? Is that what you wanted to say? Insane?
(Paces around her chair)
I hope so. Oh, God. I hope so. I am insane, right? You wanted to say it. I didn't tell you. I didn't influence that remark. But you knew; you sensed it. I agree with your judgment. Emphatically. You don't meet people like me every day, people with my ideas, with the courage of my convictions. I am insane, say it!

GLORIA

If you'd listen to me . . .

BEN

Not until I give you permission! Is that clear? Between us, between you and me, there's only one thing that counts. Power, strength, my physical superiority, this fist and this arm. Here, tonight, I say to you I am insane so that I can be human. You see how great it is? You see how everything falls into place? You don't understand anything, do you? Linguistic concepts are too much for your little female bird-brain. But that's all right. You have other assets. You're nice to touch. I assume. You're soft. Your blood is warm and alive.
(He tries to kiss her. She moves her head away. He presses his nose to her cheek)
Now? Do I end your miserable life now? Quickly and suddenly . . .
(Looks about)
All right. All right.
(Takes record out of album cover, puts it on phonograph: music, Tschaikovsky's Concerto No. I)
We'll do it. You sit there. Right there. We'll do it now and we'll do it properly. With all the trimmings. With all . . .
(She turns her head back towards him. He kisses her, daintily, on the cheek, then shuts phonograph)
That was a little better. Sometimes the tiger has to claw the tigress; then she understands what it's all about.

GLORIA

Let me tell you . . .

BEN

Did I give you permission to speak? Did I?

GLORIA

May I have your permission?

BEN

All right. You're learning. You can speak to me now if you wish.

GLORIA

I . . . I'm a married woman. I have been married for the last six years. My husband is an . . . honest hard-working man. We have our own home; it isn't fully paid. We're not what you'd call well-off by any means. We have two small children, two little girls. And you can ask anyone out on the Island where we . . .

BEN

Enough! Enough of that noise! I don't like babbling women. You can cry, but don't babble. Is that clear? Any woman who leaves her kids to go tramping around at night is a whore and she deserves, ipso facto, what she gets.

GLORIA

I wasn't . . .

BEN

What?

GLORIA

Can I please say something?

BEN

All right, now.

GLORIA

I wasn't tramping around all night. I wasn't. Every Thursday. . . I belong to a bridge club and a few other girls whom I worked with when I was single . . . It all goes to charity!

BEN

Continue. I didn't say stop, did I?

GLORIA

It's only one night a week. I'm in every other night. I get out so little, that when I get the chance . . .

BEN
(Stands behind her, strokes her hair, gently)
Your husband takes you out on Saturdays. All husbands take their wives out on Saturdays.

GLORIA

Not for some time now. I swear to you, that's the truth. He's so tired when the weekend comes and . . . It costs so much for a baby-sitter, even if you can get someone . . . reliable. Please, don't.

48

BEN
(Facing her)

I want you to kiss me.

GLORIA

No, no . . .

BEN

I said I want you to kiss me.

GLORIA

I can't, please . . .
(She lowers her head)

· BEN

Pick up your head! Pick it up!
(She raises her head; without kissing her)
I'll accept that for now. But you'd better learn and learn quickly. I'm not to be con-
tradicted. Not in word, thought or deed. I'm all your world tonight. Remember that,
lady.

GLORIA

I won't ask you to consider what you're doing for myself. It isn't myself I'm concerned
with right now. But I do have a husband and a family. All of them will suffer. It's
not only me. Why don't you consider them? Why don't you . . .

BEN

I didn't hear a word you said because . . .
(Flaring petulantly)
because you didn't have my permission to speak! You can cry whenever you want,
however. That much I allow you because you're a woman.

GLORIA

I'm not going to cry. There's no reason to cry. I believe that there's goodness in you.
I can see it in your eyes. Isn't there someone whom you love very much?

BEN

Besides myself?

GLORIA

Besides yourself.

BEN

No one.

GLORIA

There must be someone. Your mother . . .

BEN

Don't make me laugh.

49

A wife?

BEN

Do you think I'm that dumb?

GLORIA

Then friends. You must have had friends.

BEN

No one. No one. I have no one but myself and that's all that counts. Me. Myself. The fulfillment of my own body and my own primitive soul. Sometimes ... Sometimes I walk along the street at night and my feet, as I walk, my feet feel like large soft paws, and the moon, the moon shining overhead, so brightly, so primeval, I want to raise my head and ... and let loose from inside of me some wild strange ... a sound that hasn't been heard for thousands of years, but it's inside of us, you see, deep, deep inside of us ... Tonight I don't have to hold anything in. Tonight I have you. To play with. To destroy. To do whatever I want with. After that, I don't care. I want you to kiss me. Now.

GLORIA

You're driving me out of my mind.

BEN

You don't want to?

(She does, on his cheek)

Not good enough!

GLORIA

Leave me alone, leave me alone ...

BEN

(Turns on phonograph: music)

All right, prepare yourself! We don't have to speak any more. We'll be quiet and still and listen to our heartbeats, pounding, pounding ... That which is deepest in us will rise, will overcome us in a moment of blind primitive passion ... Then we will be ourselves, the essence, the primal force, free of all hypocrisy, free of all pretending, pretending to morality, pretending to sanity, pretending ...

(GLORIA kisses him lightly)

Unsatisfactory. You will hold your lips to mine until I give you the signal. Now.

(He snaps his fingers. She kisses him. He shuts phonograph)

Better. There are signs of progress. I'm glad to see that some learning is taking place.

GLORIA

My arms are sore. Can't you untie me?

BEN

Did you speak?

GLORIA

I . . . I didn't mean to. Can I ask you a favor?

BEN
(Erases board; absent-mindedly)
Was it you who wanted to say something?

GLORIA

I have a favor to ask of you.

BEN
(Reluctantly)
All right. Go ahead.

GLORIA

The blood isn't circulating in my arms. I'd really appreciate it if you untied me. I won't try to get away.

BEN

I don't believe you. Not for a single solitary minute do I believe you. But . . . I have no objection. Tonight the word fear is in your vocabulary, not mine.
(He unties her)
Of course you realize that if you do try to get away I'll have to punish you. Maybe even kill you, right here on the spot! You can never tell when I'll lose control of myself. So be careful!
(Pulls threateningly on raincoat belt)

GLORIA

Thank you. You see, there is good in you. You can be reasonable.

BEN

Take off that skirt.

GLORIA

Isn't there any way I can convince you?

BEN

No. Do as I say.
(He snaps belt in air)
Do you hear me?
(She removes her skirt, stands in loud garish slip)
Nice. Very, very nice. Let me have it. Now sit down in that chair. Go ahead.
(She sits on wooden chair. He looks at skirt, puts it on bureau. He then takes cigarette and matches from bureau, lights cigarette and sits down on steps)

GLORIA

May I have one?

BEN

No.

GLORIA

It's cold here. I'm freezing.

(He ignores her)

You could make yourself some easy money if you just let me go. My husband would gladly give it to you. Why don't you phone him? You can ask for . . . five, ten thousand dollars. He can get it. Wouldn't you be better off with all that money?

BEN

A man lives in his mind, not in a place. No use explaining it to you. I'd be wasting my time. Idiots. A world of idiots and illiterates, too damn dense to comprehend the most basic laws governing their own existence. What does the name of Plato mean to them? Or Beethoven or Spinoza or Rembrandt? Idiots. You all follow one another like a pack of sheep, one following the other. . . Up at nine, out of the house, into the subway, down the street, work until twelve, lunch, everybody eating, over the counter, munch, munch, munch . . . chock-full-a-nuts, munch, munch, munch, back at one, work until five, down the street, into the subway, out of the subway, into the house, in bed at ten . . . Sheep, millions of sheep.

GLORIA

Out on the Island where I live . . .

BEN

Did I ask your opinion?

GLORIA

I wanted to say . . .

BEN

I'm not interested in what you wanted to say. I'm not giving lessons in democratic principles. Not this semester, lady.

(Rises)

Everybody has something to say; everybody has an opinion to give you. But do they have the background, the training, the mental discipline, to give you an opinion on the facts? On objectivity? On scientific comprehension? Oh, no. Not that. But they all babble. Right?

GLORIA

Yes.

BEN

You think I'm right?

GLORIA

Yes, I do. I agree with you.

What was I right about? Do you know? Do you fathom the implications, the ramifications?

(At blackboard, writes A, B, C)

Reiterate my line of reasoning and present me with a brief summation of its salient points. Begin, now.

GLORIA

I couldn't . . .

BEN

I said begin now! This minute, begin!

GLORIA

I'll try. I think what you were saying is that in a democracy where everybody has a voice in the government, despite intelligence, despite ability, this leads to the false belief . . .

BEN

(Erases board, quickly, angrily)

Is that what you think?

GLORIA

Isn't it . . .

BEN

Who wrote *The Divine Comedy?*

GLORIA

Dante?

BEN

When was the Civil War?

GLORIA

Between 1861 and 1865.

BEN

How do you spell concatenation?

GLORIA

Concatenation. C-O-N-C-A-T-E-N-A-T-I-O-N. How do you spell pulchritude?

BEN

Pulchritude. Capital P-U-L-C-H-R-I-T-U-D-E. Physiology.

GLORIA

Physiology. P-H-Y-S-I-O-L-O-G-Y. Somnambulism.

BEN

Somnambulism. Capital S-O-M-N-A-M-B-U-L-I-S-M. Miscegenation.

GLORIA

Miscegenation. M-I-C-S . . .

BEN

M-I-S-C . . .
(Writes S C, S C on blackboard)
S-C! S-C! E-G-E-N-A-T-I-O-N. You stupid bird-brain. Don't you dare speak loosely to
me. Not unless you're willing to pay the consequences.
(Wagging finger)
That's a point for you to keep in mind.
(Erases board)

GLORIA

I will. In the future. I will. May I . . . please have a glass of water?

BEN

I'm not your servant. Maybe tomorrow, but not tonight. Oh, no. Not tonight, lady.

GLORIA

I'll get it, if . . .

BEN

Ahh, sit there and shut up.
*(BEN goes into kitchen, closing door behind him. GLORIA rises, picks up her
pocketbook, skirt, starts moving up the steps. At once the entrance door is thrown
open and BEN enters, holding a glass of water. GLORIA jumps back in fright)*

BEN

You going someplace?

GLORIA

No, I was just . . .

BEN

Never mind you were just. I know what you were just.
(He empties glass of water contemptuously into plant)
You can try those tricks on your husband, but not with me. Is that clear? I know
what goes on, all right. You're all the same. Every damn one of you.
(Touches wet feet with annoyance)
You wait until they go off to work and then it's first come, first served. You ask them
in for a cup of coffee; tell them there's no hurry . . . Oh, no. There's no hurry. There's
no one at home, you make sure they know that. I had those propositions before,
plenty of times.

GLORIA

I've never been untrue to my husband, never. I swear to you.

BEN
(Points)

Get back to your chair.

GLORIA
(On wooden chair)
I won't try to leave again. Really. I'd like a cigarette, please.

BEN
(Takes socks from bureau)
I'm running out of socks, damn it! If you try anything, it'll be the last time. I hope you had enough education to understand that. You did go to school, didn't you?
(Sits on steps, puts on dry pair of socks)

GLORIA
You probably won't believe it, but I graduated from college. So did my husband. That's where we met. We were both taking the same course. He . . . sat right next to me.

BEN
That explains your ignorance, thoroughly and completely. I remember once I walked into a class at some stupid college uptown. I thought I would listen to the wisdom of the ages, the prophets speaking through the intelligent and refined mind of a scholar, a pedant.
(Rises)
There was a young cockeyed kid standing on a high platform. He had one hand in his pocket; the other hand he was waving in the air as if he was leading a band. "The packaging of an article cannot be circumscribed, ladies and gentlemen, by a few simple rules. We must here consider not only the item which is to be packaged, but the conditions under which it must be sold, the costs involved, the packaging prevalent on the market, motivating the buyer, satisfying the producer, complying with state and federal regulations . . ."
(Laughing)
I started laughing like crazy. I couldn't help myself. I had to put a handkerchief over my face and stagger out of there.
(Grimly)
That was as far as I got in college.
(Hangs wet socks on line)

GLORIA
You mean you're not a graduate?

BEN
Did I tell you I was?

GLORIA
No, of course not. But . . . your vocabulary, the way you talk . . . I was almost certain . . .

BEN

College is for imbeciles, for sheep, for baa baa sheep. I taught myself everything I know.

(Lifts armful of books from floor)

By reading, by studying, by perusing the prophets, the philosophers, the anthropologists, the poets, the scientists. Every night I read, whatever I could lay my hands on, years and years of reading and studying until . . . until I gave myself a diploma: it was a doctorate in comprehensive ontology.

(Puts books on floor)

I understood then, I saw through the lies and hypocrisy; the truth was as clear to me as a ball of crystal. They wanted to dehumanize me, yes, yes, precisely that; they wanted to make a sheep of me, a baa baa sheep. That . . . That which was purest in me, the animal savage, innocent, primitive, childlike, that I had to save, I had to salvage and redeem; and it's for that, for the right to be human as I must be to live, that I offer you in sacrifice on this evening of May the 22nd.

GLORIA

Does it have to be a living human being?

BEN

You poor bird-brain. You poor ignorant bird-brain. What do you know about being? Being? Ha! What do you know about your own body, about the elementary physical processes of your own body? For example. Did you ever ask yourself why you're so small there?

(Points at her breasts)

GLORIA
(Looking down)

Small? Where?

BEN

There! There! Right where you're looking. The mammalian glands. Your mother was small, too, I bet. Hereditary. Genetic evolution. A fascinating field. Fascinating. Darwin, Lysenko, Dobzansky . . . In a hundred years you won't have any. There won't be any. Nobody'll have any. That's right.

(Outlines on blackboard)

The giraffe's neck, number one; the monkey's tail, number two.

(Turning)

Those things are going to disappear. Like that.

(Snaps fingers)

How does it happen? Lysenko! That's how. But you wouldn't know anything about that.

(Erases board)

GLORIA

I'm interested in it. For a number of years I subscribed to one of the science magazines, and each month they'd have articles on a particular branch of science, say, biology or . . .

BEN

Let me have your shoes.

GLORIA

My shoes?

BEN

Did you hear me?

GLORIA

Why do you want my shoes?
(Gives them to him)

BEN

We come closer and closer to the end which is the beginning. The beginning is in the end and the end is in the beginning. Time is like an egg and life ... life is like a chicken that lays the egg.

GLORIA

Is ... Is that original?

BEN

What do you think it is?

GLORIA

I like it. I do.

BEN
(Sits in upholstered chair)
Nights and nights alone in here, studying, reading the masters, looking deep, deep inside myself ...

GLORIA

Despite everything, I can't help enjoy listening to you. Before I married, you know, I was a social worker with the Department of Welfare. It was part of my job to direct people into work they were suited for, temperamentally, educationally ... It was very absorbing work. I really hated to leave. But ... Why didn't you go to college? I think you could have made a very good instructor.

BEN

At one time that was my ambition. To teach in college. To be a professor of epistemology and linguistics. Those bastards. They're not worth spitting on. I don't need them. I don't need anybody!

GLORIA

What happened?

BEN

Did I give you permission to speak?

57

I failed the damn entrance exam. I . . . I can't speak French and they don't take you unless you can speak French or some damn language.
(Almost bawling)
Oh, I tried, I tried. But I couldn't do it. I couldn't. Go ahead. Laugh. Is that what you feel like doing?

GLORIA

Not in the least. I just can't understand it. It shouldn't have been difficult for you.

BEN
(Takes books from bureau drawer, gives them to her)
See all these books? French books. I took courses in it, studied it with tutors, with Frenchmen, with whoever I could find. It wouldn't sink in. Call it an emotional block. Call it whatever the hell you want. I don't give a damn any more for that crap. I have other ambitions now. More important things to do. Life, that's what counts. Not degrees or accomplishments or being sucked in. I don't accept it. Do you hear me? I don't accept it!

GLORIA
But it isn't too late. You still can do it.

BEN
What are you talking about? Do you know how old I am?

GLORIA
I'd say thirty-six, thirty-seven.

BEN
Forty-two in August. No. I'm not interested any more.

GLORIA
But forty-two isn't old; that's where you're so wrong. You're in the prime of life and isn't that the time to get an education?

BEN
Are you deaf? I told you they wouldn't take me.

GLORIA
Only because you didn't know French. I remember the trouble I had passing my French exams.

BEN
You speak French?

GLORIA
(Coyly; as is)
Oui, un petit.
(BEN rises, angrily takes books from her and dumps them into bureau drawer)

Get back to your chair. Get back . . .

I'm in my chair. This is my chair!

Not that chair.
(Points to upholstered chair)
That chair! That chair! Get over there. Go ahead. I don't want to hear another word
out of you, understand? I want silence, complete and utter silence.
(GLORIA is reseated. BEN removes jacket)
If I lose control of myself, you're the one who's going to pay for it. So be careful. I'm
warning you. Too much damn talking anyway. Everybody has something to say. But
do they know. . .
*(Indifferently, he presses his hand on the hotwater pipe, pulls it away with an
inaudible howl, wags it furiously)*
. . . what they say? Do they care? They babble. They don't talk to one another. Oh,
no. They talk to themselves. They talk to their own egos.

That is perceptive of you. There's no communication between people any more.

Did I tell you to shut up? Listen. You might learn something.
(Slight pause)
There's no communication between people any more. Everybody's inside of himself,
inside in his own little egotistical shell. You meet somebody in the street, they say
"How are you?" Do you think they care how you are? Do you think they care? Ha!
That's a laugh. It just comes out of their mouths, drivels out; there's no feelings, no
interest, no humanity, nothing. "How are you?" Ha! What a mockery. What a
deceit. You say, "Oh, I'm fine." And they don't even listen.

They don't listen.

That's what gets me. They ask the question, "How are you?" And when you answer
them, when you say, "I'm fine," they don't even listen; they don't care. I know. I see
what's happening. A couple of days ago I met this kid who works in the A & P
where I buy my things. He stopped me and said, "How are you?" By the time I
could say, "I'm fine," he was on the crosstown bus, three blocks down the street!

They're all alike. They're not concerned with human values, only with making
money, with keeping up with the Joneses.

Are you going to shut up? I said I want silence from you, complete and utter silence!

They're not concerned with human values, only with keeping up with the Joneses, with grabbing as much as they can get their hands on. That's all they think about. Money, the bitch-goddess! They're all after it.

GLORIA

But what matters, finding one's identity, that they don't care about. That's why there are no individuals today.

BEN
(Sitting down)

That's right.

GLORIA

Everybody wears the same clothes, does the same kind of work, talks about the same subjects . . .

BEN

It's as if they were all coming out of Detroit on the assembly line.

GLORIA

You couldn't have put it better. That's precisely what all this talk on conformity is.

BEN

I know. I know. You don't have to tell me. It's getting so bad people are beginning to resemble one another. I mean, actually, physically resemble one another. You think I'm kidding? You walk along the street any day in the week and try to get somebody's attention. Try it. Go ahead. They don't look at you. They don't want to look at you. Stick your head right under their noses and they still won't look at you. Why should they? You look just like everybody else!

GLORIA

I couldn't contradict you. I see it with my own eyes.

BEN
(Rises)

I've been living in this place for seven years, seven years! Do you know what the landlady said to me when I went up to pay her the rent last time? "Sorry. No vacancies."

GLORIA

She didn't know you.

BEN

After seven years. But that's not all of it. Do you know what happened to me tonight? Listen to this. I walked into a restaurant to get something to eat when this woman with a man's hat on her head, get that, a man's hat on her head, I never saw her before in my life . . . This woman grabbed my arm and said, "You son-of-a-bitch, you're late!" I said, "Lady, what are you talking about?" She said, "You know damn

well what I'm talking about. Come on home, you little piss-pot, I want to get you home; come on . . ." She kept pulling at my arm and . . . Look.
> *(Brings her his raincoat, shows her the sleeve)*

Look what she did. Tore my raincoat.

GLORIA

Oh, that's awful. That is awful.

BEN

She kept pulling at my arm and hitting me over the head with her damn pocketbook. There was a whole crowd watching us. I don't know how the hell I got away from her. And I still didn't have anything to eat.

GLORIA

She must have been drunk.

BEN

Drunk or crazy, what difference does it make? The point is that everybody's beginning to resemble one another. That's what we're up against. Read your Mendel. Read your history books on the Industrial Revolution. It's all there. It's no secret. Try to live in this world. Go ahead. Try.

GLORIA

It's becoming impossible. I know.

BEN
> *(Seated)*

Impossible. That's just the word. And what do you think'll happen once this population explosion we're having gets moving, huh? Can you imagine what it's going to be like with three million people standing at the bus stop, all looking the same, all wearing the same hat and coat!

GLORIA

We won't even be able to use umbrellas.

BEN

You bet we won't.

GLORIA

Nobody listens.

BEN

Chaos. It'll be sheer chaos.

GLORIA

But does anybody listen?

BEN

Millions and millions of people; millions of sheep.

GLORIA

Nobody listens.

BEN

What?

GLORIA

I said nobody listens.

BEN

You put your finger right on it.

GLORIA

That's how it is. When it's too late, then they'll decide to do something about it.

BEN

I don't know. And they accept it. That's what gets me. They accept it.
(As she talks GLORIA *rises, picks up her pocketbook, returns to upholstered chair; she takes a cigarette out and then discovers that she has no matches; she goes to bureau, picks up a book of matches, returns to chair, lights a cigarette)*

GLORIA

Out on the Island where I live, that's where you really see what's happening. It's unbelievable the extent to which they all live the same dreary lives, doing the same dull things. I've seen it grow; and it gets worse and worse. People when they first move into the neighborhood always seem interested in a great many things and they seem to have a great many interests. But after six months ... All they can talk about is crab grass and bowling and what somebody else's wife is doing. That's where the danger is. It's not so much that we're all going to look alike; after all, that's only physical, but that we're all going to think alike and have the same social attitudes— that's something to keep in mind, the same social attitudes. And right there is where the real danger is.

BEN

You're telling me? Listen, lady, I've been fighting it for years!

GLORIA
(Seated)

You should fight it. We all should fight it. That's why our hospitals are filled with people who absolutely cannot function on any level. Do you know how many beds there are in our hospitals for each patient that needs a bed? You wouldn't believe it if I told you. But there are statistics that prove, conclusively, that in some hospitals there are three patients for every bed. Three patients for every bed. Think about it a minute. And it'll get worse and worse and nobody'll do anything about it. At least nearly nobody. The girls with whom I play bridge, we had raffle books printed and what we're doing is trying to get as many beds into these hospitals as we can; make every effort to get each patient a bed.
(Removes raffle book from pocketbook; rises)

It's only one dollar a raffle or a book of twenty raffles for nineteen dollars.
(A pause as she holds out raffle book; BEN *stares dumbly at her)*
You ... You can win a television set or an AM/FM radio or ... or a vacuum cleaner ...

BEN
(Another pause; then with sudden fervor, rises)
And what about the atomic bomb, huh? What about the atomic bomb? You think they know what they're doing? Those lunatics don't know from one minute to the next what they're doing. But don't say anything. Don't do anything. Let them blow us all up. What the hell, we don't count. There's a million more where we came from.

GLORIA
I never trusted any of them.

BEN
Two thousand years of civilization, two thousand years, and the only way we can survive is by digging holes in the ground and living like the lowest specie of insect life.

GLORIA
So long as they talk of what's happening in outer space and all the great progress we're supposed to be making.

BEN
Outer space. Outer space. Up theirs with outer space. What about us down here?

GLORIA
They must think we're all a bunch of fools. I had an argument with someone about this: he was so certain we have nothing to worry about. But try to argue with someone while he's pulling out crab grass. It's a joke out there. Everything's a joke.

BEN
It's that bad, huh?

GLORIA
You don't know the half of it. Most of the time I don't know what to do with myself. There's no one I can really talk to. And as for intellectual excitement or appreciation of the arts ... It's another world. I have to come to the city just for a breath of fresh air.

BEN
I couldn't live anywhere else myself.

GLORIA
We had a place downtown for a few years but we had to plan for when the children were ready for school ... You know how the schools are in the city.

BEN

Idiots. The whole system's filled with idiots.

GLORIA

They're driving out the middle class, that's what they're doing.

BEN

Ahh, what's the use of talking?

GLORIA
(Seated in upholstered chair)

It helps. It does. It's good to talk about these things.
(Slight pause)
You are making a mistake, you know. I can teach you French. There's no reason why you shouldn't . . .

BEN

Are you deaf? I told you it's too late.

GLORIA

But it's not too late. It's really not.

BEN

Like hell it isn't. Do you know how old I am?

GLORIA

I'd say . . . forty-two.

BEN

That's right. How did you know?

GLORIA

Because I know people. I know you and I know what you're capable of. Look. Sit down. We have time, don't we? There's no hurry. My husband goes to bed at nine. He never waits up for me and he never knows when I get in. What book do you want to use?
(Takes book from bureau drawer; returns to upholstered chair)
This one looks as if it'll do. We'll try it. Sit down. Please. We'll start at the beginning.
(Pulls wooden chair closer; reads first-year French, badly)
Bonjour, monsieur.
(No response)
Are you going to do it with me or not?

BEN
(Sits on wooden chair; reads, unenthusiastically)
Bonjour, mademoiselle.

GLORIA

Very good. That was very good. Je m'appelle Gloria. Comment vous appelez-vous?

BEN
Je m'appelle Benjamin.

GLORIA

No, not quite; hold your lips like this and let the words run into each other. Like this. Je m'appelle Benjamin. Try it.

BEN

Je m'appelle Benjamin.

GLORIA

Now you have it.
(Reads)
Comment allez-vous, monsieur?

BEN
(Reads)
Très bien, merci; et vous?

GLORIA

Pas trop mal, merci; mais mon frère est malade.

BEN

C'est dommage. Je regrette beaucoup.

GLORIA

Wonderful. That was really wonderful.

BEN

It didn't sound bad, did it?

GLORIA

Bad? It was absolutely perfect. Why, we sounded just like a French couple sitting in their home and chatting. You must have been joking when you said you couldn't learn French.

BEN

It seems a lot easier now but . . .
(Rises)
What the hell are we doing? Do you know how I live? How I support myself? I'm a postman, a letter carrier.
(Enters kitchen, returns with bag of tangerines, offers one to GLORIA; they are both seated, eating tangerines)
I go from door to door, ringing bells and opening mailboxes. Me, with what I know, with my education. Okay, so that's it. That's all I'm good for. They say so. They lay down the law. This is what you are. This is how you have to spend your life. Oh, no. I don't accept it. I don't accept those conditions.

GLORIA

It's criminal, that's what it is. Just look how far you've gone, with no one's help, through your own efforts. It would be a pity if you gave everything up now. I know you could be an instructor, there isn't a doubt in my mind. Try. It's for your own good, you know.

BEN

It's not as simple as you're making it.

GLORIA

I'm not saying it's simple, but why should you have to suffer because you have the courage to live your own life, without compromising, without accepting the lies? When I think of the people who are able to get ahead nowadays . . .

BEN

You don't have to tell me. But that's what they want, that's what they've geared the whole stupid society to.

GLORIA

It makes my blood boil.

BEN

Just because they've got a college degree or know how to wear those tight faggot pants . . . You wait. Russia's going to crush us like a bunch of ants if we don't wise up.

GLORIA

You don't know how right you are. My own husband, he has absolutely no talent in anything. I don't think he's ever said or done an original thing. And as for reading a book . . . Just try to get him to read a book. I tell you, if not for the children . . . But that's another story. Do you know what he is? Listen to this. An assistant executive, he's an assistant executive in one of the largest textile factories in the city, and he makes every year—wait till you hear this, twelve thousand dollars for sitting behind a desk and cutting Kewpie dolls out of scraps of material.

BEN

I bet he's a college graduate.

GLORIA

Do you know why? I watched him. I know. He used to sit in his seat all during the lecture, hardly moving, every muscle in his face absolutely rigid. He's stare up at the instructor with wide-open eyes, as if he was listening to a sermon, but there were earplugs in his ears; he hates listening to anyone but himself. At the end of each lecture he'd go up to the instructor and say, "My name is William Hamlin. I want you to know, Professor, that your lecture tonight was one of the most brilliant I ever heard."

BEN

They're not interested in the person, not in what the individual can do. All they want to know is how many years did you take this course, how many points do you have in this subject or that subject. You need twelve points in social psychology to become a supervisor in the post office. I couldn't even get that!

GLORIA

Then go for your degree, Ben. Prove to them that you're a lot better and a lot smarter than any of them. You can do it.

BEN

What makes you so damn sure?

GLORIA

Because I have confidence in you.

BEN

Do you mean that?

GLORIA
(Softly)

I do, Ben.
            (After exchanging glances, holds out book, reads)
Bon soir, monsieur.

BEN
(Reads, eagerly)

Comment vous portez-vous ce soir?

GLORIA

Good. Je me porte très bien, merci.

BEN

Comment va votre soeur?

GLORIA
(Corrects him)

Comment va votre soeur?

BEN

Comment va votre soeur?

GLORIA
(Nods)

Elle a mal à la tête.

BEN

C'est très désagréable.

GLORIA

Excellent. That was excellent, Ben.

67

BEN
(Stares intently at her, not from book)

Mademoiselle?

GLORIA
(Puts book aside)

Monsieur?

BEN

Comment vous appelez-vous?

GLORIA

Je m'appelle Gloria, monsieur; et vous?

BEN

Je m'appelle Benjamin.

GLORIA

Comment allez-vous, Monsieur Benjamin?

BEN

Très bien, merci; et vous?

GLORIA

Très bien.

BEN
(Touches her shoulder, uncertainly)

Mademoiselle . . .

GLORIA
(Rising, coyly)

Monsieur?

BEN
(Rising, heatedly)

Mademoiselle.

GLORIA
(Melting)

Monsieur.

BEN
(Hugging her)

Oh, mademoiselle, ma chérie, mademoiselle . . .

GLORIA
(Embracing him)

Monsieur; mon magnifique monsieur.

BEN
(Lifts her off her feet, carries her to bed, jubilantly)
Oh, mademoiselle, ma chérie, ma chérie . . .

GLORIA
(Kicking her feet, playfully protesting)
Oh, non, non, non, non. Non, monsieur. Monsieur . . .

BEN
Oui, mademoiselle. Oui. Oui. Oui. Oui . . .
*(GLORIA pulls cord of lamp, turning out light, throwing bed in darkness. Unseen,
BEN turns on the phonograph: the main theme of Tschaikovsky's Concerto blares
out. Shortly GLORIA turns on light, shuts phonograph. BEN is not seen.
GLORIA puts on her skirt, her shoes. BEN enters from the kitchen. They are both
vaguely uncomfortable)*

GLORIA
Will I be seeing you again?

BEN
It's up to you.

GLORIA
I'd like to, very much. I wasn't lying about anything I said.
(Putting on makeup)
You are going to try, aren't you?

BEN
Maybe. It's something I always wanted.

GLORIA
Then you'll certainly get it. I know you will. Look. I can come every Thursday night
and help you with your French. We can study together. You won't have any trouble
passing the exam this time.
(Picking up book)
Here's what I'd like you to do by next week. Read from the beginning to . . . here.
And do these exercises on pages five and six. Is that too much for you?

BEN
I can do it. What about your husband?

GLORIA
(Seated on arm of upholstered chair)
He wouldn't know if the roof fell on him. He'll think I'm playing bridge with the
girls. We can meet at the same place.

BEN
In front of the stationery store?

69

GLORIA

Seven-thirty.

BEN

Seven-thirty.

GLORIA

Do I get a good-night kiss?

(He bends over, kisses her)

That wasn't good enough.

(He kisses her again)

That was a little better.

(He kisses her a third time)

That ... That was a lot better. Next time I come I'm going to give this place a good cleaning. It's a mess.

(At top of steps)

Bon soir, my darling.

BEN

Bon soir.

(GLORIA exits. BEN sits in upholstered chair and studies his lesson in the French book as the light fades)

CURTAIN

Fragments

I broke myself into three parts and named the parts Max, Baxter, and Jax.

Ann is a facsimile of my wife.

The time of the play is prior to my marriage.

After my marriage I'm happy to say the three parts of myself came together of their own accord in a single person.

After my marriage, however, my wife broke into three parts: she gave birth to our two children.

"Is that all you have to say about the play?"

"That's it."

"Listen, if you don't treat your work seriously, no one will."

"So?"

"So don't you like it when people say you're profound and perceptive and have insight into the human condition?"

"Do you know what I like? I like to feel good."

"Is feeling good all you have to tell us?"

"No. I said feeling good is what I like. But if you want me to tell you something, I'll tell you this: there are no winners in the game of life."

—M. S.
March 9, 1983

FRAGMENTS *was first presented in New York City, by Edgar Lansbury and Marc Merson, at the Cherry Lane Theater on October 2, 1967.*

JAX	*Humbert Allen Astredo*
BAXTER	*Gene Hackman*
MAX	*James Coco*
ANN	*Tresa Hughes*

Directed by LARRY ARRICK
Set design by KERT LUNDELL
Costumes by LIZ DOMINICK
Lighting design by ROGER MORGAN

A room divided into three smaller "rooms" only by the arrangement of the furniture and a pattern of imaginary lines. Window in left wall, entrance door right wall, rear.

J A X's room is on the left: a single bed parallel to the window. B A X T E R's room is in the center: a large dilapidated upholstered chair; behind the chair is a chest of drawers with an attached mirror from which ribbons, kewpie-dolls, bric-a-brac dangle. M A X's room is on the right, a low trunk, forward, a desk and chair, parallel to the right wall; on the rear wall there are two neat shelves holding medicines, brushes and books; on the right wall is a small Vermeer reproduction, unframed; neatly arranged on the desk is a cup with pencils and pens in it, folders and papers; attached to the leg of the desk by a bicycle chainlock is an Olivetti portable typewriter.

The light is fully on.

J A X is lying in bed, supine, covered to his ankles with blankets: his shoes rest on a number of pillows at the foot of the bed, pointing upwards, several inches apart. Only the soles of his shoes can be seen.

JAX
(As he coughs weakly, then suddenly, without pain or emotion)
Oh, my God. It's here, at last. It's here. Soon. Soon it'll be over. Soon it'll be over. Come now; let it come now; come now; come now; come . . .
(He coughs again, weakly, his arms rise slightly and fall to the sides of the bed: he is silent. B A X T E R enters, flushed, panting. He is somewhat good-looking, although pudgy, dissipated, balding. His clothes—jacket, pants, unbuttoned shirt— are rumpled and dirty)

BAXTER
Jax? Jax? I'm back. I'm . . . are you playing dead again? Jax, are you . . . Don't ask me where I was. Don't ask me. I don't know. I don't know what happened to me.
(He picks up toy telescope, clings to rear wall as he goes to window, not stepping into J A X's room, he squints through telescope at room across alleyway)
Is she in tonight? Is she . . . the light's on. She has to be in. She never goes out and leaves the light on. I can't see her, though . . .
(He clings to rear wall to return to his own room: he removes his clothes, leaving them in a pile on the floor; under his clothes he is wearing a faded wrinkled pair of pajamas; from the floor, in a pile, he picks up another set of clothes just as rumpled and dirty as the clothes he has taken off; he puts them on)
What a nightmare I've been through. What a nightmare. How long was I gone? Four days? Five? I don't know what the hell got into me. I remember walking down Second Avenue, to the grocery store, I told you I was only going down to get something to eat but . . . In the street . . . did I see anything? What was it?
(Shaking his head)
I don't remember. Some dirty kids playing in the gutter, yelling . . . a car, a big yellow convertible it was, with an old man sitting behind the wheel, honking the horn . . . a woman, there was a woman sitting on a stoop . . .

(Shaking his head)

No. That wasn't it. I don't remember. But I ... I went up to Third Avenue and I had a beer. I had a beer and ... I don't remember. I don't ... Jax? Jax, are you all right. Jax?

(He moves towards JAX, *about to cross imaginary line separating their rooms)*

JAX

(Without moving, shouting)

Don't come into my room!

BAXTER

(Jumping back, apologetically)

I wasn't. I wasn't, Jax. I thought something might be wrong. Jax ... I did some terrible things, some awful things.

(Seated in upholstered chair)

I didn't want to start drinking. That wasn't what I had in mind. I was going down for a can of soup, a can of vegetable soup. Don't you remember me telling you? "I'll be back in five minutes, Jax. Five minutes. I'm just going down to get myself a can of soup. I'm ..." And I meant it, Jax. I wasn't lying. That's all I had in mind. I went down. It was beautiful out. Beautiful. I never saw the sky looking so blue, so real, not in the city ... I ... I didn't want to start drinking, Jax.

(His face creases as if he is about to cry)

Do you believe me? Do you believe me, Jax?

(No answer, he starts towards JAX's room)*

Jax? Jax?

JAX

(Without moving, shouting)

Dooon't come into my room!

BAXTER

(Moving back, angrily)

I thought so. I thought that's what you were doing. Playing dead again. Jax, you are a phony, do you hear me? You are a phony, buddy; a hypocrite, a liar, a stinking ...

(He stops abruptly, sits down in upholstered chair, brushes back his hair)

I don't know why I even bother talking to you. If you knew some of the things I did these past few days ... I'm worse than you are, Jax. I'm worse. What the hell got into me? Why did I start drinking? Why did I stop? Jax ... Jax, I can't live in this world. I can't.

(Again his face creases as if he is about to cry)

I always want to cry, did you know that? My head is filled with tears, it's bloated and swollen with tears. They drown my eyes, my tongue; when I cut my face shaving in the morning, they pour out like a cataract; and when I ... ahhh, what's the use? It's no use.

(Rises)

Jax, do you have any money? Jax ... please ... you bastard! You selfish bastard!

(He spots someone in room across alleyway, quickly gets telescope, puts it to his eye and moves to window, clinging to rear wall)

She's there. There she is, Jax. She was taking a shower. She's wearing her blue terrycloth bathrobe. I can almost smell the steam rising from her body. Ohh, she's nice, Jax. She's really nice. If I had a woman like that I'd say, "I love you. I love you. I love you."

(He presses his face to window and shouts)

I LOVE YOU!

(He quickly pulls his head back and throws himself stiffly and fearfully against rear wall so as not to be seen)

Whew, too much. I need a drink. There's no getting away from it. I gotta have a drink and that's a fact of life.

(He moves along wall, hugging it, behind imaginary line; he pulls out his pockets to make certain he has no money. He spreads out sheets of newspaper so as not to leave any possible marks on the floor before entering MAX's room)

JAX

Stay out of Max's room, Baxter. He won't like it.

BAXTER

Don't you worry about it.

(In MAX's room BAXTER searches about for money, careful not to disturb anything, first giving his attention to the shelves and then the desk)

I'll tell you something, buddy. Maybe if I could come back once, just once, and I didn't have to look at you laying there like that, maybe I'd be all right then, maybe I wouldn't have to drink to get your stink out of my nose, maybe I wouldn't have to . . .

JAX

A letter, Baxter. Write a letter for me.

BAXTER

(Without interrupting his search for money)

Go to hell.

JAX

I'm dying, Baxter.

BAXTER

If you weren't, I wouldn't recognize you.

JAX

One letter, Baxter. One last letter. Then you can divide the room in half. There'll be more room for him, more room for you.

BAXTER

(Picks up cup from desk, looks into it, then sets it down again)

How do I know you're not lying? You said all this before, buddy. What guarantees do you give me?

JAX

My will power. My convictions.

BAXTER
(With interest)

You're going to force yourself ...
 (BAXTER picks up newspaper from floor, backs out of MAX's room)

JAX

Do I have to? One dies, Baxter. Like a clock ticking. Like a pebble dropping. Now I am. Now ... where? Where am I? There. It's over. No more, Baxter. No more.

BAXTER

I've never seen a dead person, Jax. When you die, I'm going to celebrate. That's right. I'm going to celebrate.
 (Waving newspaper)
I'm going to dance in the street, set off firecrackers, wave a big flag ... you know what day it's going to be for me, Jax? The Fourth of July. Freedom day. You bet!

JAX

One letter. One last letter. They have to know, Baxter. Someone has to tell them. The truth. How it is. The truth.

BAXTER

Are you going to die tonight, Jax? Are you?

JAX

More room for you, Baxter. More room for him.

BAXTER
(Throws newspaper away)

Okay. Fine. I agree. What's the letter?

JAX

Write in ink.

BAXTER
(Protesting)

Do you want me to ...

JAX

Write in ink!

BAXTER
(Takes pad, pen from bureau)

Okay. In ink.
 (Moves to upholstered chair which he starts to lift)
Can I bring my chair into your room, next to your bed?

JAX

No. Write.

BAXTER
(Drops chair, sits down, impatiently)

Go.

JAX

"To the Atomic Energy Commission." Do you have it?

BAXTER

I have it.

JAX

Read it back to me.

BAXTER

"To the Atomic Energy Commission."

JAX

Good. Now. "To the Atomic Energy Commission. Dear Sirs. Keep up the good work. Best regards."

BAXTER

Is that all?

JAX

That's all. Sign my name. Mail it.

BAXTER
(Rises, puts pad and pen back on bureau)

And now?

JAX

And now . . . now it's over, Baxter. At last. It's over. Now, now it comes, now, now, now, now . . .

BAXTER
(Over JAX's *"nows")*

Jax, it's not out of hate I want you to die, you understand that, don't you? Sometimes, I . . . I feel very close to you and . . . I think of you a lot; an awful lot. These past few days when I was drinking, I remember I used to think about you, back here in the room, and I . . . I envied you, Jax. I envied you!

JAX
(Softly)

When we were boys on the cracked and broken streets . . .

BAXTER
(Excitedly)

That's right? That's right, Jax! What a time that was!

77

JAX

How we laughed in our secret caves . . .

BAXTER

Remember? Remember, Jax? We were always hiding; we were always finding places to hide in!

JAX

Darkness was light . . . the cold was warmth . . .

BAXTER

Under houses, under boxes and blankets . . .

JAX

What was real became make-believe . . . make-believe became real . . .

BAXTER
(Seated on left arm of chair, covering his face)

Oh, my God, my God!

JAX
(As if with his last breath but without pain or emotion)

At last. It's over. Come now; let it come now; let it be over; now, now, now, now . . .
(Slight pause.)

Baxter.
  (BAXTER *lifts his head, leans forward, expecting to hear* JAX*'s death-rattle.*
Strongly)

One more letter.

BAXTER
(Rises from chair)

For cryin' out loud, Jax. If you're gonna do it, do it already!

JAX

One more, Baxter. Just one more. Then . . . what? The same thing again? No. The smell will be gone. Write this, Baxter.
(Shouts)

Baxter, write!
  (BAXTER *picks up pad and pencil this time from bureau, sits in chair)*

"To the President of the United States." Are you writing in ink?
  (BAXTER *rises, gets pen from bureau, returns to chair)*

It has to be in ink. Let me hear it.

BAXTER

"To the President of the United States."

JAX

Anything else?

BAXTER

No.

JAX

Why not?

BAXTER
(Shouts)
Because you didn't say anything else!

JAX

Good. Now continue. "To the President of the United States. Dear Mr. President. Let's remember Pearl Harbor. My deepest love to Lynda Bird." Sign my name. Mail it.

(Slight pause, BAXTER *replaces pad and pen)*

Baxter, I despise you. I despise your tears ... your weak snivelling sentimentality ... your ...

(He coughs weakly)

your ...

(He releases a sigh. And is silent. BAXTER *at first laughs to himself at this, then enters his room, uncertainly. He looks down at* JAX's *face, covers it with blanket, solemnly, he returns to his own room where he sits in chair, head between hands.* MAX *enters. He wears a worn, shiny but pressed business suit, white frayed shirt, dark tie, carries a scarred imitation-leather briefcase. His posture is stiff, almost military in bearing: he is compulsively neat and precise. He looks carefully about his room to see that nothing has been disturbed, straightens cup on desk, then puts his briefcase on desk, removes his jacket, brushing dandruff from it and hangs it fastidiously on hanger which dangles from shelf on rear wall)*

BAXTER
(In a moment)
He's ... gone.

MAX

When?

BAXTER

A little while ago.

*(*MAX, *clinging to rear wall, starts for* JAX's *room. As he is about to lift blanket from* JAX's *face,* JAX *snaps up to a sitting position like a jack-in-the-box, and shouts loudly)*

JAX

Dooon't come into my room!

(And he falls back onto bed, out of sight)

MAX
(Laughing at BAXTER)
You are perceptive, aren't you, Baxter? Extraordinarily perceptive. Did he get you to write another last letter for him? Is that it? Another last letter, Baxter?

79

(Still laughing, MAX goes into his own room, clinging to rear wall)

BAXTER
(To JAX)
You phony! You lying hypocritical phony! Here, here are your letters! Paste them together and mail them yourself!
(He tears letters and throws them at him)

MAX
(Opens briefcase, takes out dinner)
We had it nice and quiet for the past few days. I was hoping you wouldn't come back.

BAXTER
I don't know what happened, Max; honest. I went down for a can of soup, for a can of vegetable soup, that's all I had in mind. Why would I lie to you?
(He starts towards MAX's room)

MAX
Stay in your own room.

BAXTER
(Moving back from imaginary line)
I went down. I saw nothing unusual. Nothing unusual happened. Was I singing? Max, I think I was even singing. I was feeling that good. It was beautiful out. Beautiful, Max. Spring, the taste of spring . . .

MAX
(Seated at desk, spreads out a napkin, unpacks dinner: a container of coffee and a cheese sandwich)
But you needed to taste something else, didn't you?

BAXTER
I needed it. I did. I thought if I didn't have a drink, I'd have to lay down on the sidewalk, put my cheek on the curbstone, like on a guillotine, and cry and scream and kick my legs . . . they would have had to take me away. Max . . .
(He moves towards MAX's room)

MAX
Stay in your own room.

BAXTER
Max, I did some terrible things. I must have been out of my mind.

MAX
You weren't out of your mind. Don't give yourself excuses. I can safely assume you were merely your own obnoxious self.

BAXTER
Are you going to sit there and judge me, Max? You?

MAX

Yes, me! Me! The man who pays the rent here, the man who bought you those clothes, the man who feeds that fat ugly face of yours. And if you don't like it, my friend, you can pick yourself up and get the hell out of here. And take that foul-smelling dunghill over there with you!

JAX
(Softly)

When we were boys on the cracked and broken streets . . .

BAXTER

I judge myself, Max. I punish myself. More than you ever could. In a million years. And that's a fact. So you don't have to . . .

MAX

I am eating my dinner now. Please do not disturb me.

BAXTER

You're a heartless creepy son-of-a-bitch. You don't give a damn for anyone. Not anyone, Max. No matter what you say.
(Looking to JAX)
At least he doesn't judge. He doesn't condemn.

MAX

I condemn you, Baxter. That I do. And I detest you to the core of your weak self-indulgent soul!

BAXTER

Why? Will you tell me why?

MAX

Why? You have the gall to ask me why? How many jobs have I lost because of you and your drinking and your whoring and your big vulgar mouth! What happened at Ericson's?
(BAXTER laughs to himself at thought of what happened)
That was a good job, Baxter. I needed that job, Baxter. Who asked you to keep coming in there, drunk, cursing, knocking over furniture, so that Mr. Ericson was forced to get rid of me? Who asked you, Baxter? Who?

BAXTER
(Shaking his head, grinning)

Max . . .

MAX

You don't know what it means to exercise a modicum of self-control. Humiliate me like that. Job after job. Haven't you ever heard of the word dignity, Baxter? Pride in oneself and in one's work! Why don't . . .
(Turning to desk)
What's the use? I'm just wasting my time talking to you.

Max, listen. I'll lay it on the line with you now. No conning. I respect you, Max.
I'm not ashamed to say it. I always respected you. I remember . . . there was a couple
I met, an old geezer and his wife. I told them. I said, "There's only one man I know
I respect. He works all day in some stinking office and at night he sits at his desk
until his head is too heavy for him to keep on his shoulders and he tries to write, he
tries . . ." Max, all I'm asking is for a little respect from you, too. Consideration.

(As if about to cry)

That's all I'm . . .

MAX

Ask me for nothing.

BAXTER

Pity? Not even pity?

MAX

For nothing.

JAX
(Softly)

How we laughed in our secret caves, darkness was light, the cold was warmth . . .

BAXTER
(To JAX; shouting after "caves")

Why don't you shut up! You two, you're together. You pretend you're poles apart,
but at bottom you're one and the same. You're both out to get rid of me. That's what
you want, isn't it? That I should curl up and die so you can throw all my stuff out?

(Points to pile of clothes on floor)

Forget that I was ever alive? I . . . I nearly saved you the trouble.

*(He removes six-inch blade hunting knife which remains in sheath from pocket of
jacket on floor. On his knees)*

I bought this. That's what happened. It was beautiful out. Spring. The first real day
of spring. I heard the kids yelling and an old man honking the horn of a yellow
convertible. I saw a woman on a stoop, sitting there like a piece of sculpture that had
its face washed off by the rain. Then I passed a hardware store and this knife was
in the window, its blade catching the sun and noise and the old man and the woman
. . . I bought it. Then I went for a beer. I had a beer and another beer and a . . .

(Holding knife in sheath far from his chest and hitting the top of it)

How many times did I put it against my chest and pray for it to go in, to go in . . . !

MAX
*(Having finished his dinner, he cleans up, putting thermos bottle in drawer, cup
with a little coffee in it remains on desk)*

But you didn't have the courage to use it.

BAXTER

Would it have been courage?

MAX

For you. Yes.

BAXTER

Max, did you . . . want me to use it?

MAX

I think it would have been best for all concerned.

JAX

Now, now, do it now, let it be now, now, now, now . . .

BAXTER
(Over JAX's *"nows," throws knife down, rises)*
Maybe I will. Maybe I'll surprise you. You can't tell with someone like me.
*(*MAX *uses dental floss, energetically. Almost formally)*
Max, I'd like to go down for a drink. I need a drink. Unfortunately I have no money.
If you could possibly loan me . . .
*(*MAX *rises, unlocks typewriter which he puts on desk)*
It may very well bring about the results that everyone present seems so anxious to
achieve. A dollar would be sufficient, Max. Max, a dollar . . .
(Shouting)
We're not going to spend all night together in this lousy room are we?

MAX
(Matter-of-factly)
She said she would drop in.

BAXTER

She?

MAX

Our friend across the alley. I ran into her downstairs. We stopped and talked.

BAXTER

You talked to her?

MAX
(Sarcastically)
Yes, Baxter. It wasn't difficult. Members of the opposite sex can talk to one another
without having nervous breakdowns. It's quite common, I understand. It seems that
not only have we been watching her through the window but she's been watching us
as well.

BAXTER
(Excitedly)
Then she's coming! She'll be here!

MAX

I expect her in a few minutes.

BAXTER

Why didn't you tell me before? I'm not washed or dressed . . .
*(He quickly changes his clothes, putting on the clothes he had taken off previously
and leaves the clothes he now takes off in a pile on the floor)*
How did she look? What else did she say?

MAX

Pretty. A very pretty young lady. She's a counselor, Baxter. In elementary school.
She thinks she can be of help.

BAXTER

(Moves towards MAX, with pants on one leg only, holding them up)
Help?

MAX

That's what she said.

BAXTER

Do you think . . . ?

MAX

What, Baxter?

BAXTER

You said she was a *nice* girl?

MAX

I didn't. But she is, Baxter.

BAXTER

Fine. I'm glad. It doesn't matter.
(Finishes putting pants on)
Anything so long as we're not stuck up here alone. Just let her come. Let her . . .

JAX

One letter.

BAXTER

Does he have to be here, Max?

JAX

Baxter!

BAXTER

You're not talking to me, buddy. Max, let's get him out of here. He ruins it for us.
Every time somebody comes up here. It happens every time. As soon as they get a
whiff of him they start running. Why don't we . . .

JAX

One letter, Baxter. One last letter. Then . . . darkness. Silence. Nothing.

BAXTER

Every day he sings the same stupid song. Over and over. Over and over.

(To JAX*)*

What's wrong, buddy? Can't you think of something else? You're a writer, aren't you? A man of ideas, of imagination! Remember, Max? Remember him telling us the novels he was going to write, the great enduring lovely novels?

*(*MAX *laughs,* BAXTER *holds out pad and pen to* JAX*)*

Well, go ahead, buddy, go ahead and write them!

JAX

He was in your room.

MAX

Who's he talking to?

BAXTER
(Returns pad and pen to bureau)

He's raving. Don't pay him any attention.

JAX

He was in your room.

BAXTER
(Turns, moves towards MAX*)*

No. What the hell would I be doing in your room?

MAX

You were. I can see it in your face.

BAXTER

Are you going to listen to him? That lunatic? That stinking . . .

*(*MAX *empties cup—there is only a small amount of coffee in it—in* BAXTER*'s face)*

MAX

Are you mortified, Baxter? Are you offended? Have I penetrated that thick skin of yours? There, there's the knife. You bought it. Now use it! Use it!

JAX

Now, now, do it now, now, now, do it now, now, now, now . . .

BAXTER
(Picks up knife, in a frenzy, over JAX*'s "nows")*

Who should I use it on? On me? On him? On you? Who do you want me to use it on? Just tell me! tell me!

*(*BAXTER *stares at* MAX *a moment, then drops his eyes, the knife falls from his hand)*

85

MAX

Next time you come into my room, it'll be the last time.
(MAX sits down behind desk, starts to type)

JAX
(Softly)

The snow came down all night. We stood by the window, watching, our noses pressed to the cold glass, our tongues hanging out as though to catch the snow. We crawled under the blanket, and hugged each other, tightly, tightly . . .

MAX

I'm trying to work.

JAX

In the morning we got up, we dressed, we ran out . . . into the street, the white and silver pristine street . . . the snow was as high as our stomachs. We rolled in the snow, we ate the snow, we buried ourselves in the snow . . .

MAX
(Erases typing error)

Tell him to be quiet. I'm trying to work.

BAXTER

Tell him yourself.
(To JAX, sitting on arm of chair)

I remember that morning. We built an igloo. We were at it all day, without stopping. Our gloves were frozen to our fingers.

JAX

The cold was warmth.

BAXTER

Our cheeks were like big red apples.

MAX
(Looking up from his desk)

When it got dark we sat inside the igloo and we started a fire.
(MAX rises, faces BAXTER over imaginary line. They start to laugh, hold and hit each other playfully)

BAXTER
(Rises)

Do you remember that fire? Do you remember it?

MAX

It burned a hole right through the roof!

BAXTER

We were choking with the damn smoke!

MAX

And the ice . . .

BAXTER

Melting down our heads . . .

MAX

Soaking our clothes . . .

BAXTER

We . . . were turning into icicles!
(BAXTER *turns around and falls back on his heels.* MAX *holds him up,*
laughing)

JAX

Max.

MAX
(Suddenly grim, pushing BAXTER *erect)*
I thought we weren't talking to one another.

JAX

One letter. Please.

MAX
(Seated at desk)
Ask Baxter. You can suck him in with your whining, but not me. Not me. So far as
I'm concerned you don't exist.

JAX

Max. Soon . . . soon it'll be too late. Soon it'll be over. All my studies, my contem-
plations, for nothing, nothing . . .

MAX

Your studies? You haven't picked up a book in ten years. And what are you contem-
plating over there, your navel? Your toes? The stink that rises from your rotting
corpse? Don't bother me. I have work to do.
(Starts typing again)
I have a novel to finish . . .
*(*JAX *laughs mockingly)*
You have something to say.

BAXTER

Let's cut it out. She'll be here any minute.
*(*JAX *continues laughing, mockingly)*

MAX

Say it, Jax. Say it or shut up! I said I have a novel to finish . . . I said I . . .

*(MAX rises, infuriated by JAX's laughter, he races along the rear wall, moving
towards him)*
You son-of-a-bitch!

BAXTER
(Holding MAX back)
For cryin' out loud. She'll be here soon, Max.

MAX
(To BAXTER)
Get your hands off me. Get them off!
*(BAXTER drops his hands, moves away. MAX straightens his clothes and returns
to his own room)*
All right, Jax. You had your laugh. But it'll take more than that to bring me down
to your level. I'll finish. Despite him. Despite you ... and do you know why, Jax?
Because I'm not afraid to commit myself to the world I live in and to be responsible
for it and to change it. To change it, Jax! Now you know what keeps me going,
friend. But what keeps you going? What are you hanging onto?
(He picks up knife and slides it across the floor to JAX's bed)
Here. Here it is, Jax. Use it! Use it! Don't tell me you have qualms. Not the great
Jax. Not our representative from the asylum of croaking catatonics! Come on now,
Jax. Go out with a little style. You don't want to die of bedsores, do you?
(He and BAXTER break out in laughter. To BAXTER)
We'll probably have to bury him with the bed, like an Egyptian pharaoh with all
his earthly possessions.

BAXTER
I bet he couldn't get out of that bed if he wanted to.

MAX
He couldn't. I saw him trying it one day and the mattress stuck to his back. He was
laying down even when he was standing up!
(MAX and BAXTER laugh. MAX moves to his desk where he starts typing)

JAX
Listen. Listen to him, Baxter. The voice of the left wing and the pissed-on proletariat.
He pounds his drums, making noises, noises of progress, noises of ...

MAX
Noises! That's right! And you'd better get used to it because there's going to be a
helluvalot more of it before you succumb to those bedsores of yours.

JAX
He doesn't know, Baxter. He's a baby. The world's a new toy for him. He wants to
play with it.

BAXTER
(Now ingratiating himself to JAX)
He's in the process of enlightenment, is that it, Jax?

JAX

His book will change the course of events.

BAXTER

His work contributes to the sanity and well-being of humanity.

JAX

An end to war!

BAXTER

An end to tyranny!

JAX
(Sings mockingly)

Arise ye prisoners of starvation . . .
(BAXTER *joins in, pulls out a pail from under bed and hits it as if it were a*
bongo drum)

JAX and BAXTER

Arise ye wretched of the earth . . . justice triumphs condemnation . . . a better world's
aworld's abirth . . . mine eyes have seen the glory of the coming of the Lord . . . Etc.

MAX
(Frantically, at the same time with above)

That . . . that's still valid. The . . . the idea of that is still valid. You morons! You
imbeciles! History isn't today or yesterday, mistakes are made, that's not the point,
but tomorrow . . . tomorrow . . . with decent education, with science, with, with . . .
(BAXTER *and* JAX *stop singing)*

JAX
(Rises at waist in bed, intones)

Peace be with you, my child.
(And falls back again)

BAXTER
(Intones)

Peace be with you, my child.

JAX
(Rises again, intones, gestures)

Peace be with you, my child.
(And falls back onto bed)

BAXTER
(Intones)

Peace be with . . .

MAX

Shut up! Shut up!

(Rips paper out of typewriter, hurls it at them)
Both of you! I know what's burning your tails.
(To JAX*)*
I'm not aware you exist anymore.
(To BAXTER*)*
I'm not buying you booze anymore. You're on your own and it's killing you, it's killing you!
(Inserts paper in typewriter, types)

BAXTER
(Puts down pail, moves towards MAX*)*
But you're the one that's dying, Max. Look! Look! Worms are crawling over your face. Worms are eating at your heart. Work, Max? Write, Max? Study, Max? For what? For where? For whom?

MAX
For me! For myself! To be better than you are. Better than the both of you! To triumph over your weak, self-indulgent dissipating . . .

BAXTER
There! You said it! He said it, Jax. That's what's behind all his liberal malarkey. He wants to triumph over us, Jax, over us!

JAX
I concede.

BAXTER
You concede.

JAX
They concede.

JAX and BAXTER
We all concede.

BAXTER
There you are, Max. You won. You're top man. King of the Hill. Better than the best of us. Is that it? Is that what you want? Like fun it is. Triumph over yourself, buddy. Over your mean little ambitious self!

MAX
I'm not ambitious. What I do isn't for me, not only for me. It's a lie! A lie!

BAXTER
Did you hear that, Jax? Did you hear him say he's not ambitious? Then he shouldn't mind being a flop, should he?
(To MAX*)*
Because that's what you are, buddy. A flop. Washed up. Beaten. Finished.

                                MAX
No. It's ...
                          (Visibly shaken)
I don't believe it. There's still time ...

                              BAXTER
Open your eyes! Look at yourself! A sixty-buck-a-week clerk! A writer who can't
write! Meat for the analyst's couch! Ten years gone by, buddy. The worms are getting fatter. Triumph over yourself. Here. This way.
       (Quickly he dashes into JAX's *room, picks up knife, hits desk with it)*
This way. Once and for all. Triumph over yourself, Max, over yourself!

                                JAX
Now, now, do it now ...

                                MAX
No. You're wrong. You're ...

                                JAX
Do it now, now ...

               (BAXTER *holds knife out to him, hits trunk with it)*

                                MAX
It's not only for myself. It's not for myself! I can still ...

                                JAX
Now ...

                                MAX
I won't ... no ... I won't ... no ...
       (BAXTER *tosses knife to* MAX *who catches it, holds it in his hands without
                              moving at all)*

                                JAX
Now ...

                                MAX
Please ... please ... no ...
               (The door buzzer rings. MAX *drops knife)*
Thank God.
(MAX *hurries to desk, takes shoebrush from shelf and brushes his shoes on desk
chair, then covers typewriter and uses a second brush to brush his jacket. At the
same time* BAXTER *picks up knife, returns it to his jacket on floor, moves to
bureau mirror where he turns on sunlamp, combs his hair and sprays deodorant
under his jacket sleeves.* MAX *shouts excitedly)*
I'm coming, Ann. One minute. I'll be right with you. I'll be right there, Ann. One
minute. I'm coming. I'll be right with you, right ...

(At door, opens it)
Come in. Please come in. I ... I was afraid you wouldn't make it.
(ANN enters. She is about thirty. She is all smiles and enthusiasm and speaks with a rush of words and nervous gestures)

ANN

So was I, Max. I never thought I'd get here. Just as I was leaving the phone rang. He works in the Housing Authority.
(Glances at BAXTER, smiles)
It was really embarrassing. But as you know, Max, I had already promised you I'd come up here and I didn't have your phone number to cancel this engagement so I had to get out of my other engagement with him and since he was already on the phone and I could cancel that engagement whereas I couldn't cancel this engagement ... I spoke so rapidly I don't think he understood a word I was saying!
(She laughs self-consciously)

MAX

I am glad you came.

ANN

I'm glad to be here, Max.
(Looks about)
Nice. It's a very nice place. I don't believe I met your friends, Max; not officially, that is.

BAXTER
(Putting out his hand)

Baxter.

ANN
(Shaking his hand)

We've seen each other lots of times, haven't we, Baxter? It's a shame we never got to speak to one another.
(Turns to JAX)
And this is ...

MAX

He ... he's sleeping. He's not feeling well, Ann. I don't think we should ...

JAX
(Softly)

When we were boys on the cracked and broken streets ...
(ANN turns to MAX)

MAX
(Begrudgingly)

That's Jax.

92

ANN
(Moving into JAX's *room)*
I've seen you before, too, Jax. Lots of times. It must be extremely ...
(She sniffs at air)
extremely ... difficult for you ... being in bed all the time, without getting out
or ...
(She turns away from JAX, *pinching her nose)*
Is there anything I can do for you, Jax?

JAX
Yes.

ANN
(Tries to open window, it is stuck)
I'd like to ...

JAX
Take off my shoes.

ANN
Your shoes?

BAXTER
Ann, you don't have to ...

ANN
No, no. I don't mind really. It's one of the reasons I was so anxious to come up. If I
can be of any help ...
*(She pulls up left shoe by heel: it comes right off, then right shoe: it also comes off,
easily. She looks from the bed where she sees neither feet nor legs nor contrivance
that have held shoes in place on pillows to empty shoes which fall from her hands.
She turns to* BAXTER *and* MAX *open-mouthed. They both turn away from her.
In a moment,* JAX *pulls his naked feet from under the pillows and plants them
where his shoes were)*

JAX
Ahhh, that feels better. So much better. Now a letter, Ann. Write a letter for me.
Please.

ANN
(Pulling herself together, trying once again to be of help)
Yes. Yes. Of course. I'm only too glad ...
(To MAX, *moving towards him)*
May I have some paper?

MAX
Don't bother, Ann.

93

BAXTER

We'll write it for him later.

JAX

Now. Now. Write it now!

ANN
(To MAX)

It's no bother. Really. I'd like to try.

MAX
(Gives her pad, she whispers)

You should see some of the problems I have to deal with at school. But we're considered experts in this particular field. I'll bring a chair to his bed and . . .
(She picks up desk chair)

BAXTER

No!

MAX

You can't do that.

ANN

I can't?

MAX

That's one of our rules.

JAX
(Rises at waist)

That's one of our rules.

(And falls back on bed again)

BAXTER

Furniture can't be moved. But you can sit in my room, Ann.

ANN
(Puts chair down, moves to BAXTER's room, sits in upholstered chair)

Well, if it's a rule . . . I wouldn't want to be accused of breaking any rules my first
evening here.
(Laughs self-consciously. BAXTER sits on arm of chair)

I'm sure there's a good reason for it. And it's not for me to inquire any further. We
frequently run into this sort of thing with the Board of Education. I'm ready if you
are, Jax.

JAX

In ink. Write in ink. "To the Association for the Prevention of Cruelty to Animals."
Do you have it?
(MAX is seated at desk, seemingly busy with his own work, writing with pencil)

94

ANN

I have it.
(*To* BAXTER)
It's been ages since I've taken any stenog . . .

JAX

Read it back.

ANN

"To the Association for the Prevention of Cruelty to Animals."

JAX

That's it. Are you writing in ink?

ANN
(*Holding up pen*)
Blue-black permanent recording ink; it's approved by all city agencies.

JAX

Good. "To the Association for the Prevention of Cruelty to Animals. Dear Sirs. You killed my brothers. Rats.
(*Slight pause*)
"Mice.
(*Slight pause*)
"Shit."
(*Slight pause*)
Sign it. Mail it at once.
(ANN *looks up at* BAXTER *and* MAX, *puzzled*)

MAX

I told you he wasn't well.

ANN

What's wrong with him?

BAXTER

He's not in his right mind.

MAX

There's nothing we can do.

ANN

I can't believe that.

JAX
(*Shouts, not painfully or emotionally but outrageously*)
I'm dying. Oh, God, I'm dying and I've done nothing, nothing . . .
(*At his first words* ANN *jumps up out of chair in fright*)

95

ANN

Why don't you call a doctor? Or get someone to look after him? That's no way to treat a human being.

MAX

He's only acting that way because you're here, Ann; because he has an audience. I suggest we ignore . . .

JAX
(Shouts)

Why? Why? What was it all for?

MAX

That's enough, Jax!

BAXTER

Cut it out, Jax!

JAX
(Shouts)

For this? Was it for this? No. It can't be. It can't. No . . . no . . .

ANN
(Going to him)

What is it? What's wrong?

JAX
(Suddenly calmly)

A letter. Please, Ann. One last letter.

ANN

Why don't you rest? Try to get some sleep.

JAX

A letter. Then . . . I'll sleep.

ANN

Promise?

JAX

I promise.

ANN
(Going into BAXTER'*s room)*

Very well. One letter, Jax. Then I expect you to keep your promise.

JAX

They have to know, Ann. Their lids have to be held open. Their eyes have to be made to see. What is. How it is. The truth. Are you writing in ink?

                              ANN
The same as before.
                    (To MAX and BAXTER, whispers)
Your friend is really overly suspic . . .

                              JAX
Write!

                              ANN
               (Finger to mouth, to MAX and BAXTER)
Shhhh.

                              JAX
"To the Chairman of the International Biologists Convention, Geneva." Do you have
it?

                              ANN
I have it.

                              JAX
Read it back to me.

                              ANN
"To the Chairman of the International Biologists Convention, Geneva."

                              JAX
Good. Now write. "Dear Chairman. News has just reached me that your wife is
running around with a Chinese chemist. Come home at once."

                              ANN
    (Stares up at JAX, then down at what she has written, then up at JAX again)
Are you making fun of me?
                         (She rises)

                              MAX
Don't be angry, Ann. I tried to warn you.

                              ANN
But that's . . .

                             BAXTER
I tried to warn you, Ann. You're not blaming me for what he did, are you?

                              ANN
                        (Forcing a smile)
You? Of course not. But how can you live in the same room with him?

                             BAXTER
That's why we have certain rules here.

MAX

That's why we have certain rules here, Ann.

BAXTER

Let's not talk about him.
(BAXTER takes pad from her, puts it on bureau)

ANN

That's all right with me. I'm not one who invites unpleasantness.
(Sits in upholstered chair)
What kind of work do you do, Baxter?

MAX

Ann, would you like to sit in my room? I think you'll be more comfortable here.

BAXTER

She's comfortable.

MAX

She's my guest, Baxter. Ann ...

ANN

I'll only be a minute, Max.
(She smiles, turns to BAXTER)
Whatever you do, Baxter, it must be extremely interesting.

BAXTER

Write. I'm a writer.

ANN

Really?
(BAXTER nods)
I never visited socially with a writer before. You'll have to excuse me if I sound naive
What kind of writing do you do?

BAXTER
(Takes tobacco-filled pipe from bureau, leans against back of chair, pipe now in mouth)
A novel. I've been working on a novel, Ann. If it maintains its present standard I have great hopes for it. But not commercially. I don't think the general public would care for it. It's unconventional, experimental in style and how it depicts our contemporary ...

MAX
(Seated at desk, mutters)
He said that ten years ago.

BAXTER

I'm talking. Don't interrupt!

98

MAX

Why don't you tell her how much you wrote this past week?

BAXTER

That's my affair. Butt out!

(To ANN*)*

It kills some people to mind their own business. If it wasn't for certain obligations, Ann, I would have left them long ago.

MAX

Did you hear that, Jax?

JAX

Did you hear that, Max?

MAX

I heard that, Jax.

JAX

That makes two of us, Max.

BAXTER

You see? You see what they're like?

ANN

I expected this kind of behavior from him, Max. But I'm really surprised at you. Baxter, there seems to be bad feelings. Maybe I should go . . .

BAXTER
(Shouting, standing in front of door)

Are you going to shut up now?

(To ANN*)*

They'll be quiet. The last thing they want is for you to leave.

ANN

That's hard for me to believe. Are you three related? Are you brothers?

BAXTER

We're not brothers or cousins or friends or . . . or anything. I don't want to talk about them, Ann. You work for the city, is that right?

ANN
(Nods)

A counselor. In elementary school. But it's only temporary. Another year or two at the most. Not that I don't like working with children. But, I don't know, it gets tedious. Especially when it's other people's children.

BAXTER

And you live alone . . .

ANN

I did live with a girl friend but I much prefer . . .

BAXTER

And you spend all your spare time reading Jane Austen.

ANN

How did you know that?

BAXTER
(Showing her toy telescope)

My secret eye.

ANN
(Pulling dress down over knees)
I must remember to keep the window shade down.

BAXTER

Don't. I like watching you. That's how I spend my spare time. But why you?

ANN

Oh, I get plenty of . . .
("Invites" would follow but she drops thought, shrugs)
I don't know. After awhile going out didn't seem like much fun.

BAXTER

You didn't go out with the right people.

ANN

I didn't meet any others.

BAXTER

Until recently?

ANN

Perhaps.

BAXTER

Can I ask you a blunt question? Now I want you to answer me honestly, no holding
back. When you first saw me, what image came to your mind? I mean . . . what did
I remind you of? Think now. And look at me closely.
(Hunching his shoulders, burying his head, etc., unnatural voice)
Sometimes when I look in the mirror a buffalo stares back at me. Is that it? Was it
a buffalo?
(He moans like a buffalo)

ANN
(Laughing)

No, no, really . . .

BAXTER

Hmmm. I see. Well, how about a duck? Hey, I bet that's it. A girl once told me I
had the most beautiful duck-eyes she ever saw.
(Contorting himself into shape of duck)
Look closely. Is that it? A duck?
(He waddles about, flapping his arms, quacking like a duck, he quacks at MAX
who scowls at him)

ANN

Nothing like it.

BAXTER

A good sign. A very good sign.
(Half-squats)
I have a theory on this, based on many years of practical experience. If you meet
someone and they remind you of a particular animal, whenever you see that person
in the future, you're going to think of that animal. Even if you don't want to. Spon-
taneously. Listen, I once went with a girl who first time I saw her reminded me of
a grasshopper. A grasshopper, of all damn things! And you know, I took her to the
park, the last time I saw her, I took her to a park, and while we were sitting on a
blanket, suddenly, without rhyme or reason, she lifts up her legs, raised her eyebrows,
and hopped away, plunk! plunk! plunk!
(He moves his fingers along her thigh, she playfully pushes his hand away)
I looked for that girl for hours, until it was too dark to see, but I couldn't find her. I
felt pretty sad about it. I kind of liked her. To this day, Ann, whenever I see a
grasshopper, I instinctively bend over and whisper, "Sheila? Sheila, is that you?"
(He pretends to see grasshopper hopping in front of him)

ANN
(Laughing)

And what do I remind you of?

BAXTER

You? Of a woman.

ANN

I'm flattered.

BAXTER

It's hard to believe the window isn't between us. Can I touch your face to make sure?
The closer you are, the prettier you are.
(Moving closer to her)
Ann . . .

ANN

Give me time . . .

BAXTER
(Moving still closer, not embracing her but now holding her hands)
Ann . . .

ANN

Please . . .

JAX
(Rises at waist)

Ann.

(Then falls back onto bed out of sight)

BAXTER
(To JAX)

Shut up!

MAX

Ann.

BAXTER
(To MAX)
I'm talking to her! Why do you have to butt in?

MAX
Ann, aren't you going to spend any time with me?

ANN
(Rises, frees her hands)
I should, Baxter. It isn't fair. Max did ask me up.

BAXTER
You don't have to, Ann. There's no rule says you have to. We were just getting started.

ANN
We'll have plenty of opportunities . . .

BAXTER
(Shaking his head)
It never works out like that. You have something going for you and then . . . all of a sudden something else comes up and the other thing isn't there anymore or it's different, it's . . . look, why don't I go down and get something for us to drink? Hey, that's an idea. No, no, I insist.
(Searches through pockets at door)
This is on me. I . . . that's funny. Did you see my wallet, Max?

MAX
Forget it, Baxter.

BAXTER
No. I had it. I swear. I'm sure of it. Of all the lousy luck. Look, Ann, I wonder if you could . . . I don't like asking but . . . I wonder if you could possibly loan me a few dollars. I know it isn't . . .

MAX

Baxter!

JAX

Baxter!

ANN

That's all right. I don't mind. It's only money.
(Gives him money)
That's one thing nobody can accuse me of, and that's being precious about money.

BAXTER

Thanks. I appreciate it. Don't you leave now. I'll be right back. Before you know it. I'll be . . .

(He exits)

MAX

You shouldn't have done that, Ann. He's a lush, a wino. You won't see him again tonight.

ANN

Are you serious?

MAX

I'm serious.

ANN

I'm . . . really sorry you told me. He seems like a . . .

MAX

He seems like. I know what he seems like. Don't trust them, Ann. Neither one of them. They have no scruples, no sense of what's right or wrong. They believe in nothing, in nobody. If you knew how much I despise them . . .

ANN

Then why do you live with them, Max? I don't understand.

MAX

I tried to get away. I tried. I moved from one place to another, from one city to another, like a gypsy, but they were always there, they always turned up.

ANN

And there's no way for you to live together?

MAX

No more. It's too late for that.
(He turns away from her)
Sometimes I think my only hope is if one of us dies, at least one of us. Even if that one is myself.

103

                              JAX
                            (Softly)
When we were boys on the cracked and broken streets . . .

                              MAX
                  (Murmurs, almost to himself)
We were all right then. We played ball with the sun . . .

                              JAX
We caught lightning from the sky . . .

                              MAX
                   (Excitedly, moves to JAX*)*
Remember when we went swimming in the rain, Jax? at the PAL camp?

                              JAX
We took off all our clothes.

                              MAX
When we came out of the water we . . .

                              JAX
We couldn't find them.

                              MAX
We looked for hours.

                              JAX
We found a cardboard box.

                              MAX
We put it over our heads and we walked . . .
                            (Laughing)
We walked all the way back to camp with the box over our heads.
                       (Suddenly grim, to ANN*)*
That was a long time ago. A long, long time ago.
                 (He moves to ANN, *sits next to her on trunk)*
I'm not being a very considerate host, am I?

                              ANN
I just feel that I want to help but I don't know how.

                              MAX
You can help. Don't give up on me too quickly.
                 *(*ANN *picks unwittingly at* MAX*'s tie)*

                              ANN
Giving up is a luxury I can't afford.
      (The tie, which is clipped to MAX*'s shirt collar, snaps off in* ANN*'s hand)*
Oh. Sorry.

                              104

MAX
(Pulls tie out of her hands, puts it back on, embarrassed)
That's . . . that's all right. It never stays on. Ann, isn't there anyone . . .?

ANN
Not really.

MAX
The fellow in the Housing Authority?

ANN
Who?

MAX
The fellow who phoned you. From the Housing Authority.

ANN
Oh, him. He's a cockroach exterminator. He's been trying to get into my apartment for weeks.

MAX
But there was someone.

ANN
(Nods)
There was someone. I was divorced by the time I was twenty. Does that surprise you?

MAX
What happened?

ANN
Everything I suppose. After awhile it became illogical for us to continue, so we added our assets, subtracted our legal expenses, divided by two, and presto! it was done.

MAX
You regret leaving him?

ANN
No, not leaving him. I regret not trying to stay with him. I thought . . . why didn't I think then? I thought the easiest thing in the world is to start over again, to walk away and begin as if nothing had ever happened. How wrong I was. It's much easier to lock the door and read Jane Austen.

MAX
We have a great deal in common.

ANN
You don't mean Jane Austen.

105

MAX

I mean the strength to be alone.

ANN

Don't you believe it, Max. There's nothing I dread more. I'll tell you a secret. One night last week I went to a dance, one of those public dances they advertise in the newspapers. I stood against the wall and I waited. I waited. Have you ever gone through anything like that? It's really an exercise in masochism. When someone finally came up to me and asked me to dance . . . it seemed like such an unsatisfactory reward for my standing there that I politely said, "No, thank you," and left.

MAX

I'm glad you did.

ANN

I was just being snobbish.

MAX

Some of us shouldn't try to be like the others, Ann. We're not. We don't fit in. I'll let *you* in on a secret. I'm a shipping clerk. Sixty dollars a week. With the Great Western Drug Company. Does that surprise you?

ANN

I'm sure you're not there because you couldn't get anything else . . .

MAX

It doesn't matter. I'm a writer. I write. That's my job; my profession. I know it's old-fashioned to talk about being committed to more than one's own skin and one's own material comforts, but those things aren't important to me, Ann.

JAX

Ann.

MAX

That's not what I . . .

JAX
(Raising voice)

Ann.

MAX

Be quiet!

JAX
(Even more loudly)

Ann.

ANN

Let me see what he wants.

MAX
(Stands between ANN *and* JAX, *holding* ANN's *arm)*
We can't lock ourselves in a room, Ann. We owe it to ourselves . . .

JAX
(Shouts)
Ann, forgive me.

MAX
(Turns to JAX*)*
I said be . . .

ANN
(Removes MAX's *hand from her arm)*
A minute, Max. I'll only be a minute.
*(*ANN *moves to* JAX*)*
I didn't want us to quarrel, Jax. Can't you tell me what the trouble is?

JAX
I'm dying, Ann. At last . . . at last . . .

ANN
Why do you keep saying that? There's nothing physically wrong with you.
(Turns to MAX*)*
Is there anything physically wrong with him?

MAX
Don't waste your time on him, Ann.

ANN
Is there?
*(*MAX *shakes his head)*
There. Now why don't you try to get up? Come, I'll help you.

JAX
I can't. I can't move.

ANN
(Trying to lift him up)
You don't want to move.
(Asking for help)
Max . . .

MAX
He'll suck the last drop of blood out of you, if you let him. Ann, don't stay . . .

JAX
Ann, my heart . . . see for yourself. Feel my heart.
(He puts her hand on his heart)

107

It's getting weaker, isn't it? Tell me the truth. Isn't that the truth? Soon it'll be quiet. Soon I'll feel nothing, nothing . . . Ann, put your hand on my forehead.

(He takes her hand, puts it on his forehead, holds it there)

How good that feels. How good . . . Ann, stay here; stay with me. Don't believe what they say. They're thinking of themselves. Only of themselves. They're the same, the . . .

MAX

Ann, don't listen to him.

JAX

Ann, listen.

MAX

Ann, for your own good, don't . . .

JAX

Ann . . .

(A N N rises, turns from one to the other as they call her name. At the same time from outside the room B A X T E R is heard shouting: "Ann! Ann! Ann!" He enters, flushed, disheveled, out of breath)

BAXTER

Ann . . . I . . . I was afraid you left. I suddenly said to myself, "What if she left? What if I don't see her again?" I ran like the dickens. Ann, I . . . I'm sorry about the money. I shouldn't have taken it.

ANN

You spent it drinking, didn't you?

BAXTER

Let me explain . . .

ANN
(Excitedly)

You don't have to explain it to me. For all practical purposes we're strangers. Why do you have to explain anything to me?

BAXTER

Because I want to. Because there's no one else.

ANN

I don't want to hear it, Baxter!

BAXTER

I . . . I've been on a binge, Ann, on a drunk . .

ANN

I don't, Baxter!

108

BAXTER

For the last few days. I don't know what got into me.

ANN

You're being inexcusably cruel. I've looked forward to meeting you for months ...
for a very long time ... for you to tell me all this now ...

BAXTER

I ... I went downstairs. When was it? Four days ago? Five days ago? I don't remember. I went down and everything was so right, so perfect ... then I looked around,
at the dirty kids, at an old man hunched over the wheel of a yellow convertible, at a
woman sitting on a stoop. ...

(Slight pause)

It was her eyes, Ann. That was it, I guess. Her eyes. There was so much sadness in
them, so much misery ... I wanted to throw myself down on the sidewalk and dig
my fingers into the concrete. I was so filled with her misery and my misery and your
misery that I begged for pain, begged for my flesh to be torn, for no more remem-
bering ... I ... I drank instead. And when you hear some of the things I did ...

ANN

Why do you have to tell me all this now, Baxter? I don't want to hear it!

MAX

Shut up, Baxter!

JAX

Shut up, Baxter!

MAX

Baxter!

JAX

Baxter!

MAX

Shut up!

JAX

Shut up!

BAXTER
(Quietly)

I met this couple in a bar on Third Avenue. They bought me a few drinks and ...
we went up to their place, a smelly little room near the river. They had a bottle and
we drank some more. We were having quite a party for ourselves. The old man sang,
he did a crazy jig, and then he passed out. His wife, that's what she said she was, a
fat gray-haired woman with dirty fingernails and red swollen hands ... she crawled
across the floor towards me like some mad old witch, her mouth grinning from ear
to ear and ... she started pulling at my clothes, tearing at my clothes and ... I knew
what I was doing, Ann. I knew it!

ANN
(Slight pause)
What do you expect me to say now, Baxter?

BAXTER
Just let me explain. It's important that I can tell you everything and you don't walk away. That's important to me. That you don't walk away. You see, Ann, I did it because . . .

ANN
I'm really not interested, Baxter. And I don't know that it'd do any good. We all have our problems. That's something somebody should tell you.
(She rises, moves towards door)
And I have enough of my own. More than enough at present. Thank you for asking me up. Max.

MAX
You're not blaming me for what he did, are you, Ann?

ANN
I'm tired. And I do have to get up early tomorrow.

MAX
A little while longer. Please. Sit here. In my room. We don't have to have anything to do with them.
(ANN sits in desk chair)
So far as we're concerned they're not here, they don't exist.

ANN
I must have had delusions of grandeur to think I could help. I am sorry for them.

MAX
Don't be. That's their one consolation, and they don't deserve it. I don't want to talk about them. Ann, if you're not busy one day next week, I'd like to . . .

ANN
(Nods at once)
I would, too.

MAX
You would? You know what we'll do? We'll take the 125th Street ferry to Playland. We'll ride all the rides, eat hot dogs, dance out in the open . . . we have to try everything, Ann. No excuses. No holding back.

ANN
You know, I've never been there before.

MAX
Never?

110

ANN

Never.

MAX

Wonderful. You don't know what you've missed. It's ... come to think of it, I've never been there myself!
(They both break out in laughter)
We do have something in common.

ANN

What's that?

MAX

We can still laugh.

ANN

It's not easy.

MAX

Nothing's easy.
(He moves closer to her, touches her face)

ANN

Give me time ...

MAX

Ann ...

ANN

I need time. Please. That's not being unreasonable, is it? It's the only way I can know ...

MAX

I don't want to know anything.

ANN

But I have to. I have to, Max. You haven't even told me about your writing, what you're writing ...

MAX

A novel. I've been working on a novel ...

BAXTER
(Muttering)

He said that ten years ago.

MAX
(Ignoring BAXTER, pacing)
If it maintains its present standard, I have great hopes for it, Ann. Not commercially.

I don't think the general public would care for it. It's unconventional, experimental in style and how it depicts our contemporary . . .

JAX

Don't believe him, Ann.

BAXTER

Don't believe him, Ann.

MAX
(Raising voice, flustered)
It's a long . . . a . . . a very long and involved novel. It doesn't hold with fashionable pessimism . . .

JAX

It doesn't hold with fashionable pessimism . . .

MAX
(Continues pacing, agitatedly)
But points out in no uncertain terms . . .

BAXTER and JAX

But points out in no uncertain terms . . .

MAX

That men are . . .
(BAXTER and JAX join in to complete sentence with MAX)

ALL THREE

Motivated by ideas, commitments, by love . . . and on occasion self-sacrifice and . . .
(MAX is silent, he sits down on trunk)

BAXTER and JAX

And an unselfish response to the challenge of our age . . .

MAX
(Weakly)
And an unselfish response . . . to the challenge . . .

BAXTER

Despite . . .

JAX

History.

BAXTER

Despite . . .

JAX

Mistakes.

112

BAXTER

Despite . . .

JAX

Betrayals. Greed.

BAXTER

And the inability to live together like human beings.

MAX
(To BAXTER, *shouts)*

You open your mouth again . . . !

JAX

Ask him to show you what he wrote tonight, Ann.

BAXTER

Ask him, Ann.

ANN

May I see what you wrote tonight, Max?

MAX

Nothing. Nothing. I haven't been writing lately. But once I get into it again . . .

BAXTER

On his desk.

JAX

Look on his desk.

BAXTER

On his desk, Ann.

ANN
(Pulls out paper from typewriter)

Is this it? Is this what you wrote?
(No answer, she reads from paper)

"The quick brown fox jumped over the lazy mother dog. The quick brown fox
jumped over the lazy mother dog. The quick brown fox jumped over . . ."
(Shaking her head, quietly)

I don't understand.

MAX
(Taking paper from her)

It's nothing, Ann. Nothing. I wrote it for Jax. It's his. Jax, tell her! Tell her!

JAX
(Softly)

When we were boys on the cracked and broken streets . . .

113

MAX
(Crosses to ANN)

Ann, listen to me . . .

BAXTER

Ann, let me explain . . .

JAX

Ann, forgive me . . .

ANN
(Shouting)

What is it you want from me? Will one of you please tell me what it is you want from me!

BAXTER

I did those things deliberately, Ann. I drank deliberately. I slept with that old hag deliberately . . . I wanted to be so ashamed of myself, so disgusted with what I was that the rest would have been easy.

MAX

He bought a knife.

(BAXTER *picks up knife)*

JAX

He was going to kill himself.

ANN

You weren't . . .
        (BAXTER *holds knife in hands, raises it slightly out of sheath)*

BAXTER

I wanted to see my own flesh cut. I wanted to see the blood . . .

ANN
(Pulls knife out of his hands)

Stop that!

BAXTER
(Shouts angrily)

Owwwwww!
                (Pinches thumb and stares at minute cut on it)
Now look what you've done!

ANN

You shouldn't be playing with knives. Does that give you pleasure?

BAXTER

Your anxiety gives me pleasure.

ANN
(Crosses to bed, kneels in front of BAXTER)
Let me bandage it.
(She bandages his thumb with her handkerchief)

JAX
(Softly)
We went to the park on a Sunday morning. We took our guns, our swords, and filled our knapsack with apples and a canteen of water.

MAX
(Crosses through BAXTER's room to JAX's room, sits on bed)
We walked under the tree, our arms swinging at our sides . . .

JAX
Our eyes straight ahead . . .

MAX
Our shoulders thrown back . . .

BAXTER
We buried our knapsack under a large stone and then we ran and shouted . . .

JAX
Conquering new worlds, proclaiming ourselves to be masters . . .

MAX
Over the rocks, around the edge of the lake, and up the tallest tree . . .

BAXTER
Where we sang out at the top of our lungs, "I am the King of the Universe . . ."

JAX
(Rises at waist, holds his fist up)
And I raised my fist to the sky.

MAX
And I raised my fist to the sky.

BAXTER
And I raised my fist to the sky.

ANN
(She has been wholly absorbed in bandaging BAXTER's hand. She rises)
There. It should be all right now.

MAX
Do you have to go, Ann?

115

ANN
(Moving to door, half-turns to them)
I'm tired. More tired than I thought I'd ever be.
(Nods)
I have to.
(They all turn their heads towards her as she moves closer to door)

BAXTER
Don't go, Ann.

JAX
Stay.

BAXTER
Another chance?

JAX
Ann . . .

MAX
Will I see you next week?

ANN
(At door, slight pause, shakes her head)
I don't think so. I am sorry. I have a great deal of reading to do and . . .
(Laughs weakly)
I don't only read Jane Austen, you know. I read a great many authors and . . . self-education is very important in civil service. Especially in counseling. It's . . .
(She looks around with a hopeless air)
it's not a bad life . . . Good-night.
(She quickly exits. BAXTER rises, starts to change his clothes again. MAX moves to desk, JAX falls back on the bed)

BAXTER
We shouldn't have let her go.

MAX
What would you have suggested? That we tied her up and locked her in a closet?

BAXTER
Anything. Anything but this . . . I didn't get a chance to talk to her, to explain . . .

MAX
You talked too damn much.

JAX
You talked too damn much.

MAX

You talked too damn much.

JAX

You talked too damn much.

MAX

You talked too damn much.

JAX

You talked too . . .

BAXTER
(Shouts.)

Shut up, both of you! Shut up!
(BAXTER *glares at them, throws pants down that he was about to put on, sits,*
wearily)

JAX
(Shortly)

A letter. Write a letter for me.

MAX
(Shaking his head, seated at desk)

You won't die. You won't die.

BAXTER

I need a drink. God . . . oh, God . . .

JAX

Soon. Soon it'll be over. Soon.

MAX

I'm going to work. I have work to do.
(He does nothing)

BAXTER

We shouldn't have let her go. We shouldn't have . . .

JAX

Now, now, now, now . . .

MAX

I'll finish it. Whatever you say . . . whatever you do . . .

BAXTER
(Cries out in pain)

Max!

MAX

Go away!

BAXTER

Max!

MAX

I have work to do, I said!

BAXTER

A drink, Max! I need a drink!

MAX
(Rises, fists smash down on desk)
I'll kill you! I swear I'll kill you!
(They stare at each other a few seconds)

JAX
(Softly)
When we were boys on the cracked and broken streets . . .
(Curtain starts to close as BAXTER *moves back to upholstered chair and* MAX *sits down at desk)*
How we laughed in our secret caves . . . darkness was light, the cold was warmth . . .
what was real became make-believe . . . make-believe became real . . .

CURTAIN

The Basement

Originally, you weren't supposed to see Minna, only the bottom half of her legs moving up and down the staircase. But when the play was first done in Stockbridge, I was persuaded that the audience, if they did not see her, might think she had the face of a monkey! (Or something of the sort.) I gave in and allowed her to show her face to the audience.

It was probably a mistake.

I remember when I was in rehearsal with An American Millionaire, *which was done at the Circle in the Square on Broadway, the Patty Hearst kidnapping took place. The similarity between that event and my play was spooky. Fearing that Miss Hearst might be found dead at any moment, I rewrote the second act of my play so that it wouldn't seem like a sick parody of what was actually happening.*

That was a whopper of a mistake.

Rewriting while staging a play is a treacherous business. More often than not the rewrites will do more harm than good. And yet if during previews the play you've written is not "bringing down the house," the pressures to rewrite come fast and furious from every side.

A word of advice, playwright! Don't rewrite a word unless, during a preview, your mother walks out of the theater.

—M.S.
March 9, 1983

THE BASEMENT *was first presented in New York City, by Edgar Lansbury and Marc Merson, at the Cherry Lane Theater on October 2, 1967.*

ZACH	*Gene Hackman*
MINNA	*Sylvia Gassell*
LEO	*James Coco*

Directed by LARRY ARRICK
Set design by KERT LUNDELL
Costumes by LIZ DOMINICK
Lighting design by ROGER MORGAN

The basement of an old one-family house. Right, forward, leading into the basement is a short flight of six steps and a descending angular wall fixed to the ceiling which conceals the shoulders and head of anyone standing or sitting on the steps; on the left wall there is a shelf holding a can of talcum powder, red rubber surgeon's gloves and other appropriate paraphernalia; rear, in the center wall, a paneless window, barred, arched, on a level with the sidewalk outside; forward, a large long low table on which there is a variety of laboratory equipment; seated rigidly, his arms bent in front of him, his eyes glassy, half-closed, at the left-end of the table is a dead chimpanzee; Band-Aids cover his upper arms; against the right rear wall rows of rickety shelves: they are filled with yellowed notebooks, boxes, jars, tubes, etc.; a crate is in front of the right rear shelves; a milk box is left, forward.

ZACH *is behind the table, center, angry, agitated. He is wearing a not-too-clean oversized laboratory coat.* MINNA *is on step five. She wears bulky red ankle socks that sag, scuff slippers, a nondescript housedress. She is not permitted to go below the bottom step so that we see only her legs and her gesturing hands; two or three times her head will peek out from behind the wall where specified.*

ZACH
No. No. I'm not hungry. I can't eat. Food. Food. Food. Is that all you can think of? I have my work to do. My work. You said you understood. I thought you understood. But you don't. That's the tragedy. Right there.
(Takes baseball cap off hook, puts it on jauntily, staring at cracked mirror)
You say you do, oh, yes, you go right ahead and you say you do, you probably think you do, too, but . . .

MINNA
(Comes down to step three)
You haven't had your dinner. You have to eat something. I don't want you to get sick. Your health is important. Isn't it? Isn't your health important? Let me bring you down a plate of cold chicken and corn niblets with sliced cucumbers and a glass of . . .

ZACH
(Takes clip-board from table, glances at it)
You don't understand! There's the tragedy. You never understood me, Minna. All these years . . . you pretended you understood, and I believed you, I took your word for it, but now I see I made a mistake. It was all a mistake.
(He moves to chimpanzee, feels its arms, legs, chest, carefully, slowly, then inserts thermometer into its mouth, takes its temperature, notes temperature on clip-board)

MINNA
That isn't true. How can you say that? It's because I disagree with you. Every time I disagree with you, you say I don't understand you. Is that fair? Is it fair? All I want you to do is have your dinner. For my sake, Zach. If you don't want cold chicken and corn niblets with sliced cucumbers and a glass of milk, let me make you

a tuna-fish-and-tomato sandwich with French fried potatoes or a bowl of hot asparagus soup and a couple of hard-boiled . . .

ZACH

If you understood me, if you really understood me, you wouldn't go on this way.
You'd stop and you'd say to yourself, "He wants to work. Food isn't important to
him, not when he has his mind on his work. His work. That's what counts. That's
what keeps him going. I'll let him work and exhaust himself and then I'll come down
and I'll say, 'Zach, would you like to have a cup of black coffee and a little chocolate
pudding with sweet cream?'" I'd say, "Oh, that's very thoughtful of you, Minna. I'd
appreciate that very much."
(Suddenly shouts)
And we wouldn't have to go through this every goddamn time I get ready for work!
*(*MINNA *moves to step five, then down to step four.* ZACH *sprinkles talcum
powder into pair of red rubber gloves, then puts them on; he moves to shelves,
stands on box, carefully and preciously removes large jar with red liquid in it from
shelf, carries it across room, puts it down on shelf, and at once removes red rubber
gloves)*

MINNA

But I did that last night? I did it? Don't you remember? You said the same thing
and I said, "Very well, We'll try it." I waited upstairs, watched television, read a
magazine I read twice before, defrosted the refrigerator, and then I came down and
I found you asleep on the floor. You wouldn't even think of eating. I called and called
. . . Zach, there's something else I have to tell you. Don't be angry and don't say I
don't understand. But . . . Zach, why can't I come down? I mean, all the way down
to your workroom? Why do you have to keep me out?
(On step two, sticks her head out from behind wall, looks around)
And the place is a mess, Zach. I can clean it, dust off the shelves, arrange things so
that you won't have any trouble getting at them . . .

ZACH

You don't understand. Good God, you don't, and that's all there is to it . . .
*(*MINNA *pulls her head back once* ZACH *speaks.* ZACH *takes yellow fluid from
shelf, pours it into jar of red fluid)*
This is my workroom. Where I work. Where every piece and part of it is like an
extension of my own body.
(To MINNA*)*
Would you ask to walk on my body? Would you ask to clean it, to change it? It's
private, Minna; intimate, too intimate even for you, and sometimes it's too intimate
even for me. Now go up, go upstairs. I have to start.
(Glances at wristwatch)
Time, time, it's . . .
*(He moves to rear where, dangling from a line, he takes a pen flashlight, hangs it
around his neck, prepares table for work, setting out materials before going to
chimpanzee and continuing its physical examination, noting everything on clip-
board)*

122

MINNA

No. Not yet. Please. You've said some things tonight that have hurt me. Deeply. You couldn't have meant them. I just know. Are you sorry you married me, Zach? Do you wish you hadn't married me? Has your life been so terrible with me? I must know, Zach. Tell me. Please.

ZACH

No. No, Minna. Don't think it. Never. If I sound impatient, if I sound thoughtless or inconsiderate . . . time. I don't have the time. There's so much . . . Minna, you know what I want, above everything else, you know what I have to do. You do understand, don't you?

MINNA

Of course I understand. I want you to say I understand. Your work, it means as much to me as it does to you. Your achievement, your fulfillment, what else is there for me? I understand, Zach. More than anyone. Isn't that true? Isn't it?

ZACH
(Removes small hammer from pocket and taps chimpanzee's knees several times, placing one leg over the other)
Yes. Yes. It is true. It is.

MINNA

It is true. I want you to say it's true. More than anyone, I understand. And you will do something one day that will be here long after we're gone, and it will be us, we will be here, too.

ZACH

We will. I promise. Granted the time, granted the strength . . . something that will make . . . something that will help . . . something that will go . . .
(Suddenly shouts)
Why else have I lived?

MINNA

What other meaning is there for us?

ZACH

We've given everything for it, haven't we? Nineteen years . . .

MINNA

We haven't given much, Zach. That's not true. We've kept what is most important, most valuable and precious.

ZACH

Each other?

MINNA

Each other.

123

ZACH

How good you are.

MINNA

Selfish. Selfish.

ZACH
(Moving to her)

Not you. Anyone but you.

MINNA

Yes. Yes.

ZACH

No, Minna. No. When I gave up teaching at Edgar Allen Poe Junior High
School . . .

MINNA

Selfish. I was selfish.

ZACH

When I gave up a salary, a pension, tenure, major health and life insurance benefits,
so I could have more time for my work, you never said a word.

MINNA
(Pacing on step)

I was happy. I wanted you to.

ZACH

And when we moved into this house, this rat-trap . . .

MINNA

You're exaggerating.

ZACH

This old broken-down rat-trap . . .

MINNA

It isn't that old.

ZACH

And I said we would probably remain here for the rest of our natural lives . . .

MINNA

It's not that bad.

ZACH

Because we'd have to save every penny we had . . .

MINNA

It was for your work.

ZACH

It was for my work.
(Looks about confusedly)
My work.
(He hurries to chimpanzee)
Minna, go upstairs, leave me. Please. I have so much to do.
(He examines mouth of chimpanzee, using spatula, then examines its eyes with pen flashlight, marks down findings on clip-board. MINNA *moves up to step five, then comes down to step two)*

MINNA

I'm going, Zach. I'm going. Thank you for the very nice things you've said to me tonight. Zach . . .
(Very quickly, sticking her head out from behind wall)
If you don't want a tuna-fish-and-tomato sandwich with French fried potatoes or a bowl of hot asparagus soup and a couple of hard-boiled eggs, I can make you frankfurters and baked beans with a tossed green salad and some hot seeded . . .

ZACH

Minna, if I have to . . . !

MINNA
(Pulls head back, starts up steps)
I'm going. I am. This minute.
(Slight pause)
Is there anything you want me to do upstairs?
(No answer, climbs up more steps)
Zach, is there anything you want me to do for you?
(Starts climbing down steps)
I'm going up now.

ZACH
(Mumbles, pulls crumpled slip of paper out of his pants pocket)
You can't keep yourself busy. You still don't know how. After all these years . . .
(Loudly, reading from slip of paper)
There's a button missing on my gray jacket, there's a hole in a sock in the bottom drawer of the bureau, and look up the word "solipsism" for me in the unabridged dictionary that's holding up the gas range.
(As she speaks ZACH *stares at the slip of paper, turning it in his hand, mentally checking off each item)*

MINNA

You told me to give away the gray jacket months ago. I sewed the sock in the bottom drawer of the bureau, ironed all your handkerchiefs and solipsism is a philosophical theory that a person can't know anything but his own existence. Is that right, Zach? Is it?

125

(ZACH crushes the slip of paper and tosses it over his shoulder, without answering her. She now sits on step, clasps her knees. ZACH puts on stethoscope, taps and listens to chimpanzee's chest and back. He is soon caught up in MINNA's reminiscences. He puts stethoscope aside, makes notations on clip-board. MINNA, lyrically)

You know what I was thinking this evening, Zach? I was thinking of the time when we used to walk by the river. That was before we were married. How beautiful it was. We used to walk and walk, with our arms around each other's waist ... it seemed as if everything was around us, as if we were in the very middle of the whole universe, and the clouds and the river and the sun, all of it was where it was because we were there, in the middle, I mean ... Zach, I was thinking of the time when we were sitting by the river and you looked at me and you said, "Minna," and I said, "I understand you. Why are you afraid? I want the same things you want." And you said, "Minna." And your eyes were wet and you were trembling and I took you in my arms and I said, "Zach. Zach. Zach."

(With an amused laugh, rises)

And then you said that we had to draw up a special contract before we married, that everything had to be crystal clear between us, so there'd be no mistakes, no misunderstandings, no recriminations. And I said ...

(Sticks her head out from behind wall)

"Zach, I love you."

(She pulls her head back)

ZACH
(Turning to her excitedly)

And I said, "No. We shouldn't get married!"

(He puts thermometer under chimpanzee's arm, then gets mortar and pestle and grinds powder in mortar, moving behind table)

I said, "Minna, this fellow, this bookkeeper or whatever he is, he likes you, he'd marry you tomorrow if you said the word. You'd have a normal life. He'd buy you things, he'd spend time with you, he'd take care of you ... he'd give you ... give you ..."

(Unable to complete thought he mops his brow, continues forcefully)

I said, "Minna, you don't know me. You don't know what I'm like inside; inside, that keeps me going, pushes me ahead, it's ... it's ..."

MINNA

But I said, "I know. I know, Zach. There's so much good in you. You want to do things. You want to give some of this goodness to other people."

ZACH

"I believe in the future," I said.

MINNA

"I believe in the future," you said. And I said, "You're not like other men. You're different. And that's the very reason, don't you see ..."

ZACH

You laughed at the idea of signing the contract, though, didn't you? You laughed.

You told me I was foolish. You said, "Why do we need a special contract?" And I said, "Because unless you understand what you're letting yourself in for . . ."

MINNA

I understood. I did. I said, "Isn't it enough that the two of us will be together? Isn't it enough?"

ZACH

You said that. Those were your own words, Minna. You said, "Isn't it enough that the two of us will be together? Isn't it . . ."
                    (MINNA *starts walking up the steps. Shouts*)
Minna!
                    (MINNA *starts walking down the steps*)

MINNA
(With effort)
Yes. Yes. I said it. "Isn't it enough that the two of us will be together?"

ZACH

That's what you said. And years later when we had to decide if we should have any . . .

MINNA

I don't regret it, Zach!

ZACH

Because there wasn't that much time left to you . . .

MINNA

Don't you dare think I regretted it!

ZACH

I said then, I said, "Here's where we could use a contract. Here's where we should have it all down in writing, so there'd be no mistakes, no misunderstandings . . ."

MINNA

And you said . . .

ZACH

"No, not for us," I said. "They would cost too much money, they would get in the way, they would take up too much time . . ."

MINNA

"But if you want them, if you feel that you have to have them . . ."

ZACH

I left it up to you, Minna. I left it up to you but you said the same thing I did or you didn't say anything and we agreed. Didn't we agree?
                    (MINNA *starts walking up the steps. Shouts*)

127

Minna!
(MINNA starts walking down the steps)

MINNA
(With effort)
Yes. Yes. We agreed. You left it up to me. You said, "But if you want them, if you
feel that you have to have them . . ."

ZACH
And we agreed.
*(ZACH moves to chimpanzee, glances at wristwatch, then removes thermometer
from under chimpanzee's arm, makes note of it. He prepares hypodermic needle)*

MINNA
We agreed. And we didn't need a special contract, did we, Zach? We didn't need it
in writing. You're not sorry you married me, are you? Are you sorry you married
me?

ZACH
(Pauses in his work)
No, Minna. No. It was the best thing that could have happened to me. I couldn't
have done it alone. Never. I would have given up. Years ago. If not for you . . .

MINNA
I did help.

ZACH
You helped more than I could have hoped. My work . . .
(At once he pulls down cap and returns to work)

MINNA
Your work. I helped in your work. For nineteen years I saw to it that there was no
noise, that you had all the time to yourself you could possibly have.
(ZACH lifts chimpanzee's leg and rubs some alcohol on its behind)
I saw to it that you weren't disturbed or distracted so that you could devote your full
energies and concentration to your work. And you are doing well in your work. I
know you are. You are doing very well in your work.
(ZACH inoculates chimpanzee in its behind. Slight pause)
Zach, I never asked you. But . . . Zach.
(Sticks her head out from behind wall)
What kind of work are you doing?

ZACH
(Moving away from chimpanzee, leaving hypodermic needle in its behind)
There! There you go again! That's what I get for letting you stay up there!

MINNA
(Moving up to step four, very quickly)
It was rhetorical. It was rhetorical. I know what work you're doing, Zach. Of course
I know. I mean, how is it progressing? How is it coming along?

(Coming down step)
Can you look forward to its conclusion?

ZACH
(Removing hypodermic needle)
Its conclusion?
(With hushed excitement, looking about for possible eavesdroppers)
Minna, if I told you ... I can feel it. This time it's right. I'm so close to it, you wouldn't believe it.

MINNA
How wonderful!

ZACH
Now I'm not letting myself out on a limb or anything like that, but I think ... I think this is going to be it, Minna. After all these goddamn years ... this time I feel ... it's going to be right. It's going to be right!

MINNA
Zach, Zach, I'm so happy!

ZACH
You know I never looked for any kind of profit from my work, Minna. You know that.

MINNA
(Indignantly)
Who would dare think such a thing?

ZACH
(Stilted, moving behind table)
And it can be said without any sacrifice to the truth that I never sought honors or rewards or the cheap attention that my colleagues run after with greater enthusiasm than they do the interests of their own profession.

MINNA
I can verify everything.

ZACH
(Standing behind table, facing front, as if addressing an audience)
But if the community in which I worked and if the society towards which I have made my small contribution deem it proper at this time to acknowledge my achievements, I will with proper humility and gratitude accept whatever it may be, in the spirit in which it is given, on so memorial and auspicious an occasion.
(He removes cap, bows his head)

MINNA
(In same solemn speechmaking tone)
And as the wife of Zachariah Nathaniel Miller, one who has been privileged, indeed

honored, to work by his side through all the years he has devoted to bringing to light whatever it may be . . . I want to say here and now that he has given to society not only his achievement, not only the product of his genius and his dedication, but he has given to humanity itself his love and the belief in its eternal redemption.

(Pause, a shade heavier tone)

Will you please step up here, Mr. Miller.

(Stiffly and solemnly, Z A C H *walks to step one: only his legs are seen. He faces* M I N N A *who is on step three)*

Mr. Miller, today is a day that will not be soon forgotten. What you have done, what you have set as an example to the young people of our nation, will endure wherever men pay tribute to the great, the unselfish and the good. Doctor Miller, congratulations.

(She shakes his hand)

ZACH
(Choked voice)

All I can say is . . . thank you.

(Turns his back to M I N N A*)*

Thank you all for seeing fit to . . .

MINNA
(Whispering urgently, tugging at the bottom of his coat)

Doctor . . .

ZACH
(Brushes her hand away, steps to floor level so that he is now wholly visible)

. . . to reward me so generously for what I did without any concern for personal profit or tribute . . .

MINNA
(Whispering urgently, tugging at the bottom of his coat)

Doctor . . .

ZACH
(Brushes her hand away)

. . . but with the hope, and with the prayer, yes, with the prayer, that out of my efforts something would be born, something. . . .

MINNA
(Tugs again at his coat)

Doctor . . .

ZACH
(Turns to her, whispers with great annoyance)

What is it?

MINNA

They're having a reception for you upstairs and they're serving frankfurters and baked beans with a tossed green salad and some hot seeded .

130

(Angrily)

That's it! That does it!

(Pushes her upstairs)

Get up there now, Minna. Go ahead, get up there! And stay up there, do you hear me? Stay up there! And don't come down again!

(ZACH closes door at the top of the steps, then comes back down into basement, moving to table, pulling his cap down on his head, mumbling to himself)

Don't understand. Never understand. Right from the beginning. I know it. Talk to her. Talk to her . . . explain . . . don't help. Nothing helps.

(Pours powder from mortar into red liquid, then puts on rubber gloves)

Nothing . . . all these years . . . said she understood. But she doesn't, she doesn't . . .

(Now mumbling to chimpanzee)

She doesn't know . . . nobody knows what we're doing here. Everybody expects things to come easily nowadays. No one's willing to put in the work, the sweat, the time . . . what's necessary for doing anything that amounts to anything.

(He now connects ear plugs into the chimpanzee's ears: the right ear plug is connected to a large bottle at the chimpanzee's side by a wide plastic tube, the left ear plug is connected also by a wide plastic tube to a plastic funnel several inches above chimpanzee's head)

They all look for the easy way . . . the easy way . . . but in the end it shows. The hard work shows, what you put in you take out, no more, no less. There's no faking it, no covering up.

(To chimpanzee as he prepares to pour red fluid into funnel)

Easy. Easy now. Just take it easy.

(Slight pause, nods)

Good luck.

(And pours the red fluid into the funnel connected to the chimpanzee's left ear, from the right ear a blue fluid flows into the bottle at its side. Shortly a huge face appears in the window. LEO lies full-length on the sidewalk, outside the window. Only his head is seen, now and then his hands gesture through the barred windows and he wipes his horn-rimmed eyeglasses with a handkerchief. His voice is constrained, urgent, almost a monotonous wail. ZACH removes gloves and is busy behind table)

LEO

Psssssst.

(Slight pause)

Zach.

(Slight pause.)

Pssssssst.

ZACH
(Without turning making notations on clip-board)

· Go away, Leo.

LEO

I just spoke to Minna, Zach. She won't open the basement door. She said I should ask you if it's all right. Zach, can I come down? I want to speak to you.

131

ZACH

Tomorrow. Not now. Go away.

LEO

It's important. I wouldn't bother you if it wasn't important. Zach, I can't stay here much longer. I'm stretched out on the sidewalk. People are staring at me. It's Dad, Zach. The doctor was just over to see him and he's sick, he's very sick. He's been sick all week. And you didn't phone, you didn't come over, you ...
(Raising his head, clear loud voice to someone on sidewalk)
What? What's that? No, no, I'm all right. I'm not drunk. I don't drink. I ... it's none of your business whether I drink or not, lady! I ...
(Lowers head, constrained voice, urgently)
Zach, I can't stay here. It's dangerous. Let me come down to the basement and speak to you.

ZACH
(Takes blood pressure of chimpanzee, notes it on clip-board)
Go home, Leo.

LEO

I wouldn't be here if it wasn't for Dad. I don't care if I never see you again. That's the way you want it, isn't it? But it's for Dad. He deserves this much from you. You have to see him, Zach. You won't believe how much he's changed. He's wasted away to nothing, skin and bones. And his eyes ... they're popping out of his head and his whole face it's ...

ZACH
(Turning to him)
Will you shut up! Are you blind? I'm working. I can't be interrupted. Go home, Leo. Leave me alone.
(ZACH returns to his work. Once he is done taking chimpanzee's blood pressure he fills a flask with blue fluid and lights the Sterno under it, he then makes further notations)

LEO

You're not going to hear the end of this, Zach. If I have to stay here all night, stretched out on the sidewalk, ruining my only good suit, a suit that isn't paid for yet, and suffer from severe chest and stomach pains because of your stubbornness, I will, Zach, I will. I won't go back without you. I won't. I promised. I said, "Dad, you know how Zach is. He doesn't mean anything by it. As soon as I let him know you want to see him ..." He looked at me with those strange eyes that he's got now and I thought, "Dad. Dad. How is it possible? When was it that you stood like a tower, like a colossus of strength and worldly wisdom ... when was it that I looked up at you, my mouth half-open, my heart beating with excitement because I was so close to you ..."

ZACH
(Without turning, fists clenched, shouts)
Leo! Leo!

LEO

No. No. I'm not going to stop. You're not going to make me stop. He's in bed, Zach. Dad's confined to his bed. And I sit and I listen to him, hour after hour . . . "Where's Zach?" he asks. "When is he coming to see me?" And you know what hurts? I'm there! I'm with him day and night. But it's you . . . like always. Why is that? He's living in my house, he's eating my food and benefiting by my attention and sacrifice and . . . over and over he asks, "Where's Zach? Where's Zach?" That hurts. *That* hurts. My wife is working herself sick; my kids have to walk around the house in their stockinged feet; I phone the office every day and I tell them I can't come in . . . "Where's Zach?" he asks, "Where's Zach?"

ZACH

Leo, do me a favor. Please.

(Moves to window)

It won't do any damn good talking about it. Go home. If I get the chance I'll come over and if I don't get the chance . . . my work . . . I have my work to do. My life isn't in him. Not anymore. That's how it is. If you can't under . . .

LEO

(Suddenly turns and shouts)

Hey! Hey! Get that dog away from me! Get him away!

(ZACH drops his hands with exasperation and moves to table)

Never mind, mister, this happens to be a public sidewalk and if I feel like laying on it, I'll lay on it, that's my business! You just keep moving, keep moving . . .

(LEO waves him away, then down on sidewalk again, head at window, he continues wailing as if there had been no interruption)

but his life is in you, Zach. He gave you his life. How could you forget? And it was for you . . . that's what hurts. What he did was for you, not for me. I stood by his side, always stood by the side and watched and said, "All right, let Zach go to college. I don't mind giving up my own education and getting a job." I said, "Sure, Dad; whatever you think best. I don't need a car now. It's more important that Zach has the books he needs and there are no holes in his shoes. I can wait for the car."

(ZACH covers Sterno, then opens large research book, makes notations on clipboard; he is unable to concentrate with LEO ranting on behind him; he moves to milk box, tries again for several minutes, fails, moves to crate, uses pen flashlight in order to see what he's doing, and tries once again to concentrate on his work)

And I didn't mind. I didn't. That's what hurts. I would have done anything he said, and I would have been glad to do it. I thought we were a family. I thought this is the way families have to be, giving to each other, making sacrifices for each other. When did we stop being a family? When did it happen? Even after Mother passed away, may she rest in peace, we were close together, closer together than we ever were. Her memory was there with us, holding us together, saying things to us that nobody else could hear. Dad and I . . . we tried to keep her alive. We spoke about her and we remembered the different times . . . but you. You wouldn't let us. You wouldn't have it. You're the one who buried her, Zach. Just as you're burying Dad now and just as you want to bury me and everything . . .

ZACH

(Rises, slams book and clip-board on table, moves to window)

133

You won't leave me alone! Who asked you to sit up there, buzzing in my ear, not letting me work? Tell him whatever you want. Think whatever you want. But ... Leo. Try to understand. What I'm doing. What I'm trying to achieve here ...

LEO

You haven't been over to see us in six, seven years. You have two nephews, do you know what they look like? Do you care? But when you needed money, then you came to the office and you said, "Leo, I've got to have some money right away." Did I throw you out? Did I say, "Why don't you come home? Why don't you phone me once in a while so we'll know you're still alive?" No. I said, "How much do you need, Zach?"

(At shelves ZACH *opens several empty boxes of cigars before he finds a cigar butt in one of them. He lights it, then sits on crate)*

ZACH

And I said, "I need three thousand dollars." And what did you say?

LEO

"You must be joking," I said.

ZACH
(Nods)

That's what you said.

LEO

I said, "I don't have three thousand dollars. I don't have three hundred dollars. Do you know what it costs to keep up a house nowadays, to feed two growing boys, a wife and a father who is your responsibility as much as mine?" I said, "Did you ever give a penny for Dad's support, for his medical bills and all the rest?"

ZACH

Then what did I say?

LEO

You said, and I remember your words exactly, Zach, you said, "All right. All right. How much do you need for Dad's support?"

ZACH

Then what did you say?

LEO

I said and I remember your words exactly, Zach, I said, "In view of the high cost of living ..."

ZACH

"Twenty-five dollars a month," you said. Which I sent you every month from that day I was dumb enough to ask you for a loan of three thousand dollars in the first place!

(Rises, his back to LEO *he leans on shelf)*

134

LEO

And from which day you never got in touch or phoned or as much as said thank you for all I've done for you. Was that nice? Was it, Zach? I'm your brother; your flesh and blood. What do you have against me? Why do you avoid me? It isn't natural. My wife makes fun of us. She does. She can't believe it. She says, "I can't believe it. Your brother hasn't been over to see you in years and you only live ten minutes away. It isn't natural," she says. And she's right, Zach. That's what hurts. She says, "You only have one brother, one brother and you don't ..."

ZACH

Leo, listen to me. Please.
(He pushes crate under window with his foot, stands on it so that he's on a level with LEO*)*
I can't stop what I'm doing now. I can't. I've been at it too long and I'm finally coming near the end, the finish of what I hope will be something ... what I want to accomplish, what I'm trying now to successfully conclude ... you see, Leo, that ... that chimpanzee sitting there, that monkey, he's been laying dead in my freezer for nearly nineteen years!
*(*LEO *stares at chimpanzee, then down at* ZACH, *turning from one to the other. A long pause)*

LEO

You have a freezer?

ZACH

Leo!

LEO

When did you get a freezer? I don't have a freezer! I can't afford a freezer! My wife has to chop meat in the ice-tray compartment because it sticks to the sides and we can't go out and buy a freezer. But you have a freezer? I never ...

ZACH

Listen, Leo! For one minute! That ... that's been dead for nearly nineteen years. Of a brain injury which I was able to fix and make good again. He's in almost perfect physical condition. Now if I can revive him, Leo, if I can bring him back after nineteen years in the freezer, can't you appreci ...

LEO
(Nods slowly, sadly)
I didn't get the chance to tell you, Zach. Uncle Sidney is sick, he's very sick.
(Resolved, ZACH *leans over, picks up three wide boards and nails them to the window, covering it completely. Without a pause)*
Aunt Bertha phoned from the hospital today and she could hardly speak. It was awful. It was terrible. She said, "It's serious, Leo. He's going to leave us. Your Uncle Sidney who was so good to you and your brother, Zach. Where is Zach? Why doesn't he phone us once in a while?" she asked. I didn't know what to say to her. She was hurt. She was terribly hurt. She said, "I never thought Zach would turn out to be that kind of person. Here is his uncle, a man who did so much for him, and he doesn't have the common decency or courtesy to see if he's still alive or dead or has what to

eat or a roof over his head." She said, "What's happened to your brother Zach, Leo? Did we insult him? Did we offend him? Did his uncle do one thing to him to deserve this kind of treatment from him?" You should have . . .

(As last board is nailed into place, protesting)

Zach! Zach!

(The window is completely boarded now. ZACH *steps down from crate and goes to table to continue working. He puts thermometer into chimpanzee's mouth, staring at wristwatch, smoking cigar. A long pause. Then* L E O*'s loud voice is heard from behind boarded window)*

Keep this up, Zach, and I'm leaving! I'm going! I'm not coming back! You'll never see me again. Never. Forget you had a brother. Forget you had a father. Forget you ever belonged to a family or had anyone who worried about you or cared about you or stayed up nights . . .

ZACH
(Turning to window)

Go! Go! I want you to go! You're too damn dumb to understand. You don't understand. My work . . . my wife . . . that's all I have and that's all I . . .

LEO

Your wife? Minna? We talked before. In the kitchen. I showed her some pictures I took this week of my two boys, so she'd recognize her own nephews, her own relatives. Do you know what she did, Zach? Do you know what? She cried. She held the pictures of my two boys, my sons, my flesh and blood, and she cried. I said, "Minna, why are you crying? What's wrong?" She shook her head. She said, "He said, but if you want them, if you feel that you have to have them . . ."

ZACH

You're lying! You're jealous!

LEO

What did she mean, Zach?

ZACH

You don't know what you're saying!

LEO

Want what?

ZACH

She said what I said!

LEO

Feel what?

ZACH

She said she didn't want . . . she said . . .

LEO

What did she want?

136

(Voice fading as he leaves)
What was it? Crying. I never saw anything like it.

(At foot of steps, over L E O's line)
Minna! Minna! Minna!
(No answer, he goes up steps, throws open door)
Come down here! I said come down here!
(He comes down steps, into basement)
He's lying, Minna. He's making it up. Tell him he's lying. Tell him you said what I said. Tell him . . .
(Goes up steps again, shouts)
Minna, come down here! I said come down here, Minna! You know he comes here to make trouble!
(Comes down into basement again)
I thought you had enough sense to understand that. We agreed. We agreed. Now I don't want to hear another word about it. Not tonight or any other night. Do you understand? Do you understand, Minna?
(Moves to behind the table, puts cigar aside, removes thermometer from chimpanzee's mouth, then removes ear plugs from its ears)
In the future, don't let him in the house, don't even let him lay on the sidewalk, that's all. I don't want him here. He's a troublemaker. Showing pictures of his boys. Who asked him? And you fell for it, Minna, you fell right into the trap he set for you. And you should have known better. You should have seen through it. You should have stood up to him and said, "You don't understand your brother Zach. What that man is doing so far exceeds any thought you ever had in that head of yours that any comparison is ridiculous, utterly ridiculous." That's what you should have said to him, Minna. Instead of letting him trick you that way. But I don't hold you responsible.
(Shouts)
Minna!
(No answer; half-heartedly puts stethoscope on, holds it to chimpanzee's chest)
It's not your fault. I know that man. I know how tricky he can be. We'll forget it, Minna. We'll forget he ever came here.
(Shouts)
Minna!
(No answer; he removes stethoscope, sits on milk box, stares alternately at steps and chimpanzee)
And soon . . . soon I'll be done with my work and I'll come upstairs and we'll have a couple of scrambled eggs and mashed potatoes and a little chocolate pudding with sweet cream, and everything'll be like it was again, Minna.
(Takes hat off, shouts)
Minna!
(No answer; softly, hunched over on milk box)
Everything'll be like it was.

CURTAIN

The Chinese

In my novel, Days and Nights of a French Horn Player, *I wrote the following:*

> *I talked to myself as if I was my best friend.*
> *Hi, Eddie.*
> *Hi.*
> *How's it going?*
> *Okay.*
> *You wanna go to the park?*
> *Sure. Let's go to the park.*
> *Eddie?*
> *What?*
> *If you found a million dollars what would you do with it?*
> *I'd give it to my parents.*
> *All of it?*
> *All of it.*
> *There's something I have to tell you, Eddie.*
> *What's that?*
> *They're not your real parents.*
> *You're kidding me.*
> *No. I've been keeping it a secret. Your real parents live in Manhattan.*
> *Where?*
> *On Park Avenue.*
> *You're not . . .?*
> *No. It's the truth, Eddie. Your real father's name is Nelson; your real mother's*
> *name is Amanda.*
> *When can I see them?*
> *When you're twenty-one. They'll pick you up in a limousine.*

The Chinese *is a variation of the same story. I imagine I will continue to write variations of the same story for the rest of my life.*

—M. S.
March 9, 1983

139

THE CHINESE *was first presented by Gilbert Cates at the Ethel Barrymore Theatre, in New York City, on March 10, 1970.*

MR. LEE	*Joseph Bova*
MRS. LEE	*Alice Drummond*
CHESTER LEE	*William Devane*
GLADYS HOFFMAN	*Louise Lasser*
PU PING CHOW	*Marcia Jean Kurtz*

Directed by ARTHUR STORCH
Set design by WILLIAM PITKIN
Costumes by SARA BROOK
Lighting design by MARTIN ARONSTEIN

A Chinese laundry. Street window on right with block letters on it read-ing: HO HING CHINESE LAUNDRY; *glass-paneled door also on right, down, leading into street. In the rear right to center, is a work counter. There is a hinged shelf on left side of work counter, behind it and along left wall are wooden shelves on which there are stacked brown paper-wrapped packages of shirts and linen with colored tickets attached to them, bundles of dirty linen are on the floor, left, a rectangular table and chairs, a door leading into the kitchen is in the rear wall, right, next to it is a bureau, a doorless doorframe leading to bedrooms is in left wall.*

Early afternoon.

MR. HO HING LEE *is ironing shirts at work counter. He wears a white shirt, open at the neck, dark trousers and slippers.*

His wife, MRS. TING TOY LEE, *is seated at the table, on the right, numbering shirt collars with pen. She also wears dark trousers, slippers, but has on a mandarin-style blouse that hangs over her trousers.*

It is suggested that MR. *and* MRS. LEE *are played by Caucasians. It is also suggested that* GLADYS HOFFMAN *and* PU PING CHOW *are played by the same actress.*

CHESTER *enters the laundry, a bell tinkles above the door, he moves to table, he is sullen, his posture is somewhat slouched. He turns neither right nor left but moves directly to table, sits opposite his mother and thumbs through a Chinese newspaper.* CHESTER *is about twenty-five. His physical appearance is in no way Oriental. He wears tan pants, a striped shirt, canvas sneakers, and a shapeless cotton rain hat.*

MR. LEE
(As CHESTER *moves to table, speaking to* MRS. LEE. *It is obvious, however, that his remarks are directed towards* CHESTER, *in Chinese.* CHESTER *tosses rain hat into bedroom area)*
Ah, keu do le. Ngo day hai mm hai ying goy quai lok lai do dzieh keu fan lay, heh! Keu heng lay nee do, tsen hai teu ngo day tai ho le! Keu seang yut hai been do, ah? Keu deem gai mm hai po tou pong ngo day sai yeh tong yeh, dzo dee kung dzok? Keu yee wai tsien hai shu sheung dzak lok lai ge me? Keu yee wai fan tung yee fuk hai teen deet lok lai ge me? Keu yut go seen sou yup do mo, dan hai keu gum hai nee do hang lay heu dong ngo day hai keu ge gung yun, keu wah dzo mut yeh ngo day dzou mut yeh, do dzieh yut siang do mm sai. (Oh, he's here. Well, I guess we should get down on our knees and thank him for making an appearance. It is so kind of him to reveal himself to us! Where was he all day? Why is he not in the store helping us wash and iron and do the work that's necessary? Does he think money grows on trees? Does he think food and clothes fall from the sky? He doesn't con-tribute a penny and yet he has the nerve to walk around as if we were in his employ-ment, as if we are merely his household slaves to do his bidding for which he does not even show us the slightest sign of gratitude!)

(There is a pause. CHESTER *continues thumbing through newspaper, indifferently)*

MRS. LEE
(In Chinese)
Chester, nay baba tung nay gong gun. Nay ying goy dop keu. Baba tung nay gong go dzun see, nay ying goy dop keu ge. (Chester, your dear father is speaking to you. You must answer him. It is only proper to answer your father when he speaks to you.)
(Another pause. CHESTER *turns pages of newspaper)*

CHESTER
(Grimly)
Tell him to speak in English. This is America, not China. We speak English in this country.

MRS. LEE
(To MR. LEE, *in Chinese)*
Jeung fu, nay dzee go ngo day ge dzai Chester hai deem yeung ge la. Gum yut mm ho ngai gow. Mm goy nay. Tung keu going ying mun. (My dear husband, you know how our son Chester is; let us not quarrel today. I beg you. Speak to him in English.)

MR. LEE
(Shouting angrily, in Chinese)
Ying mun! Ying mun! Keu . . . keu gum dai dom gum geel ngo gong ying mun! Ngo yeel yung ying mun lay gong ngo dzou yung ying lai gong. Dan hai ngo mm yeel! Ngo sik ge ying mun tung keu ge yut yeung gum ho! (English! English! He . . . he has the outrageous nerve to ask me to speak in English! If I wished to I would speak in English! But I do not wish to! I know English as well as he does and I can speak English as well as he does!)

CHESTER
(Answers him, in Chinese)
Gum may deem gai mm gong ne? Deem gai nay dzee hai gong jumg mun ge ne? Deem gai nee gan nguk leu been mut yeh do hai jung gwok ge? Ngo day hai may gwok yun, ying goy ho tsee may gwok yun gong ying mun! (Then why don't you? Why do you always have to speak Chinese? Why does everything in this house have to be Chinese? We're Americans and we should speak English like Americans!)

MR. LEE
(Shouts back, in Chinese)
Nee do hai go jung gwok sai gwon jung gwok ge gah ting! (This is a Chinese laundry and a Chinese family!)
*(*CHESTER *turns his back to his father, crossing his legs, folding his arms, sulking)*

MRS. LEE
(Importunately, with Chinese accent)
Chester, my son, my precious child, for my sake, for your mother's sake, let this

142

quarrel with your father be finished now. He has been standing on his feet all day. Let the rest of the afternoon pass pleasantly between us. Do it for me, Chester.

CHESTER
(To MR. LEE *moving to door, looking out)*
I . . . I'm sorry, Dad. I didn't mean to yell like that.

MR. LEE
(With Chinese accent)
That's all right, my son. I know that this is a difficult time for you. Is the young lady coming today to meet us?

CHESTER
(Nods)
She's coming. She'll be here. I think you'll like Gladys. I really think you're gonna be glad I'm getting serious about her.

MR. LEE
I would be more glad if you were serious with Pu Ping Chow. She is . . .

MRS. LEE
(Interrupts him to prevent another quarrel)
Where did you meet this girl, Chester?

CHESTER
(Staring grimly at his father at the mention of PU PING CHOW)
Oh, about five years ago. In high school.
(Now turns to his mother, losing his grimness)
That's the funny thing, Ma. Gladys was in almost all my classes and I never looked at her twice. But then when I saw her a couple of months ago at Marvin Brockman's party. Wow! What a difference. I was astonished at the difference!

MRS. LEE
Does she know you're getting serious?

CHESTER
She knows. That's why she's coming over. She's an exceptional girl. And she has a fantastic job, Dad.

MR. LEE
Still, my son, if you are thinking of marriage you will have to find a job and support her.

CHESTER
I know, Dad. I know that. I'll find a job. I was over at Madison Square Garden yesterday. They got the Ice Follies there now. I met this man, Mr. Donleavy, and he said he'd put me to work tomorrow if I wanted.

MR. LEE
Doing what?

143

CHESTER

Cleaning the ice.

MR. LEE

Cleaning the ice?

CHESTER

After they skate on it. It gets all chopped up. So three or four fellows put on ice skates and go skating around, cleaning the ice.

(Demonstrates)

MR. LEE

What kind of job is that, cleaning the ice?

CHESTER

It happens to be a good job. It happens to be a union job, so don't knock it. But it would only be temporary. I know there's no future in it. But the thing is, if I married Gladys, we'd move in and live with her parents. Talk about a deal. That's what I call a deal.

MR. LEE

And it wouldn't bother the girl's parents that you are without money and have no job?

CHESTER

Look, Dad, I spoke to her father already. I'm not playing games here. He's brilliant. Some people, he said, it takes a little longer than other people to find themselves, to know what they wanna do with themselves. Especially today, when all the kids my age have the same problem, what with the wars and the armament race and the pressures they put on us. He said, "If you and Gladys decide to get married, Chester, take your time; go back to school if you want, work at different jobs if you want, nobody's putting any pressure on you; we'll do what we can to help." I tell you, Dad, after speaking to that man for five minutes, I felt so good I didn't care if I never found another job again!

MRS. LEE

And the woman who would be your mother-in-law? Is she a nice woman, Chester? (She starts to pick up huge laundry bag. CHESTER stops her, picks up bag, puts it in her arms, then moves to work counter and raises hinged counter shelf for MRS. LEE to enter)

CHESTER

My mother-in-law? Now I'm gonna surprise you, Ma. Now I'm really gonna surprise you because as a matter of fact I happen to be more in love with the woman who's gonna be my mother-in-law than I am with the woman who's gonna be my wife.

MRS. LEE

You love the mother more than Gladys?

CHESTER
(Nods)

More than Gladys even. The truth. My mother-in-law to-be is not only good-looking, not only intelligent and sensitive, but she has a figure on her that'll pop the eyes
right out of your head!

MR. LEE

Chester!

MRS. LEE

With a young lady, you must be careful, my son. She is like a bud on a tree branch
that needs sunshine and warmth to open up into a lovely blossom.

CHESTER

Gladys and me, we get along fine, Ma. Really. I don't think we're gonna have any
trouble, unless it's . . . unless . . .
(A slight pause, he raises hinged shelf, exits, lowers shelf)
Dad, before I plan seriously about getting married, is there . . . is there anything you
wanna tell me?

MR. LEE

Tell you?

CHESTER

About me, about . . .
(MR. and MRS. LEE exchange puzzled glances)
You know I wouldn't go into this unless I had to. I stay away from this particular
subject as much as I can. But now I have to go into it. I have to. Gladys'll be here
soon and she'll wanna know and her parents'll wanna know . . .

MR. LEE

Know what? Why are you shouting? Why do you raise your voice?

CHESTER

Because you're both pretending you don't understand what I'm talking about when
you both understand perfectly what I'm talking about!

MRS. LEE

Chester, my son, listen to me, please. It's best we don't go into. . .

CHESTER

Ma, I'm not going to disown anybody. I'll always love you. And I'll always love Dad.
And I'll always be grateful to the both of you for bringing me up. But I have a right
to know who my real biological parents are, that's all!

MR. LEE
(Furiously, in Chinese)

Nah! Ngo dzee do keu wui gum lay ge! Ngo day ng fen jung ge ngon ding do mo.
Keu dzou wui . . . keu dzou hov see . . . (There! I knew it would happen! We can't
have five minutes of peace in this house! He has to start . . . He has to begin . . .)

145

MRS. LEE
(In Chinese)

Mm ho gun gun jeung. Mm goy nay. Mo ban fat ge. Mm ho gum gun jeung. (Don't get excited, my dear husband. Please. It does no good. Don't get excited.)

MR. LEE
(In Chinese)

Gun jeung! Been go gun jeung ah! Ngo mo gun jeung ah! Keu dzou wui ... keu dzou hov see ... (Excited! Who's excited? I'm not excited! He has to start. He has to begin ...)

CHESTER
(Angrily, in Chinese)

Ngo mui tsee mun nay go dzing dong hup lay get mun tai, nay dzou lun ngup yah sai, dzow lai now ngo! (Every time I ask you a perfectly legitimate and reasonable question, I get double talk, I get yelled at and insulted!)

MRS. LEE
(In Chinese)

Aiya. Aiya. Nay leung go. Mm goy nay, mm ho gum le. Ngai gow been do you yung ge ne. (Please. Please. Both of you. I implore you. Be calm. Nothing is accomplished by quarreling.)

CHESTER

Somebody's hiding something, that's all I'm saying.

MRS. LEE

My dear son, my sweetheart, no one is hiding anything from you.

CHESTER

Then why does he always start yelling at me when I ask a perfectly legitimate and reasonable question?

MRS. LEE

It causes him great pain, my son. For you to deny Ho Hing as your real father and me as your real mother, and this is not the first time you have done so, Chester, is very painful and humiliating to both of us.

CHESTER

That's not the point, Ma. If you told me right now that you weren't my real biological parents, that you adopted me or ... or got me somewhere ... Do you think I'd go running out of here looking for my real biological parents? No. I wouldn't. I don't even care who my real biological parents are. I just wanna know where you found me, that's all.

MR. LEE
(In Chinese; pointing to door)

You keu heu! Nah, moon hai go do! (Let him go! There's the door!)

146

MRS. LEE

Chester, we told you a thousand times, a thousand and one times ... would you like to hear it all again?

CHESTER
(Stiffly)

Yes, Mother, I would. I definitely would.
(Sits at table)

MR. LEE
(In Chinese)

Yow lay la! (Again!)

MRS. LEE
(With a sigh, sits at table)

Your father and I were born in Macao, off the coast of southern China. We were childhood sweethearts and when we came to the United States we lived in Los Angeles for a brief period of time and then we moved here, to the Brownsville section of Brooklyn to buy this laundry which was advertised in a Chinese newspaper. You were born here, Chester. Doctor Thomas Wong, a general practitioner, delivered you. He was a wise old man who was of great help to us when we first moved into this neighborhood where very few Chinese families lived. But you grew up here, Chester. You played in the streets with the other children, and you went to school with the other children. If we seem strange to you, my son, it is because of this: we were not born in this country, we were not raised in this country, while you were, as were most of the people you grew up with.

CHESTER
(Sulking)

There are other things, Ma. There are things you didn't go into.

MRS. LEE

Your appearance?

CHESTER

Yeah!

MRS. LEE

That your skin is not the same color as ours and your eyes are not as small?

CHESTER

Yeah! That's right!

MRS. LEE

That, too, Chester, can be explained. On both sides of the family, on your father's side and mine, there has been intermarriage. I myself can count two great uncles and a great-grandparent who are European, while your father's father came from . . . .

(She turns to MR. LEE, *in Chinese)*
Nay lo tai po hai been do lay ge? (Where did your father come from, dear?)

MR. LEE
Montgomery, Alabama.

MRS. LEE
(To CHESTER*)*
Montgomery, Alabama.

CHESTER
(Rises)
Look, Ma, like you said, we've been over this a thousand times already but . . . Let me ask you one or two questions. Then I'll be quiet. I swear. I'll never open my mouth on this subject again. All right? All right, Dad?

MR. LEE
I will not tolerate rudeness or disrespect to me or your mother.

CHESTER
All right. Ma . . . You say Doctor Thomas Wong delivered me, is that right?

MRS. LEE
Yes. Doctor Thomas Wong. He was a wise old man.

CHESTER
And if I remember, if I remember correctly, you once said that Doctor Wong died six months after I was born, right?

MRS. LEE
Yes. About six months. We attended funeral services for him.

CHESTER
Now, think carefully, before you answer this, think very, very carefully. Ma . . . Was there anyone else present besides Doctor Thomas Wong on the day I was born?
*(*MRS. LEE *looks to* MR. LEE*)*

MR. LEE
No. As far as we can remember he was the only one. It was in the bedroom that you were born. Early in the morning. At five o'clock. I ran to Doctor Wong's house and brought him back with me.

CHESTER
(Softly)
Ma.
(She looks up at him)
Why did you look at Dad then?

MRS. LEE

Look . . .?

CHESTER
(Raising voice)

At Dad! Just then! I saw you look at Dad at the exact minute I asked you if anyone else was in this house besides Doctor Thomas Wong on the day I was born!

MRS. LEE

I couldn't remember. I was . . .

CHESTER

You couldn't remember or you didn't want to remember!

MR. LEE

Chester!

CHESTER

Dad, I have a right to know if there was anyone else in this house besides Doctor Thomas Wong at five o'clock in the morning on the day I was born. Will you or will you not answer that question!

(MRS. LEE looks to MR. LEE again)

MR. LEE
(Softly)

Yes, Chester. There was someone else.

CHESTER

Who?

MR. LEE

Madame Ching from Belmont Avenue.

CHESTER

Madame Ching from Belmont Avenue! Who's Madame Ching from Belmont Avenue!

MR. LEE

Madame Fannie Ching. You did not know her. And your mother did not want you to know anything about her because Madame Ching was a woman of . . . of loose ways, a bad woman, Chester.

CHESTER

So what does all that mean?

MR. LEE

That means she was here, with your mother, when I ran to get Doctor Wong. We did not like her to be here at your birth but we had no choice. Someone had to stay

149

with your mother, and she was in the street when I opened the door. It is something your mother did not wish you to know.

CHESTER

Where is Madame Ching now?

MRS. LEE

Dead.

MR. LEE

Dead.

CHESTER

She's dead too, huh?

MR. LEE

She died soon after Doctor Wong.

MRS. LEE

That is the truth, Chester.

CHESTER

What did she die of?

MR. LEE

Hepatitis.

MRS. LEE

Yes, hepatitis.

CHESTER

And Doctor Wong, what did he die of?

MR. LEE

Inflammation of the lungs.

CHESTER

And there was no one else who saw me on the day I was born except Madame Ching who died of hepatitis and Doctor Wong who died of inflammation of the lungs?

MR. LEE
(Nods)

Now you know everything, Chester.

CHESTER

Now I know everything! Now I know there was an epidemic in this city the day I was born, that's all I know!

MRS. LEE

It's the truth, Chester.

150

CHESTER

Didn't you have one single friend or one single neighbor or even one single stranger who saw me on the day I was born who didn't die of hepatitis or inflammation of the lungs?

MR. LEE
(Wagging his finers)

Chester, it's not for you to . . .

CHESTER
(Moves to door)

Boy, this is all very convenient for you, isn't it? Like losing my birth certificate, that was also convenient. Gladys'll be here soon and I don't know how I'm gonna explain . . .

(He stops himself. A pause)

MRS. LEE

She does not know we are Chinese?

MR. LEE
(In Chinese)

Keu mm dzee? (She does not know?)
(CHESTER shakes his head)

MRS. LEE

What did you tell her?

CHESTER

What's the difference?

MRS. LEE
(Rises)

Chester, I want to know what you told her!

MR. LEE
(In Chinese)

Nay wah dzo bay keu talng mut yeh ah! (Tell us what you told her!)

CHESTER
(Slight pause)

I told her we were Jewish.

MR. LEE
(Screams)

Jewish!
(He takes off his slipper and chases CHESTER through secret opening in work counter, in Chinese)

You tai! Keu fat sun ging ge me? Hai ma? Keu fat sun ging ge me? Ngo deem ho yee dzou ngo ge gung dzok, dan hai tenag keu gong duk gum bum gum sun ging mm

151

sheung sat keu ne! (Jewish! Is he out of his mind? Is he? Is he out of his mind? How can I get my work done and not want to kill him when I am forced to listen to him speak so . . . stupidly and insanely!)

MRS. LEE

Please, please, my husband. Let me take care of this. For once. Please.
(To CHESTER)
Chester, my son, my only child, why did you tell the young lady we were Jewish? Are you so ashamed of us and of all our ancestors?

CHESTER

It's not that, Ma. You don't understand what it was like growing up in this neighborhood and going to school here and everything. Everybody here was Jewish. I just got into the habit, that's all. People used to stop me and ask me what I was, so I'd say, "I'm Jewish," and right away they'd pat me on the head and they'd give me things. Flags, hats, candles, raisins. Once I even got a chopped herring sandwich.

MR. LEE

You think your mother and I are such fools? You never brought home any of your friends to introduce to us. You never invited us to visit you in your school like other parents. But we kept our mouths closed. We said nothing. We did not wish to embarrass you despite your shameful conduct.

CHESTER

I didn't tell you to move into this neighborhood, did I? What did you want me to do? Explain to them something I didn't believe myself?

MR. LEE

That we are your parents?

CHESTER

I was only a kid, Dad.

MRS. LEE

But what will you tell the young lady when she comes here?

MR. LEE

Chester, if you would be interested in Pu Ping Chow . . .

CHESTER
(Shouts at him)
But I'm not interested in Pu Ping Chow!

MRS. LEE

She is a lovely girl, Chester.

CHESTER

She's a foreigner, that's what she is. She's been in this country only three months. She can hardly speak two words of English yet. Every time I meet her in the street she bows down in front of me as if she just had a hernia operation!

MR. LEE

Don't speak ill of Pu Ping Chow!

MRS. LEE

Chester, Pu Ping Chow . . .

CHESTER

I don't want to hear any more about Pu Ping Chow. I got Pu Ping Chow coming out of my ears already! She's not gonna help me out of my predicament. Gladys'll be here any minute and I still don't know what I'm gonna tell her! If you could just give me the name of anyone who was . . .
(GLADYS enters, interrupting CHESTER in mid-speech. She is a girl in her twenties, mini-skirted, brown tights)

GLADYS

Hello, Chester.
(Looking around)
Why did you want to meet me in a Chinese laundry?

CHESTER
(Turns to her)
Hi, Gladys.

GLADYS

Is this where you bring your shirts?

CHESTER

Come on in. Come on in. I . . .
(Takes a deep breath)

GLADYS
(Sniffing)
I think I smell rice burning.

MRS. LEE
(Sniffs at air, runs into kitchen, mumbling in Chinese)
Fan, fan, fan. (Rice, rice, rice.)

GLADYS
(Takes CHESTER's arm)
Let's go, Chester. There's a lot I have to tell you. I ran into Marvin Brockman this morning and he told me.
(As they move towards door, suddenly stops)
Aren't you taking your shirts?

CHESTER

My shirts? That's right. My shirts. I almost forgot.
(Moves to counter, to MR. LEE. Deep formal voice)
I'd like my shirts, please.

MR. LEE
(In Chinese)
Ngo bay sut sam bay nay. Ngo bay nay da yut bah! (I'll give you your shirts. A broken head I'll give you.)

CHESTER
(Turned away from GLADYS, *in Chinese)*
Baba, mm goy nay. Bay gay geen sut sam bay ngo. Nog tsee dee dzoy dai Gladys fan lay. (Dad, please. Give me some shirts. I'll bring Gladys back later.)

MR. LEE
(Mutters, in Chinese)
Ngo mm lay nay dai mm dai keu fan lay. (I don't care if you never bring her back.)

CHESTER
(In Chinese)
Baba, mm goy nay. Ngo seen tung keu gong gui wah. (Please, Dad, I wanna speak to her alone first.)

MR. LEE
(In Chinese)
Dzou hoy! Dzou hoy! (Go! Go!)
*(*GLADYS *moves up to them)*

CHESTER
(In Chinese)
Ngo day tsee . . . (We'll come back . . .)

GLADYS
(Tapping CHESTER *on the shoulder, interrupting him in mid-speech)*
Are you speaking Chinese to him, Chester?

CHESTER
I . . .
(He nods vigorously)

GLADYS
Why, that's wonderful. When did you learn to speak Chinese?

CHESTER
I . . . I could speak it since I was a kid.

GLADYS
You could?
*(*CHESTER *nods)*

CHESTER
Gladys, there's something I have to tell you.

GLADYS

Let me hear you say this in Chinese: The rain in Spain stays mainly in the plain.

CHESTER
(In Chinese; unhappily)

Sai ban nga yu lok hai ping day.

GLADYS
(Delighted)

Now let me hear: Jack and Jill went up the hill. They each had a buck and a quarter.

CHESTER
(In Chinese)

Jack tung Jill pa sheung san Mui yun you yut go yee ho boon.

GLADYS
(Pleased)

Jill came down with two and a half. Do you think they went up for water?
(MR. LEE *bangs down the iron, angrily mumbling in Chinese, and turns his back
to them)*

What's wrong with him?

CHESTER

Gladys . . .

GLADYS

Is he crazy?

CHESTER

Gladys, listen . . .

GLADYS

Tell him to give you your shirts and let's get out of here.

CHESTER

Gladys . . .

GLADYS
(Knocking on counter)

Hey! Are you deaf behind there!

CHESTER
(Turning her towards him)

Gladys, listen to me, will you!

GLADYS

Don't you want your . . .

155

CHESTER

Forget that! There's a lot I didn't tell you that I wanna straighten our right now!
(He looks over at his parents)
Gladys . . .
(Takes a deep breath)
Gladys, I want you to meet my mother and father.

GLADYS

(Looks around the room then at MR. *and* MRS. LEE *and finally at* CHESTER *)*
Where are they?

CHESTER
(Moves between parents)
Dad, this is my friend, Gladys Hoffman. Ma, this is Gladys.

MRS. LEE

We are delighted to have you visit with us, Gladys.

GLADYS

I . . . I . . .
(She stares dumbly at CHESTER *)*

MR. LEE

We welcome you to our home.

GLADYS
(Turns to him)
I . . . Thank you. Thank you very much. I . . . Chester, may I speak to you privately
for a minute!
*(To parents as she moves backwards with Chester, in confusion, bowing almost to
floor)*
Your pardon. I beg your pardon. Your forgiveness. I beg your pardon and your for-
giveness and your forgiveness and your . . .
(Grabbing CHESTER *pulling him close to her)*
Chester, you're kidding. Tell me you're kidding.

CHESTER
(Whispers)

I'm not kidding.

GLADYS

They're your parents?

CHESTER

They're my parents.

GLADYS

You're Chinese?

(CHESTER *nods*)
Why did you tell me you were Jewish?

CHESTER
It was a habit.

GLADYS
A habit? What kind of habit is it to tell people you're Jewish?

CHESTER
I guess I just wanted to be like everybody else.

GLADYS
Lee. Chester Lee, It never occurred to me ... Now I remember seeing you in school once wearing a black hat and carrying a Jewish flag. I thought that was peculiar.

CHESTER
People kept giving me those things. I didn't ask for them.

GLADYS
I know. I did it myself. I once gave you my chopped herring sandwich!

CHESTER
Was it you?

GLADYS
It was me.

CHESTER
Chopped herring on pumpernickel, right?

GLADYS
I think it was pumpernickel.

CHESTER
It was. I remember. And it was delicious. I bet your mother chopped the herring.

GLADYS
(Angrily)
Will you stop talking about my mother so much! I'm the one who's suffering here!
(She glances towards MR. and MRS. LEE)
I still can't believe they're your parents.

CHESTER
You wanna know something, Gladys?
(He moves to other side, pulls her with him)

GLADYS
What?

CHESTER

I can't believe they're my parents, either.

GLADYS
(Slight pause)

Who do you think they are?

CHESTER

I don't know.

GLADYS

Do you have any idea?

CHESTER

Maybe they adopted me or found me someplace.

GLADYS

Couldn't you take blood tests? Wouldn't that prove if they're your real parents or not?

CHESTER

I couldn't ask them to do that.

GLADYS

There must be some way you can find out.
(MRS. LEE enters kitchen, returns shortly with tray on which there are a pot of tea, four cups and a dish of cakes, all of which she sets out on the table)

CHESTER

And you wonder why I can't get a job. Try spending your whole life with something like this inside you and see how far you'd go!

GLADYS
(Snaps her fingers)

I got it! I got it, Chester!
(Tapping his shoulder)
The birthmark on your shoulder. The big brown one. Those are inherited charac teristics. One of your real parents has the exact same birthmark.

CHESTER

Are you sure?

GLADYS

I'm sure. I'm sure.
(Glances towards MR. and MRS. LEE out of the corner of her eye)
Did you ever see them naked?

CHESTER
(Shakes his head)
They always walk around fully dressed.

GLADYS

How about on the beach?

CHESTER

On the beach, too.

GLADYS

They're always fully dressed on the beach?

CHESTER

What d'you want from me, Gladys? I can't tell them to walk around naked, can I?

GLADYS

All right, look, leave this to me. I think I have a way of finding out.

CHESTER

But be tactful. Don't just come out and say they're not my real biological parents to their face. I've been doing that all my life.

GLADYS

Okay. I'll be tactful. Let's go.
(They move to parents)

CHESTER
(To parents)
Gladys was just telling me how glad she is to meet the both of you, finally.

GLADYS

I've been looking forward to it for a long, long time.
(She looks to CHESTER who nods approvingly)

MRS. LEE
(to MR. LEE)
My dear husband, please join us. You have worked enough for now.

MR. LEE

There's still plenty to do but I will stop for a little while.
(Moves out from behind counter)

GLADYS

It must be very interesting working in a Chinese laundry, Mr. Lee.
(MR. LEE turns away from her with an expression of dismay. CHESTER changes the subject)

CHESTER
(To GLADYS)
The tea is good, isn't it?

GLADYS

Yes, yes, it looks delicious. Really delicious, Mrs. Lee. And so do the cakes. And that blouse you're wearing. I haven't been able to take my eyes off it since I walked in. Where did you get it?

MRS. LEE

I don't think I remember . . . I have it for years.

GLADYS

I'd love to get one like it.
(Rises)
Do you mind if I look and see if the store label is still on it? I really like it and if I can find out where you bought it . . .
(She stands behind MRS. LEE and pushes her hand under the blouse)

MRS. LEE
(Squirming, arching her back)
No, no, that tickles, Gladys . . .
(She squeals with laughter)

GLADYS

Chester, why don't you see if there's a store label on your father's shirt so you can get one, and I'll get this blouse . . .
(She hits CHESTER on the arm)

CHESTER
(Rises)
Good idea, Glad. Excellent idea. Gladys is right. I should get one just like it. It's a beaut.
(Starting to unbutton MR. LEE 's shirt)
Let me unbutton it so I can . . .

MR. LEE
(Slaps CHESTER's hand, snaps)
Get your hand off me!

CHESTER

All right, all right, you don't have to get sore . . . If you don't want me to unbutton it, I won't unbutton it. I'll get a look at it from under here, it doesn't make any difference. Sit still, Dad, I'll just get under here and see what it says on the label so I can go out and get the same shirt for myself and we'll both have . . .
(CHESTER pulls MR. LEE's shirt out at the waist and pushes his head under it)

MR. LEE
(In Chinese)
Nai ta me kwai? (What the hell are you doing?)
(MR. LEE rises, struggles to free himself of CHESTER who is caught under his shirt. He slaps at him as they turn around in a circle. CHESTER frees himself and runs behind the counter. MR. LEE, slipper off and in hand, pursues him. In Chinese)

Cheun choy, wai dan! Yeuk gwo ngo jook do nay ... Nay dzou mo hong le! (Idiot! Imbecile! If I get my hands on you ... It will be the end!)

CHESTER

I don't know what he has to get so excited about! What did I do that was so terrible?

MR. LEE
(In Chinese; moving towards CHESTER*)*
Ngo dzou wui dah bung nay ge tou, ngo mm hai tung may gong seel ge! (One more word from you, and I will split your head open, snot-nose!)

GLADYS
(to CHESTER*)*
What did your father say to you?

CHESTER

He called me a snot-nose!

MRS. LEE

Forgive us, Gladys. My husband and Chester have been quarreling about one thing or another all day.

GLADYS

I understand, Mrs. Lee.
(Clapping her hands)
Say, I got an idea, everybody? Why don't we play cards? We're all so wrought-up and anxious ...

CHESTER
(Shaking his head)
I don't wanna play.

GLADYS

With your parents, Chester. Poker. Strip poker.

CHESTER

Strip poker! What an idea! That's a great idea, Gladys. I'll get the cards ... Don't move, anybody ... Dad, you'll like this. It's not for money. It's not gambling. Ma, you'll love this game too. It's really a lot of fun.
(Getting a deck of cards from the bureau)
You explain it to them, Glad.

GLADYS

It's simple Chester will give us each one card and the person who gets the lowest card loses and has to remove one piece of clothing or jewelry, but shoes or socks or gloves or earrings will count as one thing.
(To CHESTER, *who has been shuffling the cards)*
Is that okay? It'll go quicker.

161

CHESTER

Good. Excellent. Here we go.
(He deals the cards: first to GLADYS, *then to* MR. LEE, MRS. LEE, *and finally to himself. His parents watch everything with mouth slightly open, eyes wide and uncomprehending)*
Four, nine, Jack, six.
(Picking up dealt cards at once, putting them underneath deck)
You lose, Gladys.

GLADYS
(Removes her shoes)
This game is lots of fun. When I went to high school I used to play it almost every day.

CHESTER

All right. Here we go again. Five, nine, six, three. I lose.
(He kicks off his sneakers, he wears no socks)
It starts off slow but it gets more interesting as it goes along.
(He deals)
Seven, nine, Queen, ten. You lose. Glad.

GLADYS
(Takes off her wristwatch)
My parents bought me this watch for my last birthday. $59.95 downtown. You know what you would pay for this watch uptown?

CHESTER

Gladys!

GLADYS

Go ahead, go ahead!

CHESTER
(Deals)
Seven, Jack, eight, Queen. You lose again, Glad.

GLADYS

This is becoming ridiculous.
(She removes her blouse, without a pause. She is wearing an extraordinarily small and tight red brassiere; the rest of her torso is bare. CHESTER, MR. *and* MRS. LEE *stare at her bosom. Aware of their intense staring,* GLADYS *flips her pigtails over her bosom)*

CHESTER
(Dealing again)
Nine, eight, Jack, four. Damn it!
(He rises, pulls off his shirt)
You're not gonna believe this but I never lose at this game.

162

GLADYS
(Gathering cards together)
You had your chance. It's my turn to deal.
(She deals to MR. LEE, MRS. LEE, CHESTER, *then to herself)*
Three, three, three, two. For cryin' out loud!
(She stands, removes her skirt, and places it on the work counter. She is in tights)

MR. LEE
(In Chinese)
Mm dzz been go sai keu ge yee fuk ne? (I wonder who does her laundry?)

MRS. LEE
(In Chinese)
Mm dzee. (I wonder.)

GLADYS
(Clutching her rear end, turning about quickly)
What? What did they say?

CHESTER
They wanna know who does your laundry.

GLADYS
Oh.
(Sits down, deals)
Once again. Nine, Queen, three, eight. You, Chester.
(CHESTER pauses a moment, then he removes his pants. He is naked save for his jockey undershorts)

CHESTER
(Sits, embarrassed by his parents' presence, tries to cover himself)
Let me deal now, huh?

GLADYS
No. I'm still dealing. You're getting mad because you're losing, aren't you?

CHESTER
I'm losing! You're not doing so hot yourself.

GLADYS
I'm doing as well as you are.

CHESTER
We'll see about that. Now if you're gonna deal, deal; come on!

GLADYS
(Deals)
King, nine, Ace . . .
(Gives herself a card but is silent)

CHESTER
(Jumps up, hits table)
Six! Six! All right, Gladys, take it off!

GLADYS
Chester . . .

CHESTER
I don't wanna hear any excuses, Gladys. You lost. Now take it off, come on!
*(*GLADYS *turns to* CHESTER*'s parents who stare back to her dumbly. She rises, quickly slips out of her brown tights: she is wearing a pair of red tights underneath)*

GLADYS
(Sits down, stiffly)
Shall we continue now?

CHESTER
(Picking up the cards)
I'm dealing.

GLADYS
Deal.

CHESTER
Since when did you start wearing two pairs of leotards?

GLADYS
Since I started going out with you.

CHESTER
Thanks.

GLADYS
For nothing.

CHESTER
(Deals)
Here we go. This is it now. Ten, nine, Jack . . .
(He hesitates a moment)

GLADYS
Go ahead, Chester, deal it. And not from the bottom either.
*(*CHESTER *slowly throws out a card for himself.* GLADYS *claps her hands, shrieks)*
Seven! It's a seven! He loses. Chester loses. Oh, I'm dying! This is a riot!
(She doubles over with laughter. Points at CHESTER*'s jockey shorts)*
A seven! He's got a seven!
*(*CHESTER *stares at her, sick-looking)*
We're waiting, Chester.
(Pause)

Go ahead, Chester.
(CHESTER removes a Band-Aid from his leg, holds it up hopefully. GLADYS
shakes her head. CHESTER picks shyly at his undershorts)

MR. LEE
(In Chinese)
Ngo day wan yun le. (I think this game has gone far enough.)

MRS. LEE
(In Chinese)
Hai. Yeet lay yuet so. (Yes. It's becoming silly.)

GLADYS
What? What did they say?

CHESTER
(Picking up his pants quickly)
They said the game's over. They're afraid the police are going to raid the joint.

GLADYS
Oh, now the game's over. But when I was losing, it wasn't over, was it?

CHESTER
What's the difference? We're not getting any place.
(MR. LEE returns to ironing shirts, GLADYS starts to get dressed, MRS. LEE
clears the table)

GLADYS
Did you want to get any place?

CHESTER
What does that mean?

GLADYS
It just seems to me that somebody isn't as anxious to prove something as he says he
is.

CHESTER
I'm as anxious as you are, Gladys.

GLADYS
We'll see about that.
(She suddenly grabs CHESTER by the hair and pulls him down on the table
before he can get his shirt on.)
Mr. Lee! Mrs. Lee! Look! Look what's on Chester's back!
(MR. and MRS. LEE hurry to the table. MR. LEE is carrying a large
flyswatter)

MRS. LEE
What is it, Gladys?

165

GLADYS

Look at this!

(She points to the birthmark on CHESTER's *shoulder.* MRS. LEE *breaks into a smile.* MR. LEE *returns to the work counter, mumbling under his breath)*

MRS. LEE

Oh, that. It's a birthmark, Gladys. Chester can have it removed if he wishes.

GLADYS

I . . . I got scared for a minute. Did he get it from you, Mrs. Lee?

MRS. LEE

From me?

CHESTER
(Trying to get up)

Forget it, Gladys.

GLADYS
(Pushing him down)

Things like that are inherited characteristics, Mrs. Lee. You get them from your parents.

MRS. LEE

I don't think that's so, Gladys. Neither Mr. Lee nor I have a birthmark like Chester's. And we're . . .

GLADYS

Mrs. Lee, are you and Mr. Lee Chester's real biological parents?
*(*MR. LEE *angrily tosses pieces of laundry up in the air)*

MR. LEE
(In Chinese)

Nee go dou lay! Geel deu dzou. Moon hai go do! (This one, too! Tell her to go. The door is there!)

MRS. LEE
(In Chinese; placating MR. LEE*)*

Jeung fu, mm ho gum yeung, mm goy nay. Sai mun dzai mm sik see. (My sweet husband, control yourself, please. She is a young girl. She doesn't know better.)
*(*MR. *and* MRS. LEE *continue to talk in Chinese.* CHESTER *puts on his shirt.* GLADYS *puts on blouse, boots, knotting brown tights around her throat like a scarf)*

CHESTER

I asked you not to say that, Gladys. I especially asked you not to say it!

GLADYS

I don't care. I can't be tactful or beat around the bush when something as important

166

as this comes up. I'm the one who's on the spot. If we ever got married and had a wedding I wouldn't know what table to put them at.

CHESTER

So why are you making such a big deal out of it for? So my parents are Chinese. So I'm Chinese. So what's the big deal!

GLADYS

You lied to me, that's the big deal.

CHESTER

You never lied?

GLADYS

Not about something like this.

CHESTER

Why don't we just forget it, Gladys?

GLADYS

Because I can't. Because this is too important to me and just shows there's no honest relationship between us.

CHESTER

So there's no honest relationship between us.

GLADYS

So let's not pretend.

CHESTER

So let's not!

GLADYS

So you can take your problems and solve them yourself, Chester Lee! And stay away from my mother!
(To MR. *and* MRS. LEE *as she exits, grabbing skirt from counter covering herself in confusion with skirt, bowing)*
I beg your pardon and your forgiveness . . . your pardon and your forgiveness . . . your forgiveness and your pardon . . .
(She exits, slamming the door behind her. A pause. MR. *and* MRS. LEE *move to* CHESTER*)*

MRS. LEE

Chester, your father and I are sorry that you quarreled with the young lady.
(CHESTER nods)

MR. LEE

You know that your mother and I are very fond of Pu Ping Chow.
(CHESTER nods)

167

MRS. LEE

She is a lovely girl who is well brought up. She would be a wonderful wife to someone who . . .

CHESTER

Ma!

MRS. LEE

Only speak to her. That is all your father and I ask. And it would be good for you to do it now. While the memory of Gladys is fresh in your mind so that you can see the virtues of Pu Ping Chow.

MR. LEE

Only speak to her, Chester.

MRS. LEE

That is all we ask.

MR. LEE

Do it for us.

MRS. LEE

For your dear father and me.

CHESTER
(Rises)

All right, I'll speak to her. I'll speak to her! But I'm not promising anything else. She's such a creepy weirdo.

MRS. LEE
(To MR. LEE)

My dear husband, please call Pu Ping Chow down. I know she's at home. I will prepare more tea.

CHESTER

Do me a favor, Ma, and don't bother with the tea. This is gonna be short and sweet.

MR. LEE
(Goes out into street and calls upstairs in Chinese)

Chow Pu Ping, tsean nay lok lay yut dzun. Chester seang tung nay gong gay geu wah! (Pu Ping Chow, do us the honor of visiting with us. Chester would like to speak to you!)

PU PING
(From upstairs we hear PU PING's voice answering, in Chinese)

To jieh. Lay pok. (I will be honored.)

MR. LEE
(Enters)

She is coming. She'll be right down.

168

MRS. LEE
(Carries a shirt and tie to CHESTER*)*
Here. Put these on, Chester.

CHESTER
What's that?

MRS. LEE
A fresh shirt and tie.

CHESTER
Why do I have to wear a fresh shirt and tie?

MRS. LEE
Chester, Pu Ping Chow . . .

CHESTER
(Takes shirt and tie from her)
Boy, what am I letting myself in for!
(He exits into the bedroom. Both parents busily prepare the room for PU PING.
From the kitchen area, MR. LEE *produces an upholstered chair,* MRS. LEE
brings out a small Chinese tea table)

MRS. LEE
(In Chinese; as she goes behind the work counter to get a Chinese lantern)
Gum ho dee ge. Keu geel dzee gay fat kok Chow Pu Ping hai sik hup keu ge. (It is
better this way. He must discover for himself that Pu Ping Chow is the one who will
make him happy.)
*(*MRS. LEE *turns on the light switch, which illuminates the overhead bulb.* MR.
LEE *goes into the kitchen and returns with an ornamental screen which he sets
up)*

MR. LEE
(In Chinese)
Hai me, hai me, Gladys . . . Gladys . . . Chester ngan hai mm hai you dee mo bang.
(Yes, yes, Gladys . . . Gladys . . . Chester had a defect in his eyes.)
*(*MRS. LEE *covers the naked light bulb with the Chinese lantern. She and* MR.
LEE *admire the effect.* CHESTER *returns from the bedroom. Moving to the work
counter)*
Dong yun-zun . . . dong yun-zun! (Wait . . . wait!)
(As he lowers the window blind)
Lai taiee. (Watch.)
(The room is transformed)

MR. *and* MRS. LEE
(In Chinese)
Dhun long. (How pretty.)
*(*PU PING *enters from street, closing door behind her. She wears black trousers, a
gold mandarin blouse. Her hair is long and black. She carries a large colorful
shopping bag)*

PU PING
(In Chinese; taking a deep bow in a sing-song voice)
To jeah nay day foon ying ngo do nay ga ting. (I thank you for welcoming me to your home.)

MR. LEE
(In Chinese)
Mm sai, Pu Ping. (You are welcome, Pu Ping.)

PU PING
(In Chinese; bowing to MRS. LEE *)*
To jeah nay day foon ying ngo do nay ga ting. (I thank you for welcoming me to your home.)

MRS. LEE
(In Chinese)
Mm sai, Pu Ping. (You are welcome, Pu Ping.)

PU PING
(In Chinese; bowing to CHESTER*)*
To jeah nay day foon ying ngo do nay ga ting. (I thank you for welcoming me to your home.)

CHESTER
(Without bowing, curtly)
Terrific!

MR. LEE
(In Chinese; motioning for PU PING *to sit in the chair)*
Tseang tso, tseang tso, Pu Ping. (Sit down, Pu Ping. Make yourself comfortable.)

PU PING
(In Chinese; sits in chair which faces front)
Do jeah. (Thank you.)

MRS. LEE
Your father and I have work to do, Chester. We will leave you alone.

CHESTER
Thanks a lot!

MRS. LEE
(In Chinese; to PU PING *)*
Tui mm ju, Pu Ping. (Excuse us, Pu Ping.)

PU PING
(In Chinese)
To jeah nay day foon ying ngo do nay ga ting. (I thank you for welcoming me to your home.)

Ho foon hay. (It is our joy.)
(M R. and M R S. L E E start for the kitchen. M R. L E E notes that C H E S T E R
makes no attempt to approach P U P I N G. In Chinese; indicating place beside P U
P I N G)
Choree she, Chester. (Sit over here, Chester.)
(C H E S T E R turns his back. M R. L E E moves to him, pinches him on the rear.
C H E S T E R jumps up. M R. L E E takes the stool he's been sitting on and places it
beside the tea table. He and M R S. L E E exit into the kitchen)

CHESTER
(Looking over at P U P I N G)

Hi.

PU PING
(In Chinese)

Ngo ho go hing you gay wui lay nee do. (I am delighted to be here.)

CHESTER

Hi again.

PU PING
(In Chinese)

Ngo hay mong ngo mm wui man fan nay. Ngo hay mong nay jung yee ngo lay nee
do. (I hope that I do not cause you any unhappiness. I hope you like my being here.)
(She removes a castanet and a small bell from her shopping bag. Then, she starts to
sing, in Chinese. The song is taken from a recording by the Chinese Opera
Company. First Pu Ping clicks the castanets, then, suddenly, she howls an
improbably long and loud note: "Tse nooooooooo ..." And proceeds to sing two
more bars, improvising vowels on any pentatonic scale. Castanets click. Again she
howls: "Tse nooooooooo ..." But C H E S T E R has had enough. He shouts at her)

CHESTER

All right, that's enough singing, Pu Ping! Did you come here to sing or to talk to
me?

PU PING
(In Chinese; returning the castanet and bell to shopping bag)

Nay seung dzou mut yeh ngo dzou dzo. (I come to do whatever is your desire.)

CHESTER

That's very nice of you, but I don't know what I'd like to do myself.
(Calling)

Dad?

MR. LEE
(Offstage)

Yes, Chester?

171

CHESTER

What would you like me to do with Pu Ping?

MR. LEE
(Offstage, in Chinese)

Aiya! (Good heavens!)

(He hurls a dish against the wall)

CHESTER

Never mind. Nobody around here helps me.
(He turns to PU PING. *She is weaving straws together to complete a straw basket
she has taken out of shopping bag. She hums song as she weaves)*
What are you doing?

PU PING
(In Chinese)

Ngo jik gun tso lam. (I am weaving a straw basket.)

CHESTER

What are you weaving a straw basket for? Will you put that thing away? Nobody
weaves straw baskets in this country. It just isn't done, Pu Ping!

PU PING
(Putting straw basket into shopping bag, in Chinese)

Tu mm ju, Chester. (I am sorry, Chester.)

CHESTER

Can't you just sit there and talk to me like a human being?

PU PING
(In Chinese; rapidly)

Ngo ho seung. Nay yeel deem . . . (I would be delighted to. Whatever you wish . . .)

CHESTER

In English! In English!

PU PING
(With an accent)

My English is . . . very bad.
(Pulls out small fan from under right sleeve, covers her face with it)

CHESTER

That's all right. Get used to it. My English isn't so hot either.

PU PING

Your English is . . . lovely.

CHESTER

That's because I use it all the time. Pu Ping, you have to get with it. You can't just sit back and live the way you did in Hong Kong. The kids today swing. They don't follow in their father's footsteps. They make their own rules. Everything's wide open. You have to learn how to . . .

(PU PING *has removed a large orange from shopping bag and is peeling it with her fingernails. Her back is to* CHESTER)

What are you doing now?

PU PING
(Holding out the orange to him)

I prepare an orange for you.

CHESTER

Who asked you to prepare an orange for me? You're a nut, Pu Ping!

PU PING

I put it away.
(She throws orange into shopping bag, folds her arms, angrily)

CHESTER
(Sitting beside her)

I'm trying to explain something to you. We have nothing in common. I don't know how we're supposed to get together. I really don't.

PU PING

I will do . . . whatever you desire.

CHESTER

You mean that?

PU PING

Yes.

CHESTER

How about you and me making out?

PU PING

Making out? What is that?

CHESTER

You don't know?
(PU PING shakes her head)
Wait. I'll show you.
(He rises)
Stand up. Come on. Now get up on this table. Go ahead. Get up on the table.
(She does so)
Now turn over on your back and lie flat, your arms at your sides.

PU PING
(On her back on table)

Like this?

CHESTER

Lik-a dat! Very good. Now right arm, right leg up . . .
(She does so)
Right arm, right leg down. Left arm, left leg up . . . Left arm, left leg down.
(She does so. And hereafter when she raises one side she mechanically lowers the other side)
Very good. Now. Right side up. Left side up.
(He claps his hands rhythmically, interrupts to wave his hand as though leading a band. PU PING *performs the bizarre exercise in tempo)*
Right side up. Left side up. I-make-out. You-make-out. We-make-out. They-make-out. Da-da-da. Da-da-da, etc.
*(*CHESTER *continues to perform.* MR. *and* MRS. LEE *appear at the top of the screen. Shouting at his parents)*
Do you mind if I have a little privacy?
(Their heads disappear behind the screen)
Boy, I can't do anything in my own house.
(He turns, sees PU PING *still throwing her arms and legs into the air. He moves to her)*
All right, Pu Ping. Stop it already or you'll have to get another hernia operation.

PU PING
(Breathlessly)
Is making out finished, Chester?

CHESTER

Yeah, it's finished, Pretty good,wasn't it?

PU PING

It was very . . . pleasant. I feel . . . happy now.

CHESTER

The man who marries you isn't gonna have much trouble. I'll tell you that, Pu Ping.
*(PU PING *sings.* CHESTER, *shouting)*
All right already, Pu Ping! I don't know what I'm going to do with you. I really don't.

PU PING

You do not like me?

CHESTER

It's not you. It's me. You're a good kid, but I got so much on my mind . . . We'll just have to let it go for now.
(Shouts)
Ma! Dad!
*(*MR. *and* MRS. LEE *suddenly appear from behind the screen)*

MR. AND MRS. LEE

Yes, Chester?

174

CHESTER

Pu Ping is going.

(PU PING hastily picks up her shopping bag)

MRS. LEE
(In Chinese; to PU PING)

Ngo hay mong wui see see geen nay, Pu Ping. (I hope you enjoyed your visit, Pu Ping.)

PU PING
(In Chinese; bowing to MR. LEE)

To jeah nay day foon ying ngo do nay ga ting. (I thank you for welcoming me to your home.)

MR. LEE
(In Chinese; to PU PING)

Ngo hay mong wui see see geen nay, Pu Ping. (I hope you enjoyed your visit, Pu Ping.)

PU PING
(In Chinese; bowing to MR. LEE)

To jeah nay day foon ying ngo do nay ga ting. (I thank you for welcoming me to your home.)

(To CHESTER)

Chester, there is an old Chinese proverb that says: "Man who puts girl on table, ends up on floor."

(She locks her left foot behind CHESTER's right foot, pushes him, and sends him tumbling to the floor)

Goodbye, Chester.

(She exits)

MRS. LEE
(In Chinese)

Tai ee hoy. (See what she did.)

MR. LEE
(In Chinese; laughing, flexing his arm)

Wah Pu Ping chung hai chong. (I didn't know Pu Ping was so strong.)

MRS. LEE
(In Chinese)

Lou a sai Chester. (Chester will be angry.)

MR LEE
(In Chinese)

You hoy lou. Yun why ngo fu tan eego kah. (Let him be angry. I pay the bills in this family.)

(MR. LEE goes behind the work counter and raises the window blind.

CHESTER *rises, exits into the bedroom and returns immediately with a suitcase,*
which he places on the table. He is wearing rain hat. Referring to the suitcase)
What is that for, Chester?

CHESTER
(Getting shirts, shorts, undershirts, etc., from the bureau)
I'm packing.

MRS. LEE
Why? Where are you going?

CHESTER
Marvin Brockman. I'll stay with him for a while. He's got plenty of room and he's
invited me to stay with him plenty of times.

MRS. LEE
But why?

CHESTER
Because I have to straighten things out in my mind. Because I can't do it here, that's
why.

MR. LEE
Chester, anything I said to you before in anger was not meant to be taken seriously.

CHESTER
I know that. It has nothing to do with you. I'll be better off at Marvin's.

MRS. LEE
And Gladys, Chester? Will you be seeing her?

CHESTER
I guess so. I don't know. That's one of the things I have to think out by myself.

MR. LEE
Chester.
(CHESTER turns to him)
Can we say or do anything that will make you change your mind?

CHESTER
No, Dad. It's about time I stood on my own two feet, anyway.
(MR. LEE pulls out some bills from his pocket. Taking the money, slipping it in
his pocket)
Thanks, Dad.
(To both of them)
I'll give you a ring later in the day and tell you what's happening so let's make this
clean and quick and no hysterics. Ma . . .
(He kisses her on cheek)
Take care of yourself. I'll be all right.

(To M R . L E E*)*

Dad . . . Stop working so hard. And try to get out a little more. I'll call you both this afternoon.

(He moves towards the door)

M R S . L E E

We can tell him now, my dear husband.

M R . L E E

Yes, my lovely wife, we can tell him.

C H E S T E R

(Puts his suitcase down at door, turns to them)

Tell me? What can you tell me?

M R S . L E E

We were not allowed to do so before, my son.

M R . L E E

Not until you left our home.

M R S . L E E

Not until you left us of your own accord.

C H E S T E R

(Shouting jubilantly, removes rain hat)

I knew it! I knew it! Didn't I say so? For how many years did I say so? I felt it inside, since I was a kid. I knew it all along.

M R . L E E

You tell him, dear.

M R S . L E E

No, my sweetheart. It is only right for you to tell him.

(She sits)

C H E S T E R

Tell me, somebody! Did you promise my real parents you wouldn't tell me who they are until I left the house, is that it, Dad?

M R . L E E

No, no, that is not it, Chester. Doctor Thomas Wong. We promised him. On the day you were born.

C H E S T E R

Was he the in-between man?

M R S . L E E

Doctor Thomas Wong. He was a wise old man.

CHESTER

All right. Fine. I'm glad. Now will you please tell me who my real biological parents are?

MR. LEE
(Stands beside MRS. LEE *)*

Your real biological parents?

CHESTER

My real biological parents! Who are they?

MR. LEE

Why, we are, Chester.

CHESTER

You are?

MR. LEE

We are, but . . .
(He nods to MRS. LEE. *She nods)*
On the day you were born . . . Your mother and I . . . We were not man and wife.

CHESTER

You're kidding.

MRS. LEE

No, Chester. We did not marry until after you were born. That is why we threw away your birth certificate.

CHESTER

Then I'm really Chinese?

MR. LEE

Yes, Chester. Legally speaking, you are a Chinese bastard.

CHESTER

I knew you were hiding something from me.

MRS. LEE

We would have told you sooner, but we promised Doctor Wong to say nothing until you left us of your own accord.

MR. LEE

That is the truth.

MRS. LEE

We have no more secrets from you.

MR. LEE

Now go, my son. Go into the world and take upon yourself the responsibilities of a man. Marry the woman you love, whoever she is, and do not be ashamed of your ancestors, do not be ashamed of your parents who love you very much . . . and above all else, for everyone's sake, get yourself a regular job.

CHESTER

Thanks, Dad. Thanks for telling me . . . I don't know what I would have done if you didn't tell me. Well, I guess I should be going . . .
(MR. and MRS. LEE nod. Puts on rain hat. Picking up his suitcase)
I think I can handle the future now. I think so.
(He starts out the door. MR. and MRS. LEE watch him. He stands outside the window, looking in. They wave at him)

CURTAIN

The Pushcart Peddlers

The immigrant experience is one I'm close to, since both my parents came to this country from Eastern Europe in the early part of the century.

My father had no formal education; my mother, a few years of elementary school. My father worked in the garment industry, pressing vests.

He once lost his salary (he would put his salary money in his pants pocket and tie a string around the pocket; nonetheless he lost it). I remember that evening.

My father never told me what he wanted out of life.

He thought many thoughts but he kept them all to himself.

Over the years my mother worked in a dozen different places. Her last job was as a computer operator in a Wall Street bank, from midnight to eight in the morning. She says the job saved her life. They gave her a pension. She now lives in Florida.

My father, Abraham, is dead.

—M. S.
March 9, 1983

THE PUSHCART PEDDLERS *was first produced in November 1979 at the Ensemble Studio Theatre, Curt Dempster, Artistic Director.*

CORNELIUS J. HOLLINGSWORTH III   *Fred Kareman*

SHIMMEL SHITZMAN   *Bernie Mantell*

MAGGIE CUTWELL   *Mary Catherine Wright*

Directed by PETER MALONEY
Set design by BRIAN MARTIN
Costumes by MADELINE COHEN
Lighting design by MARIE LOUISE MORETO

Waterfront, New York City.

Many years ago.

A backdrop on which there is painted, almost photographically, a symmetrically designed Customs House, side and front view: smaller buildings nearby.

Several kegs and wooden crates at both sides of backdrop. Lidded trashcan, downstage.

Sound: waterfront noises, steamship whistle.

Music: in the style of the Ragtime section of Zukerman/Bolling "Suite for Violin and Jazz Piano."

C O R N E L I U S, *in vest, collarless shirt, baggy pants and a soiled derby, is seated on a wooden box beside his banana-filled pushcart; his legs are crossed and a newspaper is spread in front of his face.*

S H I M M E L *enters, looks about, and proceeds across stage. He carries a battered suitcase, wears a threadbare suit, open-necked shirt and wilted tie, a soft cap on his head.*

Music out.

CORNELIUS
(As S H I M M E L *passes, peeks out from behind newspaper)*

Bananas.
*(*S H I M M E L *stops, turns to* C O R N E L I U S, *waits in vain for him to speak further, then moves on.* C O R N E L I U S, *peeking out from behind newspaper)*
Bananas.

SHIMMEL
(Stops again)

Excuse me.

CORNELIUS
(Rises; folds and puts newspaper on pushcart; expansively)

What a day. What a beautiful day. When I got up this morning I said to myself, "This is going to be one rotten day." But look at it. Look for yourself. It's a beautiful day. Absolutely beautiful. It just goes to show you. You can't be too smart in this world.

(Snaps open paper bag)

IIow many?

SHIMMEL

How many what?

183

CORNELIUS

How many bananas do you want?

SHIMMEL

I don't want any bananas.

CORNELIUS

You don't want any bananas?

SHIMMEL
(Shakes his head)

No.

CORNELIUS

Then why did you disturb me?

SHIMMEL

I thought you were talking to me.

CORNELIUS

You thought . . .? Why should I talk to you? Are you a millionaire?
(SHIMMEL shakes his head)
Are you a politician?
(SHIMMEL shakes his head)
Are you a celebrity?
(SHIMMEL shakes his head)
Then why should I talk to you?

SHIMMEL

I . . . I'm sorry. I made a mistake. It is a beautiful day. A wonderful day. Excuse me.
(He starts off)

CORNELIUS
(Returns paper bag)
The nerve of some people. Coming over and making a spectacle of themselves. Hey, you!

SHIMMEL
(Runs to him)

Yes?

CORNELIUS

Who are you, anyway?

SHIMMEL
(Removes cap, pushes it into jacket pocket)
Shitzman. Shimmel Shitzman.

You're Shimmel Shitzman?

SHIMMEL

Do you know me?

CORNELIUS

Why should I know you? Are you a millionaire?
         (SHIMMEL shakes his head)
Are you a politician?
         (SHIMMEL shakes his head)
Are you a celebrity?
         (SHIMMEL shakes his head)
Then why should I know you?

SHIMMEL

I thought you . . .

CORNELIUS

Where are you from, Shimmel Shitzman?

SHIMMEL

From the vicinity of Kovno-Vilna.

CORNELIUS
(Amazed)

You're from the vicinity of Kovno-Vilna?

SHIMMEL

Are you from the vicinity of Kovno-Vilna?

CORNELIUS
(Dusts bananas with feather mop)

As a matter of fact, I'm not. I'm from the vicinity of Minsk-Pinsk.

SHIMMEL
(Enthusiastically)

Minsk-Pinsk! Why, that's practically walking distance from the vicinity of Kovno-Vilna. We're practically neighbors!

CORNELIUS

Does that surprise you?

SHIMMEL

In all honesty, it does. You're the first person I talked to since I got off the boat. And to talk to someone who was practically my neighbor in the old country, that's what I call a stroke of good luck. Can I ask you a few impersonal questions, neighbor?

CORNELIUS
(Sits)
So long as you don't take up too much of my time, neighbor. You happen to have
caught me during my rush hour.

SHIMMEL
Business is good?

CORNELIUS
Business is excellent. Couldn't be better.

SHIMMEL
When did you arrive from Minsk-Pinsk?

CORNELIUS
Is today Tuesday or Wednesday?

SHIMMEL
Wednesday.

CORNELIUS
Then I arrived yesterday.

SHIMMEL
(Puts suitcase down)
You arrived yesterday from Minsk-Pinsk?

CORNELIUS
That's correct.

SHIMMEL
And you're in business for yourself already?

CORNELIUS
That's correct.
(He lights a cigar butt)

SHIMMEL
Why, that's wonderful, marvelous!

CORNELIUS
You think that's wonderful, marvelous? I heard of a man from the vicinity of Ozro-
kow-Pruszkow who arrived here in the morning and owned two factories, three
warehouses and a hotel in the Catskill Mountains before he sat down for lunch!

SHIMMEL
Fantastic. What a country this is. What a great country. I can't wait to get started
myself, but . . .

CORNELIUS

But what?

SHIMMEL

I don't know where to begin.

CORNELIUS

Well, since we're practically from the same vicinity . . . maybe I can give you a hint or two.

SHIMMEL
(Sits on suitcase)

I would appreciate that more than anything in the world.

CORNELIUS
(With emphasis)

Are you listening?

SHIMMEL

I'm listening.

CORNELIUS

Are you paying attention?

SHIMMEL

I'm paying attention.

CORNELIUS

First thing you have to do . . .

SHIMMEL

Yes?

CORNELIUS

Is buy yourself an American name.

SHIMMEL

Buy myself an American name?

CORNELIUS

That's absolutely essential.
(Steps on cigar butt; takes slips of papers from vest pocket)
And I'll tell you something else, neighbor: this is your lucky day. It so happens I have several American names that are up for sale.

SHIMMEL

But what's wrong with Shimmel Shitzman?

CORNELIUS

Shimmel Shitzman? They'll laugh you out of the country with a name like that. Do you know what my name was when I got off the boat?
(SHIMMEL shakes his head)
Elias Crapavarnishkes.

SHIMMEL

Crapavarnishkes. That's not a bad name. There was a judge from the vicinity of Lvov who had the name Crapavarnishkes. He was a very respected man.

CORNELIUS

Your Judge Crapavarnishkes couldn't get a job as a street cleaner here. The first thing I did when I got off the boat was to buy myself a brand new legitimate name. And since then I've been prospering beyond my wildest dreams.

SHIMMEL

That's fantastic. What is your American name?

CORNELIUS
(Slight English accent)
Cornelius J. Hollingsworth.

SHIMMEL

Wow!

CORNELIUS

The Third.

SHIMMEL

The Third?

CORNELIUS

That's correct. It cost me fifteen dollars with the middle initial and the Third thrown in. It was the only one like it they had. I could have gotten John Smith for fifty cents, but I wouldn't have any part of it. Well, what do you say, Mr. Shitzman?
(Reading from slips of paper)
I have Andrew Hamilton for five dollars, Sylvester Peterson for six-fifty, Thomas Hathaway, six dollars and fifteen cents, Roger Williams Carnegie, five seventy-five, Samuel P. Stone, five dollars without the tax . . .

SHIMMEL

I'm sorry, Mr. Hollingsworth. I couldn't change my name. It's been in my family for generations. I was born a Shitzman and I guess I'll have to die a Shitzman.

CORNELIUS
(Returning slips of paper to vest pocket)
Have it your own way. But don't say I didn't try to help you. It just goes to show: mind your own business and you're better off.
(Indignantly he spreads newspaper in front of his face)

SHIMMEL
(Rises; lifts suitcase)

Mr. Hollingsworth?

CORNELIUS
(Behind newspaper)

What is it now?

SHIMMEL

Can I ask you one more question?

CORNELIUS
(Behind newspaper)

I told you I was busy! I don't have all day to sit here and chat with you!

SHIMMEL

One more question and I won't bother you any more, I promise.

CORNELIUS
(Puts newspaper aside)

Go on. What is it? What is it?

SHIMMEL
(Puts suitcase down)

Where do you think I should look for a job?

CORNELIUS

A job? Why do you want to look for a job?

SHIMMEL

To work. To earn money . . .

CORNELIUS

Ridiculous. Nobody comes to this country to look for a job. There's no future in it. You have to go into business for yourself. It's the only decent way to make a living here.

SHIMMEL
(Sits on suitcase)

But I don't know anything about going into business. I'm a worker. I have experience as a tinsmith, a carpenter, a . . .

CORNELIUS

You people from the vicinity of Kovno-Vilna are all a bunch of blockheads! What did I know about going into business when I got off the boat? Nothing. Absolutely nothing. I was a shoemaker, a leather stitcher. But did I let that stop me? Not on your life. I used my head and here I am: in business for myself!

189

SHIMMEL

But what kind of business could I get into? I don't have much capital . . .

CORNELIUS

Ohhh, there are plenty of good profitable businesses you can go into. Why don't you open your eyes and look around and see what's available?
(As SHIMMEL *rises and "looks around,"* CORNELIUS *plants a* FOR SALE *sign on his pushcart)*
If I were you, Mr. Shitzman, I'd grab the first business up for sale and get right to work. I wouldn't waste any time. Things happen fast in this country. Very fast. You have to stay up on your toes and use your old noodle!
(He spreads newspaper in front of his face)

SHIMMEL
(Turns to see sign on pushcart)

Mr. Hollingsworth?

CORNELIUS
(Behind newspaper)

Yes?

SHIMMEL

Is your . . . business up for sale?

CORNELIUS
(Folds newspaper; stares at FOR SALE *sign)*

Hmmmmm. As a matter of fact, it is.

SHIMMEL

Do you think I could make a go of it?

CORNELIUS
(Puts newspaper aside; rises)

You?

SHIMMEL
(Nods)

Me.

CORNELIUS

Hmmmmm. That's a *tough* question. Let me hear you say: bananas.

SHIMMEL

Bananas.

CORNELIUS

Hmmmmm. You're not without talent. Let me hear you say: bananas, bananas, get your fresh ripe bananas!

190

SHIMMEL
Bananas, bananas, get your fresh ripe bananas!

CORNELIUS
Try it a little louder and try to speak out of this side of your mouth so your voice has a distinctive quality: bananas, bananas, get your fresh ripe bananas!

SHIMMEL
(Imitating him: from the side of his mouth, jerking his head)
Bananas, bananas, get your fresh ripe bananas!

CORNELIUS
No, no, your arms have to swing out, from the side, as if you own the whole street. And kick your leg up a little. Like this.
(Demonstrating: throws arms out, kicks up one leg, tips derby on last word)
Bananas, bananas, get your fresh ripe bananas!
(To SHIMMEL)
Try it.
(He puts derby on SHIMMEL's head; sits on trash can)

SHIMMEL
(Imitating him)
Bananas, bananas, get your fresh ripe bananas!
(Tips derby)

CORNELIUS
Excellent. Excellent. How did it feel?

SHIMMEL
Fine. It felt fine.

CORNELIUS
Were you relaxed? Were you comfortable?

SHIMMEL
I was very relaxed and comfortable.

CORNELIUS
(Rises)
I'm going to tell you something now, Mr. Shitzman: between the two of us and the pushcart, you'll make a fortune in this business.

SHIMMEL
(Excitedly)
You think so?

CORNELIUS
(Takes derby from SHIMMEL's *head; puts it on)*
I know so. It's a definite positive.

SHIMMEL
How much would it cost me?

CORNELIUS
(Moves to pushcart; arms outspread)
The whooole business?

SHIMMEL
(Nods)
The whole business.

CORNELIUS
Hmmmmm. I could ... no, no, I couldn't do that. We're practically from the same vicinity. Let me ask you this, Mr. Shitzman: How much do you have?

SHIMMEL
I have exactly ...
(Takes out change purse)
Forty-three dollars and twenty-five cents.

CORNELIUS
Could you raise another six dollars and seventy-five cents by five o'clock?

SHIMMEL
(Sits on trash can)
How? I don't know anyone here.

CORNELIUS
(Sits on box)
What a shame. I couldn't possibly sell for under fifty dollars unless ...
(Rises)

SHIMMEL
(Rises)
Unless what?

CORNELIUS
Unless I took a bunch of bananas to make up the difference.

SHIMMEL
A bunch of bananas is worth six dollars and seventy-five cents?

CORNELIUS
(He picks up a bunch of bananas)
Are you serious? Do you know what they call a bunch of bananas in this country?

*(SHIMMEL shakes his head. CORNELIUS holds out bananas, pointed
upwards)*

Goldfingers.

SHIMMEL

That's fantastic! Here you are, Mr. Hollingsworth.
(Gives him money)
I'm anxious to get right to work. Do I need any papers to prove ownership?

CORNELIUS
(Bananas under arm)

You'll find them under the fifth banana in the fourth row from the left.
(Shakes his hand)
Congratulations, Mr. Shitzman. And the best of everything to you.

SHIMMEL

Thank you. Thank you, Mr. Hollingsworth.

CORNELIUS
(Moving off)

I have to be off now. If you sell out, go to Pier 26 and ask for Pete. He'll give you a
fair shake.

SHIMMEL
(Shouts after him)

Thanks again, Mr. Hollingsworth. And drop around and say hello once in a while!
*(Music. SHIMMEL puts on cap, carries suitcase behind pushcart, places FOR
SALE sign on top of it; he then examines pushcart, proudly, with proprietary air, he
dusts off bananas with feather mop, dusts off his jacket, looks about as if he owns the
whole street. He suddenly shouts, swinging his arms, kicks up a leg, in imitation of
CORNELIUS)*
Bananas, bananas, get your fresh ripe bananas!
*(He runs to pushcart, snaps open a paper bag, as if expecting an avalanche of cus-
tomers. Undismayed he returns paper bag, sits on box, crossing his legs, and
spreads the newspaper in front of his face. Offstage, CORNELIUS shouts,
"Bananas, bananas, get your fresh ripe bananas!" SHIMMEL lowers his newspaper and gapes in astonishment as CORNELIUS rolls in a second pushcart, an
exact replica of the one he sold to him, shouting, two or three times more,
"Bananas, bananas, get your fresh ripe bananas!" CORNELIUS stops his pushcart
parallel to SHIMMEL's, removes a wooden box from it, sits down and unfolds a
newspaper in front of his face. Music out. SHIMMEL removes his cap, speaks
softly, uncertainly)*

Mr. Hollingsworth?

CORNELIUS
(Behind newspaper)

Yes?

SHIMMEL

You're not staying here, are you?

CORNELIUS
(Behind newspaper)

Of course I'm staying here.

(Reads aloud)

Hmmmmm. This is interesting. "Bride hurls wedding cake at groom for criticizing her dress. Brawl ensues."

(He hawks a laugh)

SHIMMEL

But . . .

CORNELIUS

But what?

SHIMMEL

But can we both make a living selling the same merchandise at the same location?

CORNELIUS
(Puts newspaper aside; rises)

Unfortunately we can't. The competition will force us to lower the price and we'll probably have to begin bankruptcy proceedings in a matter of days.

(Shouts)

Bananas, bananas!

SHIMMEL
(Rises; desperately)

Mr. Hollingsworth!

CORNELIUS

What is it now?

SHIMMEL

I don't want to sound rude, but if we both can't make a living here, why don't you be considerate and go somewhere else?

CORNELIUS

Why don't I . . .?

(Sharply)

Why don't you be considerate and go somewhere else?

SHIMMEL

It was my understanding when you sold me this business that I would be the only one at this location. Otherwise I can assure you, I would have thought twice aobut buying it!

CORNELIUS

Ohhh, it was your understanding! But I didn't say anything to that effect, did I?

SHIMMEL

You didn't have to . . .

CORNELIUS

This is a free country, Mr. Shitzman, and I have as much right to sell at this location as you have!

(Shouts)

Bananas, bananas!

SHIMMEL

Can't we talk about it?

(Shouts in a panic)

Bananas, bananas!

CORNELIUS

Talk, who's stopping you?

(Shouts)

Bananas, bananas!

SHIMMEL

I'm new here, Mr. Hollingsworth. I don't know this city!

(Shouts)

Bananas, bananas!

CORNELIUS

Mr. Shitzman, I have to make a living, too. My customers expect to find me here and I'm not disappointing them! Not for you or the King of Siam!

(Shouts)

Bananas, bananas!

SHIMMEL

Mr. Hollingsworth, I gave you my last penny! I trusted you!

(Shouts)

Bananas, bananas!

CORNELIUS

I can't help you more than I did, Mr. Shitzman!

(Shouts)

Bananas! Bana . . .

(Suddenly turns to SHIMMEL*)*

Unless . . .

SHIMMEL

(Eagerly)

Unless what?

CORNELIUS

Unless we went into partnership.

SHIMMEL

Partnership?

CORNELIUS
(Nods)

The two of us.

SHIMMEL

Why, that would be wonderful, Mr ...

CORNELIUS
(Grins)

Call me Cornelius.

SHIMMEL

Cornelius. Cornelius, that would be wonderful! It would solve all our problems! We could work together, cooperate ...

CORNELIUS

There's only one thing that stands in the way.

SHIMMEL

What's that?

CORNELIUS
(Sits on trash can)

Money.

SHIMMEL

Money?

CORNELIUS

That's correct. Money. You don't expect us to become full and equal partners with all my experience, do you?

SHIMMEL

But I don't have any money left, Mr ... Cornelius. I gave you my last penny, word of honor.
(He raises his hand)

CORNELIUS

Can't you borrow some from friends or relatives or a philanthropic organization?

SHIMMEL
(Sits on box)

Impossible. I told you, I don't know anyone here.

CORNELIUS
(Rises)

Then there's only one thing for us to do.

SHIMMEL
(Rises)

What's that?

CORNELIUS

Negotiate.

SHIMMEL

Can we negotiate without money?

CORNELIUS

Of course.

SHIMMEL

How do we do it?

CORNELIUS
(Using his hands)

It's simple. You make an offer. I refuse your offer and make a counter-offer. You refuse my counter-offer and make a counter-counter-offer of your own. I refuse your counter-counter-offer and I make what is called a proposal which leads you to make a counter-proposal and so on and so forth and so on and so forth until we whittle the difference to nil and come to equitable terms.

SHIMMEL

But I still don't have any money.

CORNELIUS

Who's talking about money! Jesus Christ, you are a dumb-dumb. We negotiate percentages!
(Throws arms out at one pushcart, then the other)
How much of the business do you own in contradistinction to how much of the business do I own!
(He sits on box, crosses legs, puts newspaper in front of his face)
Make me an offer.

SHIMMEL

On a percentage of the business?

CORNELIUS
(Behind newspaper)

That's correct. Do it formally.

SHIMMEL

Yes, sir.
(Puts on cap, brushes jacket; clears throat)
Excuse me, Mr. Hollingsworth.

CORNELIUS
(Newspaper on lap innocently)
Did you wish to speak to me, sir?

SHIMMEL
Yes, sir. About the possibility of our going into partnership, sir. I make an offer that you receive fifty percent of the business and I receive fifty percent of the business ... sir.

CORNELIUS
What about my superior experience, sir?

SHIMMEL
I can learn the business very quickly and if I work twice as hard that will offset the difference, Sir.

CORNELIUS
No deal, sir. I respectfully decline your offer.
(Newspaper in front of his face)

SHIMMEL
(Clears throat; whispers)
You make your counter-offer now.
(No response)
I make my offer, fifty-fifty, you're supposed to make a counter-offer.
(No response; loudly)
Aren't you going to make me a counter-offer, sir? Did I do anything improper, sir?
(Desperately)
Mr. Hollingsworth, we have to reach an agreement. You yourself said we both can't make a living here! For God's sake, make me a counter-offer!

CORNELIUS
(Lowers newspaper)
Bananas, ripe lovely bananas here!
(Newspaper in front of his face)

SHIMMEL
This is crazy! You're being unfair, unreasonable! I ...
(Resigned to it)
All right, sixty-forty! Sixty for you, forty for me. Is it a deal, sir?

CORNELIUS
(Puts newspaper aside; shouts)
Bananas, get your ripe lovely bananas here!
(Without looking at him; coaching him)
Get down on your knees. Beg me. Tell me how hard-up you are. Tell me your family depends on you for support. Get to me emotionally.

(Shouts)
Bananas, bananas here! Get your ripe bananas!

SHIMMEL
(On his knees)
Mr. Hollingsworth, I beg you to consider my offer. I think it's very equitable.
Besides, I'm broke. I don't have a penny. I don't have money to buy dinner tonight
... I don't have a roof over my head ...
*(CORNELIUS rises, paces. SHIMMEL is emotional indeed, on the verge of tears,
building his lines to a crescendo)*
Mr. Hollingsworth, my family is still in the old country. They're depending on me
to send them something each week. I have an elderly father who's confined to his
bed. My mother suffers from arthritis and bursitis. My two little sisters don't have
clothes to wear to school. My baby brother, my little baby brother ...
(He breaks into sobs)

CORNELIUS
(Tears streaming down his cheeks)
What a terrible story. What a tragedy. How old is your little baby brother?

SHIMMEL
(Weeping)
Who knows? Who knows?

CORNELIUS
(Weeping)
What disease, what affliction does he have?

SHIMMEL
(Weeping; louder)
Who knows? Who knows?

CORNELIUS
(Weeping)
Your two little sisters ...

SHIMMEL
(Weeping still louder)
My two little sisters ... without clothes!

CORNELIUS
(Weeping)
Don't say another word, Shimmel. Please, please don't! Not another word! I'll help
you. I'll do whatever you want.

SHIMMEL
(Rises)
Does that mean we're partners?

199

CORNELIUS

Sixty-forty?

SHIMMEL
(Nods)

Sixty-forty!

CORNELIUS
(Embracing him)

Partner!

SHIMMEL

Thank you, Cornelius; thank you.

CORNELIUS
(Breaks away, takes out handkerchief, blows his nose)
Oh, boy, that was a good cry. Oh, boy. I have to admit . . . enjoyed it thoroughly.

SHIMMEL
(Wiping his eyes)
I did, too. I didn't know that negotiations could be so emotional.

CORNELIUS

There's a lot you have to learn, partner. But don't worry. I'll teach you every aspect of this business. From now on your gain becomes under contract my profit. Okay, now let's get to work. No more horsing around.
(Music. CORNELIUS sits down on box, crosses legs, spreads newspaper in front of his face. SHIMMEL, imitating him, does likewise. CORNELIUS soon rises, yawns, stretches his arms over his head, shakes out one leg, then the other, looks around, then flaps handkerchief over top of wooden box before sitting down, spreading newspaper in front of his face. SHIMMEL does likewise, but before spreading newspaper in front of his face, speaks. Music out)

SHIMMEL

Cornelius?

CORNELIUS
(Behind newspaper)

Yes?

SHIMMEL

How's business?

CORNELIUS
(Newspaper on lap)
Excellent. Excellent. If it keeps up at this rate, I think we should buy another pushcart.

200

SHIMMEL

Can we afford it?

CORNELIUS

What a question.

SHIMMEL

I didn't know we were that successful.

CORNELIUS

If I told you how successful we were, Shimmel, you'd get a swollen head, so let's not discuss it and just keep working.

SHIMMEL

I will. I promise. You'll get nothing but hard work from me.

CORNELIUS

That's what I expect from you. Now let's get to work.
(They both spread their newspapers in front of their faces. Romantic, lyrical music. MAGGIE CUTWELL, *a young, very pretty girl, in a shapeless black frock, enters, carrying a tray of small bunches of colorful flowers strapped around her neck. She walks with her hand held slightly in front of her)*

MAGGIE
(In a sweet, angelic voice)
Flowers. Flowers. Pretty flowers for sale. Fresh, pretty flowers.
(She doesn't turn to the men but stands at the side of SHIMMEL's *pushcart, staring forward. She wipes her perspiring face with a rag. Music out)*

SHIMMEL
(Whispers; puts newspaper aside)
Cornelius? Do you see that?

CORNELIUS
(Puts newspaper aside)
Oh, yes.

SHIMMEL

She's beautiful, isn't she?

CORNELIUS

I've seen better heads on cabbages. But it's a pity, just the same.

SHIMMEL

What's a pity?

CORNELIUS

She's blind.

201

SHIMMEL

Is she?

CORNELIUS

All the flower girls are blind in this country.

SHIMMEL

That is a pity. She looks destitute. She looks like she hasn't had a piece of food in her mouth all day. Cornelius, can I get a credit for one banana?

CORNELIUS
(Makes an entry in notebook)
If you want to be extravagant . . .

SHIMMEL

Thank you.
(He takes banana from pushcart and moves to MAGGIE. *She doesn't turn to look at him. Gently he places the banana on her flower tray; returns to his seat)*

MAGGIE
(Looks down at banana; shouts)
Get your fucking banana off my fucking flowers!

SHIMMEL
(Jumps up, retrieves banana)
Forgive me. I . . . I thought you were blind.

MAGGIE

I'll give you blind in a minute. I'll poke out both your eyes and feed 'em to the cats!

SHIMMEL

But I . . .

MAGGIE

I know what you're after, Buster! If I wanted to be a whore, I wouldn't be selling these fucking flowers!

SHIMMEL

You're mistaken, believe me. I only wanted to help you.

MAGGIE

Yeah, and how the hell were you gonna do that? By slipping me a banana?

SHIMMEL

I thought you were hungry.

MAGGIE

I don't need your lousy banana. If I'm hungry, I know where to eat. I've been taking care of myself since I'm six years old and I haven't starved to death yet!

202

SHIMMEL

You're an orphan?

MAGGIE

You bet your sweet ass!

SHIMMEL

I'm sorry. Life must have been difficult for you.

MAGGIE

I got no complaints. How about buying a bunch of these stinkweeds for your girlfriend?

SHIMMEL

I'm afraid I have no money.
(Laughs self-consciously)
I have no girlfriend either.

MAGGIE

That figures, you crumb-bum, you creep. Wasting a girl's time for nothing. I oughta call the police. I oughta bop you in the nose.
(Shouts as she forces him back so that he sits on trash can)
Get away from me! I hate your lousy guts!
(Suddenly in a sweet, angelic voice)
Flowers. Pretty flowers for sale. Fresh pretty flowers.
(CORNELIUS rises, derby in hand; he moves to MAGGIE, speaks with great formality)

CORNELIUS

Allow me to apologize for my partner, ma'am. He's new here. He has no sense of propriety.

MAGGIE

They should send him back where he came from, the creep. Doesn't he have the decency to introduce himself like a gentleman? Did his parents name him before they dumped him into a garbage can?

CORNELIUS

His name is Shitzman. Shimmel Shitzman.
(SHIMMEL stands as if expecting an introduction)

MAGGIE

Shitzman! Shimmel Shitzman!
(She breaks out into laughter)
It fits him. It fits him perfectly.
(To SHIMMEL)
Shitzman. Mr. Shitzman!
(And she laughs again. SHIMMEL sits down on trashcan, dejectedly)

CORNELIUS
(Bows)
Perhaps you'd be good enough to permit me to introduce myself to you, ma'am. I am Cornelius J. Hollingsworth, the Thrid.

MAGGIE
(Curtsies a bit)
Please to make your acquaintance, Mr. Hollingsworth. I am Maggie Cutwell and although I find it necessary to sell flowers in order to sustain myself, I am by profession an actress, a thespian, a tap dancer, a toe dancer, and a highly regarded chanteuse.

CORNELIUS
All good fortune to you, Miss Cutwell. I am myself in the banana business at present, but it is merely transitional. My one true and genuine ambition is to gain a seat on the Stock Exchange and invest substantial sums of money in musical comedy productions.
(Puts on derby)

MAGGIE
Am I to believe that it is your intention to become a theatrical producer?

CORNELIUS
Precisely, Miss Cutwell.
(Picks up a banana)
May I offer you a banana?

MAGGIE
(Takes it from him)
I will be happy to take your banana, Mr. Hollingsworth, but I will never take his banana.
(To SHIMMEL)
Never! Not even if it was covered with diamonds!

CORNELIUS
I am doing all I can for him, Miss Cutwell, but it's a sad, a terribly sad and tragic story.

MAGGIE
I'm sure it is.

CORNELIUS
How much are your flowers, Miss Cutwell?

MAGGIE
These are ten cents a bunch, and those wilted ones on the side are three cents a bunch.

CORNELIUS
I would like to purchase two ten-cent bunches, please.

(She hands them to him; he gives her the coins)
Thank you. Here's your money and these ... these are for you.
(Gallantly he hands her back the flowers. He then passes SHIMMEL, *extending his arms as if to say, "See how easy it is")*

MAGGIE

You are a very kind person, I can see that right away. Mr. Hollingsworth, it may be premature of me to suggest, but in the event you actually become a theatrical producer in the foreseeable future, could you possibly keep me in mind for a part in one of your musical productions?

CORNELIUS

To be frank with you, Miss Cutwell, I don't know whether you're talented or not.

MAGGIE

Can't I show you? Won't you at least give me the opportunity to show you what I can do?

CORNELIUS

Ordinarily I would say yes immediately, without reservation, but you've caught me during my busiest day of the week. It's impossible. I can't. I have obligations.
(He puts foot on box, ties his shoelace)

MAGGIE

Please, Mr. Hollingsworth. This is extremely important to me. If I don't succeed in my chosen profession, I'll have to go on selling flowers for the rest of my life, or marry some beerbellied creep who'd beat me every night just for the exercise. I'll be forced to kill myself, Mr. Hollingsworth!
(CORNELIUS turns to her as she gets down on her knees)
I couldn't go on living like that, I couldn't, I couldn't ...
(She weeps)

CORNELIUS
(Tears streaming down his cheeks)
What a tragedy. What a terrible, terrible story. How long have you been selling flowers?

MAGGIE
(Weeping)
Ever since I was six years old.

CORNELIUS
(Weeping)
Tragic. Tragic. Have you experienced no pleasure, no happiness, no joy in all your young years?

MAGGIE
(Weeping)
No. Nothing but pain and heartache.

CORNELIUS
(Weeping)
Ohhhhh, pain and heartache. And you would take your own life?

MAGGIE
(Weeping)
Yes, yes, I have the pills at home and today there was a sale at Woolworth's and I bought . . . I bought six bottles of iodine!

CORNELIUS
(Moves away; she follows him on her knees)
No more, Miss Cutwell. No more. I can't take it. I can't. It's too much for a human being to bear. If you'd like to perform for me, go home, change, rearrange your appearance, prepare yourself, and come back when you're ready. But, please, hurry. I don't have the time! I have a business to run here!

MAGGIE
Thank you. Thank you. You're my light in the darkness. You're my savior.
(Rises)
Two minutes, Mr. Hollingsworth.
(Turns to SHIMMEL)
Two minutes . . . Sh-Sh-Sh-Sh-Shitzman? Shitzman? That's a riot. Shitzman.
(And she exits)

CORNELIUS
(Sits on box)
Well, what do you think?

SHIMMEL
(Rises; looks after MAGGIE)
I . . . I think she's beautiful.

CORNELIUS
Good. I'm glad you feel that way because I'd like you to get her off my hands.

SHIMMEL
But I thought . . .

CORNELIUS
(Rises; moves to him)
Don't think, Shimmel. You can be arrested for it. Feel, feel, start feeling and start expressing your feelings, your fantasies, your dreams! Use your imagination! You're a very repressed person. If I had known that before, I would never have gone into partnership with you!

SHIMMEL
But why do you want me to take Miss Cutwell off your hands? Aren't you attracted to her?

Attracted, retracted, contracted. Who has time for those shenanigans? It so happens, be it as it may, willy-nilly, hocus-pocus, I'm a married man.
(Moves toward his box; stops)
I also have three brats.
(Moves; stops)
And a gypsy girlfriend.
(Moves)
It's unprofessional for me to get further involved.
(Sits on box)

SHIMMEL
I'd be very glad to take her off your hands.

CORNELIUS
Excellent. Excellent.
(Rises)
Unfortunately one problem remains.

SHIMMEL
What's that?

CORNELIUS
Our partnership name. Hollingsworth and Shitzman. It's out of the question. Didn't you hear how Miss Cutwell laughed at it? We'll get the same treatment from everyone who hears it. We'll be the laughing stock of the banana business.

SHIMMEL
But I told you . . .

CORNELIUS
(Shouts)
I know what you told me! I know what you said! But don't I count for anything? Shimmel, please! Consider someone else for a change? There's no limit to how far we could go together, but you're destroying everything we created with your ridiculous name! It's like a cancer preventing our full growth and prosperity!

SHIMMEL
Even if I wanted to . . . I don't have the money . . .

CORNELIUS
(Sits on box)
We'll negotiate. I'll take an I.O.U. I'll place a lien on your forty percent. Don't worry about it.
(Pulls out slips of paper)
Now what will it be? Thomas Hathaway. Roger Williams Carnegie. Samuel P. Stone . . .

SHIMMEL
(Pleading)

Cornelius, my family name . . .

(Sits on box)

CORNELIUS

Which one, Shimmel? Which one?
(S H I M M E L doesn't reply. C O R N E L I U S rises; hands him slip of paper)
Samuel P. Stone it is! Five dollars even. Hollingsworth and Stone. Perfect. It couldn't
be better. Congratulations, partner.
(Sits; makes entry in notebook)
Well, do you feel any differently, Sam?
(S H I M M E L shakes his head)
You have to feel differently. A Crapavarnishkes isn't a Hollingsworth and a Shitz-
man isn't a Stone.

SHIMMEL

Samuel P. Stone. I am Samuel P. Stone.

CORNELIUS

Sam Stone!

SHIMMEL
(Rises)

I am Sam Stone.

(He faces up)

CORNELIUS

That's it. Feel Stone. Feel rock. Feel hard. Feel firm. Feel strong. Feel . . .
(M A G G I E rushes back in, wearing a Shirley Temple dress and tap shoes)

MAGGIE
(Panting)

I'm here, Mr. Hollingsworth. I'm ready to perform for you.

CORNELIUS
(Rises)

Yes, yes, but before you begin I'd like to introduce you to my partner, Sam Stone.

MAGGIE

But that's Mr. Shitzman. I met him . . .

CORNELIUS

I beg to differ with you, Miss Cutwell. That was Mr. Shitzman. But he has changed
considerably since you last saw him.
*(S H I M M E L turns, posture straight, hand in pocket; speaks with pronounced
certainty and sophistication)*

That's correct, Miss Cutwell. And if you've come to perform for us, please begin.
We don't have all day to dilly-dally.

*(Both men nod to each other, curtly, and return to sit on their boxes. M A G G I E
looks about to make sure no one is about, then breaks into a bright song and tap
dance, something in the style of "I Don't Care." She sings intro without moving,
merely bouncing up and down, hands clenched as if riding a horse. She tap dances
as she sings the chorus, moving around the peddlers, posing beside them—a
nightclub performance of sorts. This is followed by a tap dance as she da-da's tune
of chorus. She ends by whirling around several times, almost stumbling. Her talent
is not noteworthy. When she is done, she turns to them, waits breathlessly for their
verdict)*

CORNELIUS

Sam?

SHIMMEL

Yes, Cornelius?

CORNELIUS

What do you think of her performance?

SHIMMEL
(Rises; fervently)

What do I think? Do you have to ask? Are you blind? Are you deaf? Do you have
a heart to feel with? I have just witnessed a performance of such precision, of such
exquisiteness and beauty, that if I were in the producing business today, this young
lady would be a star tomorrow!

MAGGIE
(Embracing him)

Oh, Mr. Stone! You don't know how much I needed to hear that! You made me so
happy!

SHIMMEL
(Circling around her)

Enough of this, enough! You have a lot of work to do, Maggie. I am not now in the
producing business, but I have every hope of being in the producing business in the
very near future. Go home and practice! Practice! Practice! Day and night! Twenty-
four hours around the clock! I'm going to be relentless with you, I give you fair
warning. I'll pay the bills; I'll see to it that you have the necessities . . .
(Stops circling; holds her chin in his hand)
But I want you to be the best there is, the absolute best!

MAGGIE

I will be! I will!

(Starts off)

And Maggie . . .

MAGGIE
(Returns)
Yes, Mr. Stone?

SHIMMEL
No intimacy. No personal relationship. This is strictly a professional deal, is that clear?

MAGGIE
Yes, Mr. Stone.

(Starts off)

SHIMMEL
Where did you say you lived?

MAGGIE
(Returns)
Number eleven Perry Street.

SHIMMEL
I'll be up this evening to formalize our contractual arrangement.

MAGGIE
I'll be home. I'll be practicing.

SHIMMEL
Have a bite for me to eat. I'll be hungry and tired.

MAGGIE
I'll put a tuna fish casserole in the oven. Thank you. Thank you, Mr. Stone. I have hope. You gave me hope. God bless you!
(She kisses him on cheek, runs off, singing a line or two of song ending with "2, 3, 4!")

SHIMMEL
(Staring after her)
What a girl. What an incredible girl.

CORNELIUS
So you've become fond of her.

SHIMMEL
Fond of her? I'm in love with her! I'm head over heels in love with her! Cornelius, Cornelius, I never felt this way before. I never thought I could feel this way. My

heart is in my mouth. I have a temperature of over a hundred. My legs are shaking. My stomach is bubbling. It's too much. I can't breathe. Is all this happening to me or am I dreaming? Did I meet someone named Maggie Cutwell or did I make it up? Pinch me, Cornelius, pinch me! I have to know the truth!

CORNELIUS
(Rises)

Hold it, Sam, just hold it a minute! I have to ask you: are you rich enough to support yourself and her, too? After all, you just started in business, this is your first day here ... I don't understand. How can you ...

SHIMMEL

You don't understand! Of course you don't understand! You don't look, you don't listen, you don't pay attention! I met a woman I love, Cornelius. I'm going to marry her. She is going to appear in a musical that I am going to produce ...
(Points)
with you! Now I have the inspiration, the dedication to succeed in a big way. Nothing can stop me. Nothing! Now, come, no more horsing around. This is a matter of life and death to me. Let's get to work.
(He sits on box, crosses legs, puts newspaper in front of his face)

CORNELIUS
(Stares at him, incredulously; then sits on box, takes newspaper)

How's business, Sam?

SHIMMEL
(Behind newspaper)

Good, Cornelius. Excellent.

CORNELIUS

You know, I think it's time we started a corporation. What do you think?

SHIMMEL
(Newspaper down)

I don't know why we waited so long.

CORNELIUS

If I have one fault, it's being too conservative.
(SHIMMEL puts newspaper in front of his face)

CORNELIUS

Sam?

SHIMMEL
(Newspaper down)

Yes, Cornelius?

CORNELIUS
(Simply)
Welcome to America.
*(Music as they both lift newspapers in front of their faces, simultaneously uncross
and cross their legs—left over right, then right over left—with music punctuating
their actions and ending abruptly. Blackout)*

CURTAIN

The Flatulist

My instinct is always to be outrageous, to surprise, to try something new, something I haven't done before. And yet I'd like to reap the rewards of my labors as much as anyone else.

If I had to choose between writing a masterpiece and a million dollars, I would choose the million dollars.

Unfortunately, one can't choose either.

We write what we are.

Now and then what I write falls in happily with a general audience.

It's almost an accident.

Writing this play was fun, and having it done off-off-Broadway was fun, too.

One evening a florid-faced man with a string tie walked out during a performance of The Flatulist. *I went up to him.*

"Excuse me, I wrote the play and I can understand your not taking to it. I'd like to give you your money back."

"Never mind, I don't wan' my money back," he snapped at me.

"But I'd like to—" I began.

"I don't wan' it, mister, you deaf? An' let me tell you somethin'. I loved that play. I really loved it, that is until that guy on stage started fartin'!"

—M. S.
March 9, 1983

THE FLATULIST *was first produced in February 1980 at the Sanctuary Theatre, in New York City, Rip Torn, Artistic Director.*

JACK KOHANE   *Joseph Leon*

GREGORY HOROWITZ   *David Margulies*

Directed by TONY PETITO
Set design by BOB YODICE
Costumes by JANE TRAPNELL
Lighting design by LINDA THURMAN
Crepitations by ZACHARY SCHISGAL

JACK KOHANE's *office in an East Side town house: an antique French provincial table on which there are a splendid desk set, framed photographs, telephone; two Windsor chairs; a sofa and coffee table; a bar cart; a bentwood hanger with* JACK's *homburg on it; a fireplace with mantelshelf above it holding a row of first editions; an expensive oil painting on wall; overhead an ancient blade fan.*

Afternoon.

JACK *is standing with his back to the entrance door, staring out between the slats of a Venetian blind at the street below; then fills attaché case with legal papers.*

The entrance door is opened and closed by GREGORY HOROWITZ. *He is dressed in a dark suit, the jacket of which is buttoned and oddly abbreviated, ending just beneath his waist; a broad-collared shirt and a very wide, dog-eared, black bowtie; he carries a small, bruised, old suitcase. His movements are extraordinarily deliberate, stiff, inflexible, as if he is exercising the greatest restraint to keep his emotions in check.*

JACK *turns to the door with surprise.*

JACK

Greg!

GREGORY

Good afternoon. It was nice of you to see me today ... Mr. Kohane. I frankly expected to hear from your secretary, informing me that my appointment with you had been cancelled.

JACK

We ... can I level with you?

GREGORY

Please.

JACK

My secretary has been trying to get you all week.

GREGORY

Get me?

JACK

Your appointment has been cancelled.

GREGORY

But ...

JACK

You're not staying at the number you gave us, are you?

215

GREGORY

No, I . . . left. I'm . . . in between hotels now.
(Slight pause)
I'm staying with my mother. In Mamaroneck.

JACK

Well, we had no idea where you were so we couldn't get in touch with you. In any
event, I am sorry. I have a meeting with my attorney and I can't . . .
(He starts out)

GREGORY

Mr. Kohane, I've been waiting for this appointment for . . .

JACK

Mr. Kohane? Why so formal? You've called me Jack for more years than I care to
remember. For God's sake, Greg, I was your father's best friend; I was almost your
father-in-law!
(Wincing)
Mr. Kohane?

GREGORY
(Who hasn't moved at all since he entered)
Jack. Yes, Jack. Jack, will you give me five minutes, please? I won't take more than
five minutes, I promise.

JACK

I'll give you twenty minutes; I'll give you as much time as you want, but not today.
I already committed . . .

GREGORY

Five minutes, that's all I'm asking. I didn't want to bring this up, but you did say in
the past, to me and to others on innumerable occasions, you did say that if not for
my father you never would have succeeded as an agent, you did say that he was the
first name client you had and that if not for him . . .

JACK
(Sharply)
All right, all right, there was no need for you to say it! I thought we had more of a
relationship than that! Why are you acting like a stranger toward me?

GREGORY

I was . . . merely being polite.

JACK
(Sits behind desk)
Then be polite; suit yourself. Five minutes, go ahead, talk. You barge in here after I
haven't seen you or heard from you in more than three years and you expect me
to . . .

216

(Softening)

I loved your father, Greg; you know I loved him.

(GREGORY nods)

I'd do anything for his son. No matter what happened between us, I would never turn my back on his son; never.

GREGORY

Thank you.

JACK

Sit down. Get comfortable. I don't know what you're being so formal about. I used to carry you in my arms, like you were my own kid.

(GREGORY puts aside suitcase; sits in second chair, stiffly. He crosses his leg, fastidiously, showing a white sock. JACK stares at him a moment, curiously, perhaps apprehensively)

You look pale, thin, Have you been taking care of yourself?

GREGORY

I'm fine. Thank you.

(GREGORY inserts a cigarette into a cigarette holder and lights it with a plastic lighter. JACK rises, places an ashtray stand near him, returns to chair behind desk)

JACK

Where have you been? I told you to keep in touch, didn't I?

GREGORY

I've been very busy . . .

JACK

The last I heard you were going out to California to do some writing for television.

GREGORY

Yes.

JACK

And?

GREGORY

I'm not a writer. I'm a performer.

JACK

I could have told you that three years ago, but did you ever listen to me or anyone else?

GREGORY

I had to try it. I did.

JACK

How long did it last?

GREGORY

Only a couple of months. I lived in Santa Fe for a while, in Tucson, San Francisco ... I had to be by myself and ... think. I have a new act.

JACK
(Smiling)

I guessed as much. Is that a costume you're wearing?

GREGORY
(Brushing lapels)

Yes.

JACK

It reminds me a little of what Pinky Lee used to wear. I like it. Between the two of us you couldn't have come back at a better time, Greg. Everything's booming. They're dying for new acts. Here, Las Vegas, Atlantic City, Miami ...

GREGORY

You can find me something?

JACK

Haven't I always? If there's been a problem, It's been with your ... attitude. I'd get you work and you'd walk away, or you wouldn't show on time, or you'd break your contract without a phone call, or you'd be fighting with the owners, the stage managers, the electricians, the ...

GREGORY

No more. It won't happen any more.

JACK

You mean that?

GREGORY

Yes. I want to work. Nothing else matters to me.

JACK

That's what I was waiting to hear.
(Dials phone)
Would you tell Mr. Greene I'll be about fifteen minutes late. That's right. Thank you.
(Rises)
A drink, Greg? Can I get you a drink?

GREGORY

I don't drink any more.

JACK

Good for you. That was something else that got you into a lot of trouble.
(Pours himself a drink)
How's your mother?

GREGORY

The same. Fine. She's . . . she hasn't changed anything since Buzz died. The house is filled with his stuff. There isn't an inch of wall space that isn't covered with photographs of him and his friends, with posters and Playbills and awards, certificates, plaques . . . it's . . . a mausoleum.

JACK

He was a great man, your father. I said a great man, Greg. I didn't say one of the greatest comics or one of the greatest entertainers we've ever had. I said a great man. A humanitarian and a sensitive, giving human being. I remember the first time he came into my office. It wasn't this fancy place. It was a closet in the old Paramount building. He wore that checkered suit of his with the baggy pants, and he had on his blond wig, and he held a balloon in his hand, that's right, a big, red, Mickey Mouse balloon, and I remember . . .
(Laughing)
I just looked at him, he didn't say a word, but the expression on his face was so sad and tragic . . .
(Laughing)
I laughed, laughed so hard that the guy upstairs started screaming and banging on the ceiling with a broom . . . oh, God . . .
(Laughing)

GREGORY
(Restrained)
He was usually like that at home, too. Developing new material, working for the punch line or the funny bit . . . in everything.

JACK

Don't I know it. The times we had together . . . there was no one who came close to him. No one then and no one since . . .
(Adding quickly)
But you, Greg; you. You had some of his stuff. At the beginning. I thought for sure we had another Buzz Harris. You'd be sooo funny, hilarious, hil-ar-i-ous! You'd have the audience eating out of your hand, and I thought for sure . . .

GREGORY
(Lights a fresh cigarette in cigarette holder)
I wasn't . . . comfortable.

JACK

The phone calls I'd get, the offers, my God, it was incredible. Everybody wanted you. Everybody. And I tried to warn you, tried to force you to take advantage of what was being offered to you . . . a once-in-a-lifetime . . .

(Shakes his head)

It was no use. You wouldn't listen.

GREGORY

It wasn't . . . right.

JACK

I know. I know. I heard it before. What your father had, what you had at the beginning, that wasn't right for you; convulsing an audience wasn't right for you. You were that rarity among rarities, an artist, a perfectionist. You had to do, what's the expression? Your own thing?

GREGORY

Yes.

(He takes a folded handkerchief from his pocket and pats his face with it, a gesture he frequently repeats)

JACK

You broke your father's heart, you know that, don't you? He used to come in here and he'd ask me what was wrong with you, why you were throwing away your career. He'd be crying, his eyes pouring tears. "I don't understand, Jack," he'd say to me. "What is he trying to do? He has it made; it's all there for him." And what could I tell him? I didn't understand it myself. And the truth is I still don't understand it!

GREGORY

I'd rather not . . . go into it.

JACK

He knew something, though. Your father knew you were mocking him. He knew that you were looking down at him as if he were some cheap Catskill comic, some down-and-out second-banana vaudeville clown. He knew that, and you hurt him, Greg, you hurt that man very, very much.

GREGORY

That wasn't my intention.

JACK

It was heart-breaking, to see a man that was loved and revered by millions of people, all over the world, to see him being put down by his own son.

(GREGORY pats his face with handkerchief)

Are you sure you don't want a drink?

(GREGORY shakes his head)

If we're going to work together again, everything has to be out in front. From now on, that's how it's gonna be.

GREGORY

Please. Say whatever's on your mind.

JACK

You didn't ask me about Eva. Is that on purpose?

GREGORY
(Slight pause)

How is Eva?

JACK
(Brightening)

Wonderful. Couldn't be better. I've never seen her so ... you know she married, don't you?

GREGORY

Yes. I heard.

JACK

Look. Look at this.
          (He hands GREGORY a framed photograph from desk)
My grandson. Six months and two weeks old. Tomorrow.
          (GREGORY glances at photo, forces a smile, and returns it to him)
Isn't he something else? Did you ever see a kid with a smile on his face like that? He's ...
          (Gives it up)
Eva talks about you, Greg. She's always asking what you're up to.

GREGORY

Please give her my congratulations.

JACK

After what you two have been through, you should remain friends.

GREGORY

Yes.

JACK

Why don't you phone her?

GREGORY

I will. Soon.

JACK

It's none of my business, but are you ever sorry you broke off with her? Do you ever think about it?

GREGORY

At times. Yes.

JACK

You don't regret it, though. I mean, it's water under the bridge, right?

221

GREGORY

Jack, can I show you what I've been working on? I would genuinely appreciate it if you could get me a couple of bookings, anywhere would be fine. I'm anxious to get my career going again.

JACK

Something tells me your attitude has improved.

GREGORY

Yes.

JACK

I feel you're more mature now, more settled and responsible.

GREGORY

I believe so.

JACK

That makes me feel good, very good. All right, Greg, let's see what you've got.
(He sits behind desk. GREGORY *rises, puts his suitcase on sofa and opens it)*
What is it, a stand-up routine? A magic act? Songs? Whatever it is, I can guarantee there won't be any trouble booking you. Most people forgot how you carried on in the old days.

GREGORY

I changed my name.

JACK

What's that?

GREGORY

I changed my name. Legally. I'm Gregory Horowitz.

JACK

What did you do that for? The son of Buzz Harris means something to an audience. It's money in the bank. Why the hell are you throwing it away?
*(*GREGORY *removes three candles in holders from suitcase and places them on coffee table. Everything is done methodically, as if it's been rehearsed a million times.)*

GREGORY

Horowitz was our real name. Buzz changed it to Harris to avoid any religious prejudices. There's no reason for that today. In fact audiences respect entertainers who keep their family name.

JACK

Maybe out in Hollywood, with the superstars, but in the boondocks there's still plenty of prejudice going on. Your father's name . . .

222

GREGORY
(Lights candles with plastic lighter)
Horowitz is my father's name. Jack, once you see my act, none of this will be important.

JACK
You create problems, that's what worries me. What are those candles for? Is it a magic act?

GREGORY
No.

JACK
Is it funny? Will they laugh?

GREGORY
They shouldn't, not if it's done well. To my knowledge this act was done only once before, in France. It was an enormous success.
(He places a wooden toy soldier in the same line with the candles on the coffee table)

JACK
Where did you hear about it?

GREGORY
San Francisco. I was browsing in a used book store and found this old magazine. Inside it I read a story about this Frenchman. I knew immediately that if I could do what he did and make it my own, I'd have an act that no one could come close to.

JACK
Just the same, I wish you could work some humor into it. Laughs don't hurt.

GREGORY
You're the audience; the stage is here; the M.C. introduces me.
(He turns on tape recorder in suitcase: his voice, music and sound effects are on tape. As the tape plays, G R E G O R Y does a great many exercises: knee-bends, jogs in place, squats, etc. He exercises with almost fanatic concentration)

TAPE RECORDER
(Appropriate introductory music from large nightclub band; then G R E G O R Y's *voice, background noises)*
Ladies and gentlemen, quiet, please, quiet. I know you're all very anxious to hear our next entertainer, and I'm going to bring him on the minute we have a little quiet. Please, please, ladies and gentlemen.
(Applause, cries for G R E G O R Y; *nervous laugh)*
This is wonderful; this is truly a great reception for a great entertainer, an entertainer who has climbed to the top of his profession within such a short period of time. May I have quiet, please!

(Noises dwindle)

Thank you. Thank you. Thank you. Oh, this promises to be one of the most exciting evenings we've had in a long, long time. I will ask you one favor, ladies and gentlemen, and that is that you lean back in your chairs, enjoy yourself, and do not, please, interrupt the performance and do save your applause until it's all over.

(Applause and drum-roll)

Thank you. Thank you. And now without further ado, ladies and gentlemen, the most novel, the most original and artistic performer anywhere on the stage today, Mr. Gregory Horowitz!

(Wild applause and shouts; music, like "When the Moon Comes Over the Mountain"; G R E G O R Y exits; enters; raises his arms)

GREGORY
(Shuts recorder)

Thank you. Thank you.

(Slight pause)

I would like to begin by asking anyone in the audience if there's a favorite song of theirs they'd like to hear. Anyone?

(He waves for J A C K to name a song)

JACK

Ahhh . . . "Home on the Range." Do you know "Home on the Range?"

GREGORY

Yes, sir. Thank you. Ladies and gentlemen, "Home on the Range."
(Meticulously, swiftly, he unbuttons a flap at the rear of his pants and bends over, facing the audience so that his behind is not visible; his hands are clasped on his bent knees; his expression changes but is never unpleasant, grotesque or indicative of a bowel movement. He breaks wind to the tune of "Home on the Range." Speakers placed around the office are used to accomplish this: the sound will fade and rise at whatever place G R E G O R Y is at. J A C K's face is a mask of absolute amazement. He can't believe what he's hearing and seeing. He looks around, cheeks flushed, mouth hanging open. He's afraid to stare directly at G R E G O R Y but he finally does so)

JACK
(He shakes his head, covers his eyes, turns away in repulsion)

Greg . . . stop . . . don't . . .

(G R E G O R Y waves him to be quiet, intent on continuing his act)

GREGORY

Thank you, ladies and gentlemen, thank you. And now if you'll kindly keep your eyes on that table over there . . .
(Points to coffee table, then quickly bends over, breaks wind three times; the three candles go out, one, two, three; as an afterthought he breaks wind again, knocking over the toy soldier)

JACK
(Shouts, angrily)
I said enough, enough, that's enough!
(He grimaces, stumbles to the window to raise the Venetian blinds and open the window)

GREGORY
No, leave it! I'll do it!
(He bends over, breaks wind: the Venetian blinds zoom to the top of the window; he breaks wind again, and the window flies open; he now changes his position, aims at the blade fan on the ceiling, breaks wind: the blade fan whirls about, soundlessly, speedily. He rises, feeling very pleased with himself)
Thank you, ladies and gentlemen. Thank you. And now . . .

JACK
(Shouts)
Do you want me to leave this room? Is that what you want? I am not your father! I do not have to stand here and be mocked and made a fool of!

GREGORY
(Buttons flap on pants)
Jack . . . you're mistaken. I wasn't . . . I wouldn't . . .

JACK
Have you lost your mind? Have you gone completely insane? That . . . that was your act? That's what you've been working on for three years?
(GREGORY holds up his "flute")

GREGORY
You didn't let me finish. I would be grateful if you would allow me to finish.
(JACK stares hard at GREGORY, as if trying to read his mind. He gives up)

JACK
I am sorry. I'm late for my meeting.

GREGORY
But . . .

JACK
Perhaps another time.

GREGORY
Is this what you meant by never turning your back on Buzz's son?

JACK
You go too far, too far. You don't know where to draw the line. I really think you need help, Greg, professional help. I'm not equipped to deal with it.

GREGORY

Respectfully, I'd like to suggest that you're out of touch with today's audience ... Jack.

JACK

I am? That's news to me. And everybody else in the business.

GREGORY

I'm not referring to the audiences in Las Vegas and Atlantic City. I'm referring to the young people, the students on college campuses and the kids who go to small clubs that provide entertainment that expresses their political and social opinions and their ...

JACK

You're not saying your act ... ?

GREGORY

Yes, They'll understand it and appreciate it.

JACK

Obscene filth, that's what it is!

GREGORY
(Patting his brow)

You're mistaken. It's as much an art form as any other.

JACK

Art, huh? What you just did was art, huh?

GREGORY

Yes, Perhaps the highest. To create out of one's physical self something that is capable of amazing us.

JACK

Sit down. Go ahead, sit down!
(They both sit)

I'll give you one last chance. Use your father's act. Use the same material he did, stand up there and deliver a string of one-liners, and I'll get you all the bookings you want. You'll have a career for yourself, a future, you'll have something. Don't let me walk out on you, Greg. I'm begging you, for your sake.

GREGORY

Why won't you allow me to use my own material? I've been working at it day and night. It took practice and discipline. I gave everything I had to achieve the tone and the pitch and the ...

JACK

It's vile and I'm not discussing it with you. It's out of the question! Greg, why don't you listen to me? Your father was an artist, too. What he did was art. It was. Millions of people ...

226

GREGORY

My father was a clown.

(Slight pause)

He dropped his pants for laughs.

(Slight pause)

He stuck his face in custard pies.

(Slight pause)

I was humiliated watching him.

JACK

All right, go on, get it out. Let me hear what you didn't have the guts to say to his face!

GREGORY

He was a vulgar and obscene little man. His act was an abomination, an insult to the intelligence. He groveled and whined to please his audience. That, I submit respectfully, is not the . . . attitude of an artist.

JACK

But he had an audience. That's more than can be said for you. He used to stand up there for hours and he played that audience as if it were an instrument, as if . . .

GREGORY
(Suddenly losing control)

Could he do this? Could my father do this?
(He rises, quickly unbuttons flap, assumes posture: he breaks wind, several times, knocks the books off the mantelshelf, tosses JACK's homburg into the air, starts a roaring blaze in the fireplace, as painting whirls around on wall)
No one can do that! No one! No one in the entire world but me! Me!
(Abruptly JACK rises, takes his briefcase and moves to exit from office. GREGORY stops him; emotionally)
No, please, don't . . . walk out, please. I'm . . . I'm in a bit of a jam. I need your help. I do. Please. I can't stay with my mother any longer, it's impossible, and I'm broke, Jack, I . . . I had to borrow carfare to come down here.

JACK

I'll be happy to loan you whatever money you need.

GREGORY

I don't need money. I need work! I . . . I . . .
(Pinches his face together as if in great pain)
I have to have an audience or I'm dead; I'm dead!

JACK

I'm not the only agent in New York. Maybe someone else will be . . . responsive to what you're doing.

GREGORY

I've tried already, here and in California. You're the last one.

227

(Takes photo from desk)

You asked me if I ever thought of Eva and what I gave up to . . . to work on my new act. Yes, Jack. Every day. Every night. Before I go to sleep, I bury my head in the pillow and I say to her, "It's for you. What I am doing is mostly for you."

(Returns photo)

JACK

I am sorry. Will you shake hands with me? I really have to go.

(JACK holds out his hand but GREGORY doesn't take it)

GREGORY

Couldn't you send me out on a few auditions? I won't say you sent me. They don't have to know.

JACK

They'd know. It's a small business. And I make it a practice never to send out a client whose work I don't approve of. Goodbye, Greg. If you need anything else of me . . .

GREGORY

Wait, wait. Don't go yet, please. There's one more thing and then . . .

(He closes window, turns to him)

I do thank you, Jack, for giving so freely of your time and being so patient with me. I do appreciate it.

(Points to chair behind desk)

Sit down. One minute, I promise. I won't take more than a minute.

(Reluctantly JACK sits in chair. GREGORY, very talkative now)

Oh, I forgot to ask you. My mother wants to know what happened to my father's poster when he played the Sahara Dunes.

JACK

I'm having it framed for her. She should get it next week.

GREGORY

Thank you. She'll be very pleased to receive it. What I wanted to tell you . . . Jack?

(Grins)

Is it still Jack?

(JACK nods, grimly. GREGORY, returning "properties" to suitcase; snaps it shut)

What I wanted to tell you . . . Jack, I know what your answer will be, but I have to ask you once again: you wouldn't just get me an audience and let them decide if my act's any good or not, would you?

(JACK shakes his head, grimly)

Fine. I had to ask, for the record so to speak. Anyhow, you do understand that there's a lot in my act that I didn't show you. I know the more I talk to you the more crazy you must think I am, but . . . anyhow, in working on my act I discovered—I don't know whether it was due to sound frequency or toxicity or what—but I discovered, you're not going to believe this, I know . . .

(Takes a breath)

I discovered I could . . . kill things, living things. I'd find small animals, snakes, cats, mice, skunks, squirrels ... I'd find them dead in the area where I was rehearsing. Isn't that strange?

JACK

Greg, I've been as patient ...

GREGORY

Thirty seconds, that's it. I'll be done and I promise you won't have to put up with me any more. Word of honor. You know, you've been a little insidious in our conversation today. For example, I didn't precisely "break off" with Eva. She gave me an ultimatum. It was something like six months to make it as a performer or get into some other line of business. That was your idea, Jack. She told me. Frankly you exercised a great deal of influence over your daughter's life.

JACK

As it turned out, she did well by taking my advice.

GREGORY

Yes, yes, I have no doubt about that, but you do understand that my position, vis-a-vis Eva, was completely untenable. It was an either/or ultimatum and I had no choice. I had to walk away.
(Grins)
In fact, I walked three thousand miles away. You do understand that, don't you?

JACK

You made your choice; now live with it.

GREGORY

Yes, yes of course. I'm not saying differently. As for my father, though, as for Buzz Harris, you must remember that the first time he went up to your office he wasn't wearing baggy pants and carrying a Mickey Mouse balloon ... Jack. You must remember that he went up to your office carrying his fiddle, his Stradivarisburg as he called it, and that he played for you some melodies from Dvorak and Moussourgsky. It was only between melodies that he cracked a few jokes which you said he should work on and for him to forget the fiddle. You must remember that ... Jack.
(JACK stares at him, expressionlessly)
I remember it. My mother remembers it. We remember it because the same day my father, Buzz Harris, came home in tears, his eyes were pouring tears. He told us what you said and right there in front of us, while he was crying buckets of tears, he smashed his fiddle, his Stradivarisburg into a thousand tiny bits and pieces, and he started cracking jokes like a lunatic, like a man devoid of his senses. You must remember that ... Jack.

JACK

Are you done?

GREGORY

Yes, I am. I'm done. I'm finished. But before I go, before I say goodbye, I have to reiterate my ... complaint that you have much too much ... influence over the lives of others. Who would have believed that an agent, a middleman, an entrepreneur of entertainers and performers, of fiddlers and clowns, who would have believed that he enjoyed so much . . . influence. But that isn't what I want to say before I go. I want to ask you, once again; I want to get down on my knees and ask you, Mr. Kohane, please, let me do my act in front of an audience and let them decide if it has merit or not. Please. Please. I'll be eternally grateful to you. I'll do it for nothing, without pay, without a contract, without terms or conditions. Ple-ease. Pl-ease.

JACK

No.

GREGORY

Thank you. Thank you for listening to me. Thank you for being so patient and forbearing. You know, I wasn't kidding about the dead animals, the snakes and cats and mice and skunks and squirrels. My . . . ability, my talent, what I am capable of doing, is far greater than you can imagine. I am an artist, sir! Did you hear me, sir? I am an artist! And an artist has influence, too. He has power, too. You should not take lightly his complaint. You don't believe me? You think I'm talking through my hat? Mr. Kohane, watch, watch what an artist can do! It will amaze you, absolutely amaze you!

(JACK *starts for door.* GREGORY *swiftly unbuttons rear flap, turns his backside at* JACK, *and breaks wind four or five times, huge, thundering wind blasts that shake the office furniture and reverberate against the walls.* JACK *is "shot," again and again, stumbles across room gasps chokingly, clutches his throat, flails his arms, as the air around him fills with noxious, toxic gases, his face turns purple and he collapses on the desk.* GREGORY *picks up* JACK's *homburg, puts it on his own head, tilts it at a rakish angle. He takes his suitcase, looks back at* JACK's *lifeless body, and with a jaunty step exits quietly from the office, singing the lyrics of "Home On the Range.")*

CURTAIN

Twice Around the Park

— A Need for Brussels — Sprouts

After working in the theater for over twenty years I was finally commissioned to write a play for two actors. (Why hadn't I ever written for a particular actor before? Up until now my work has grown out of a need to say something rather than a need to find a play for an actor. Why do I say "up until now"? Because I've learned a thing or two: I go where the action is.)

The actors I wrote Brussels Sprouts *for influenced not only who the characters were in the play but the substance of the play as well. That men and women wish for a "third something" to relate to is a thought I've had for a long time; that the thought would be played out by a policewoman and an unemployed actor of a certain age and temperament and vulnerability were dictated to me by the actors chosen to be in the play.*

It's quite common to hear (most often from producers) actors spoken of pejoratively. What is heard frequently is that actors are "babies," "infantile," "psychotic," "crazy," "irresponsible," etcetera, etcetera. The ingratitude of these parasites boggles the mind.

I believe a talent for acting is one of the greatest gifts God has given to mankind. Anyone who can with his bare bones and craft stand in front of an audience and transport that audience into other realms of being is deserving of our everlasting praise and admiration.

—M.S.
March 9, 1983

TWICE AROUND THE PARK *was produced by Peter Witt, Margo Korda and Warner Theatre Productions in association with the John F. Kennedy Center for the Performing Arts, and opened at the Cort Theatre, November 4, 1982.* A NEED FOR BRUSSELS SPROUTS *was first presented at the John Drew Theatre, in East Hampton, New York.*

MARGARET HEINZ   Anne Jackson

LEON ROSE   Eli Wallach

Directed by ARTHUR STORCH

Set design by JAMES TILTON

Costumes by RUTH MORLEY

Lighting design by JUDY RASMUSON

Sound by DAVID S. SCHNIRMAN

The basic box set is the same for both plays. Only the furniture, proper-
ties, and set dressing are changed.

A living room in a West Side apartment building. The present tenant has
still to unpack all his belongings.

Spring; late afternoon.

We hear a record playing, an aria from the opera Tosca : *"Quale occhio*
al mundo puo star do paro."

L E O N ROSE, *wearing a trim, pin-striped shirt, brown slacks and*
brown loafers, standing center stage, sheet music in hand, singing along
with the music; at times miming it, gesturing. After a few beats, we hear
someone banging on an upstairs radiator. L E O N *dismisses the interrup-*
tion and continues singing. After a few more beats the telephone rings.
L E O N, *annoyed at the interruption, sets his music sheet down on a*
speaker and lifts the needle off the record player. He runs to the phone
which he thinks is on the desk. The telephone rings again and he stops
short and runs to the phone which is on the floor next to the Duncan Fife
table. He sets the phone on the table and answers it.

LEON
(Into phone)

Leon Rose speaking here.

(Slight pause)

One second, Cindy. One second.

(He picks up pencil and prepares to write on pad)

Yes, Cindy. What was the message?

(He writes)

Phone ... ah-ha, ah-ha ... I have it. Thank ... just a second. Isn't Jacobson a
producer?

(Slight pause)

Would you look him up in the ... that's all right. I understand. I'll call him
immediately.
(He hangs up the phone, rips off the sheet with the number on it and quickly sits
at the sofa. He takes a deep breath and begins to dial the number carefully. After a

pause.)

Hello? This is Leon Rose returning Mr. Robert Jacobson's call.

(Slight pause)

Yes, Mr. Jacobson. My service just communicated your message to me. Fortunately
I'm in town ...

(Pause. His tone changes)

What? What's that?

(He rises)

Now you listen to me. The sole purpose of the actors' photographs in the Players
Guide is for the benefit of producers, directors and casting people. It is not for the
purpose of solicitation. If you continue in this practice, sir, you will be hearing from
the Better Business Bureau. And I do not need a hairpiece!

235

(He slams down the receiver and returns the phone to the desk with the pad and pencil. He crosses to the phonograph and pauses to look in the mirror. He touches his hairline and then dismisses the idea. He puts the needle on the record again and picks up the cavalier's hat from the ladder. He begins singing again but after a few beats the doorbell rings and knocking is heard from the front door. He tries to ignore it but the ringing and banging continue furiously. Unable to ignore it any longer, he crosses to the door)

All right! All right! I'm coming! I'm not deaf! You don't have to knock the door down! Where's your common . . .

(He opens the door)

. . . sense.

MARGARET
(Offstage, shouting)
Are you the tenant in this apartment?

LEON
(Shouting)
Yes.

MARGARET
(Offstage, shouting)
Do I have your permission to enter the premises?

LEON
(Shouting)
Yes, yes, you do.

(He steps back and MARGARET HEINZ *enters. She is a policewoman wearing a complete uniform with hat, badges, blue shirt and pants, belt with pistol in holster, nightstick in ring, summons book and pen, handcuff holder and ammo belt.*
LEON *closes the door)*
Is there something the matter?

MARGARET
(Shouting)
Would you kindly shut off that phonograph?

LEON
(Crossing to phonograph)
Right away. I'll be glad to do it.

(He sets down his hat on the audio speaker and takes the needle off of the record. She, meanwhile, has taken out the summons book and pen and is preparing to write. He turns to see her doing this)
One . . . one second, miss. I mean Officer. Officer. I mean Policewoman Officer, that's what I mean. You're a Policewoman Officer, am I correct?

MARGARET
(Businesslike)
Name.

LEON

Can't we talk before you write out that ticket? By the way, I do not own a car, I do not drive a car, so if you're up here because of a double-parked car, there is a terrible injustice being perpetrated, and I have always fought against injustice, and that includes fascism, nazism, racism . . .

MARGARET

Do you give me your name, mister, or do I have to take you in?

LEON

May I ask, respectfully, what a tax-paying citizen is being accused of in the privacy of his apartment when he does not even own or drive a car?

MARGARET

You're in violation of a city anti-noise ordinance for playing your phonograph too loudly. Does that answer your question?
(She starts to write)

LEON
(Looking upwards)

Not quite.
(She stops writing)
Because I know who put you up to this, Officer, and now I'm getting mad. I am definitely getting mad. I recently moved into this apartment and I get along with all my neighbors except for this crazy old hag upstairs. Every time I sneeze, she starts banging on the ceiling and hitting the radiator with an aluminum frying pan. She has to be a genuine crackpot.

MARGARET

Do you know the crazy old hag who lives upstairs?

LEON

No, I don't . . .

MARGARET

You're looking at her, mister!
(She pulls up her trousers)
Name!

LEON
(Like a schoolboy)

Rose. R-O-S-E. Leon. L-E-O-N. Leon Rose.

MARGARET
(Writing)

Leon Rose. Residence is . . .

LEON

One second, please. I . . . I owe you an apology, miss. I mean Officer. Officer. I sincerely apologize. The truth is that I had no logical way of knowing that you were the crazy old hag who . . .

(He realizes he's ruined it; crosses to kitchen)

Would you by any chance care for a glass of Perrier water with a wedge of lime?

MARGARET
(Writing again)

Residence is 925 West End Avenue . . .

LEON
(Coming back)

Wait. Hold it. Let's not act precipitously. I have a single question to ask you. How much is that ticket going to cost me?

MARGARET
(Continues writing)

It's a summons, not a ticket. The fine is a hundred dollars.

LEON
(Shocked)

A hundred dollars? For playing my phonograph too loudly? That is ridiculous. That is highway robbery. How much would it cost me if I screamed at the top of my lungs? Like this.

(He screams loudly)

MARGARET
(Flipping to next summons)

It'll cost you a hundred dollars for each violation.

LEON

It was an example. I was merely giving you an example!

MARGARET

Look, Mr. Rose, I just finished a twelve-hour tour of duty. I made three arrests, gave out fifteen parking tickets, nine summons and I just chased a nude man from Fifty-sixth Street to Forty-fourth Street where I lost him in a movie house. So don't give me a hard time, huh?

(She puts her foot on box to write easier)

LEON

I wasn't . . .

MARGARET

All I want to do is get out of these clodhoppers and soak my bones in a hot tub of water.

LEON

I understand.

MARGARET
(Moving to him)
Do you understand? Do you know what it's like to be out there on those streets? Did you ever wear a uniform and try to break up a sidewalk crap game or collar a pimp in a massage parlor?

LEON
No. Not that I can recall.

MARGARET
We're understaffed, undersupported, underpaid, and we still have to buy our own lousy bullets with our own lousy money!
(She writes again)

LEON
Personally, I think the police department is doing a wonderful job; wonderful.

MARGARET
Do you? Did you ever write to the mayor and ask him to give us a little extra consideration?

LEON
I was planning on doing that this evening.
(She stops writing)

MARGARET
I bet you were.

LEON
(Sits on hassock)
I was. I was. Look, Officer, I wouldn't be making such a to-do about a crummy hundred dollar fine if you didn't catch me at a particularly awkward time vis-a-vis my cash flow.

MARGARET
Your what?

LEON
My financial situation. It normally isn't a problem with me but I recently had to pay the landlord two months rent in advance, plus $900 . . .
(He rises)
to the moving people to carry my belongings from the East Side to the West Side.
(He crosses to phone)
I had to install a phone . . .

MARGARET
Mr. Rose, you can explain that to the judge. Just let me finish . . .
(She writes again)

239

LEON
(Crosses to her)
I insist that attention must be paid!
(She stops writing)
After all, we are neighbors. That's what neighbors are for. To help one another. To stick together. To be friends.

MARGARET
So you want to be friends.

LEON
Yes, I do. If neighbors can't be friends, there's no hope for civilization. We might as well pack our suitcases and move back to the Dark Ages.

MARGARET
Some people should pack their suitcases so some other people can have some peace and quiet. Where do you get off playing your phonograph so loudly? Do you think I like banging on the ceiling? Do you think I have nothing else to do when I come home from work?

LEON
I can explain. . . .

MARGARET
I have been living in this building for seven years. For seven years I didn't hear a sound from this apartment. There was a nice, elderly woman living here and she knew what it was like to be considerate of other people. She died, poor woman, but she. . . .

LEON
She died? In this apartment?

MARGARET
That's right. She was. . . .

LEON
What room did she die in?

MARGARET
In the bedroom.

LEON
She died? In my bedroom?

MARGARET
There was a big brass bed in there.

LEON
The landlord sold me that bed for a hundred and thirty dollars.

MARGARET

That was her bed. She was so quiet, nobody knew she was dead for more than a week.

LEON
(Rises)

She was dead in my bed for more than a week?

MARGARET

I found her myself.

LEON

I'll tell you something. Every time I get into that bed, I have the feeling that I'm not alone.

MARGARET

Is that why you play your phonograph so loudly in the middle of the night?

LEON

No, no. I can explain.

MARGARET

Go ahead. Explain. I'm listening.

LEON

I am an actor, Officer. A trained, professional actor.
(He crosses to speaker and picks up hat and music sheet)
I'm preparing for an audition that requires I pantomime an opera singer. And when I'm preparing for an audition, I lose all sense of everything else. I lose myself in my work.

MARGARET

And that's why you're getting a summons. I have two kids up there, Mr. Rose; two kids who go to school. Do you know that since you moved in they haven't been able to study or get a regular night's sleep?

LEON

No, I. . . .

MARGARET

Why don't you lower that thing when I bang on your ceiling?

LEON

I didn't realize. . . .

MARGARET

Last night was the last straw. Where's your dog?
(She takes out nightstick and moves to kitchen door)
Do you know he was barking until one o'clock in the morning?

LEON

In that regard your're incorrect, Officer. I do not own a dog. I did own a dog. I bought him after my East Side apartment was burglarized the second time. But the third time they burglarized it, they took the dog with them. This is the dog you heard.
(He sets down hat and sheet music on speaker and picks up eight-track tape and inserts it in stereo. We hear a dog barking and growling viciously. After a few seconds, he pulls it out. Holding up tape)
I put this on whenever I go out.
(She moves away, hands in air, exasperated. He returns tape and moves down)
It doesn't do that much good. I was burglarized four times in my East Side apartment. Besides my dog they took my television set, my cameras, my silverware . . . They wiped me out. The fourth time they broke in, there wasn't anything to take so they left me a book of food stamps.

MARGARET

That still doesn't excuse those barking noises until one o'clock in the morning when my kids are trying to sleep.

LEON

I agree. It was thoughtless of me. I'm sure as a police officer you sympathize with the fact that your everyday citizen is inadequately protected.

MARGARET

We sympathize but how can we do the job if we don't have the personnel?

LEON

I'm not criticizing. You guys are doing everything humanly possible. I know it's a jungle out there.

MARGARET

A jungle is what it is. The minute we collar one bum, two bums take his place. And do you think the bum we collar goes to jail? Oh, no. Not on your life. The judge pats him on the back, gives him a speech and in an hour he's on the street again.

LEON
(Moves to her)
I know. I read about this prostitute that a judge took home with him because she had no place to stay for the night.

MARGARET

You think that's something? I once brought in a prostitute and the judge married her!

LEON
(Sits)
Nooo.

MARGARET

I'm telling you he married her. They're living in Oyster Bay now. They have a house, a car, a sailboat, a Jacuzzi. . . . That hooker's living a better life than I am.

LEON

Disgusting.

MARGARET

It's worse than disgusting. Did you ever visit one of those minimum security prisons?

LEON

I was planning on doing that this summer.

MARGARET

They're not prisons; they're country clubs. During the day, they play baseball, volleyball, tennis, golf, and in the evening they have concerts or Las Vegas entertainment, and they sleep in separate bedrooms with no bars on the windows.

LEON

How do you like that. Do you know I have bars on my bedroom windows?

MARGARET

I couldn't sleep if I didn't have bars on my bedroom windows.

LEON

We have to have bars and the criminals don't have to have bars.

MARGARET

We're the ones in prison, not them.

LEON

What we should do is change places. We'd be a lot safer and a lot happier living in those prisons of theirs.

MARGARET

You can't get into those prisons. They're so popular, they have a five-year waiting list.

LEON

What a sad, sad commentary on the state of our society.

MARGARET

It makes me sick just to think about it.

LEON

Look, Officer, now that we're better acquainted, let me introduce myself to you, properly. Leon Rose, your neighbor and I hope, in the future, your friend.
(He extends his hand, she shakes it)

MARGARET

Margaret Heinz.

(He steps back, picks up pillow)

LEON

Why don't you sit down? Relax. Can I get you anything?

MARGARET

It has been a long day for me. I wouldn't mind a beer, if you have one.
(He resets pillow on sofa)

LEON

Absolutely.
(He moves to kitchen)
One ice-cold beer coming up for my upstairs neighbor. How old are your children?
*(He exits into kitchen. MARGARET crosses to sofa, sits, removes hat and wipes
forehead with bandana from under hat)*

MARGARET

I have a girl fourteen and a boy eleven.

LEON
(Offstage)

It must be difficult for you, having a full-time job and raising two children. What
does your husband do?

MARGARET

He's dead.

LEON
(Offstage)

That is difficult.

MARGARET

It was more difficult when he was alive.
(To herself)
The lying, sneaky bastard.

LEON
(Enters with beer can and glass on tray)

Is it all right if I call you Margaret? I don't like being formal. Especially with a
neighbor.

MARGARET

I don't usually get this kind of treatment when I write out a summons. You're not
trying to bribe me, are you?

LEON

Why do you even think such a thing? Drink up. It's imported. From China.
*(MARGARET takes beer can from tray, ignoring the glass. He discreetly takes
away glass. She puts the can to her lips and drinks beer without removing the can
from her lips until it is finished. He moves away)*
I'm surprised the name Leon Rose doesn't mean anything to you. I assume you're

not much of a theatergoer. Anyone who attends the theater with any regularity would certainly be familiar with the name Leon Rose . . .

(He turns to see her still drinking)

Do you go to the theater with any regularity?

(She finally finishes drinking the entire can)

Can I get you anything else, Margaret? A six-pack perhaps?

(They both laugh)

MARGARET

No, thanks. It's not bad, Chinese beer.

LEON

It's not.

(She unwittingly crushes beer can and hands it to him. Reacting he takes it and moves back. She wipes her hands with bandana)

It goes extremely well with a couple of T-bone steaks.

MARGARET

I'll have to try it sometime.

LEON

I'm surprised you haven't seen me perform anywhere, Margaret. I've been in dozens of plays.

(He exits into kitchen with tray)

Broadway, Off-Broadway, Regional Theater, Summer Stock . . .

(He enters empty handed)

MARGARET

What plays you been in?

LEON

Oh, I've done so many, I can't keep track.

MARGARET

When I was a kid, I was kind of interested in acting.

LEON
(Moving to her)

You were?

MARGARET

In high school I took a course in it and I'd go to the movies every chance I . . .

(He starts to sit next to her)

. . . Wait a minute! I recognize you.

LEON
(Stepping back)

Well, I . . .

MARGARET

You do a T.V. commercial. It's for a cat food, isn't it? What's the name of that cat food? Tabby Chow? Kitty Tidbits? Pussy Grub! That's it. You're the meow-meow man on the Pussy Grub commercial!

LEON

What difference does it make? That's not my work. I'm an actor.

MARGARET

You're famous . . .

LEON

Actors do all sorts of things to . . . supplement their incomes. It's quite acceptable nowadays.

MARGARET

Do you know you're the only celebrity living in this building?

LEON

I am?

MARGARET

The only one. It's a weird feeling. I can't wait to tell my kids, the meow-meow man is living under them. If they come down, would you give them your autograph?
(She sits on sofa and puts on hat; picks up summons book)

LEON

Sure, I'd be glad to . . .

MARGARET

I'm really sorry I have to give you this summons.

LEON

Margaret, you don't have to give me a summons, do you?

MARGARET

I already wrote your name and address and once I do that . . .

LEON

Can't you erase it?
(He moves to desk)
I have some excellent correction fluid. It doesn't leave a trace.
(He looks on desk and picks up a bottle of Liquid Paper. He moves down to her)

MARGARET

My record's clean in the department. I don't like messing with it. You can plead guilty with an excuse. Maybe the judge'll take into consideration who you are.

LEON

Margie, it's not only the money. It's not. It's ... the principle. I mean paying for more tennis courts for prisoners. That's what's upsetting me.
(He gives up)
But whatever happens, I'm glad we're becoming friends.
(He returns the bottle to desk and turns on charm)
I didn't know I had such an attractive upstairs neighbor.
(He moves down to her, slowly)
There's something very exciting about a woman in a policeman's uniform. The way her small, soft face shines and glows at the top of her blue shirt; the way her billowy hair curls around her pink, little ears when she's wearing her cap; the way she carries a gun on her hip emphasizing the full roundness of her plump buttocks.
(He sits close to her, arm around back of sofa)
I find it very, very, very exciting.

MARGARET

Do you?

LEON

I do. You're a beautiful woman, Margie. You're like a combination of Goldie Hawn and Ethel Barrymore.

MARGARET

Who is Ethel Barrymore?

LEON

She was an incredible actress with a magnificent stage presence.

MARGARET

I remind you of her?

LEON

Your eyes in particular. "Her eyes through the airy regions would stream so bright, that birds would sing and think it were not night."

MARGARET

What would your wife say if she walked in here now?

LEON

She probably wouldn't say anything. But I'd probably faint. She's been dead for eight years.

MARGARET

Were you married long?

LEON

No, no. I've been an extremely fortunate man. I've been married three times and they were all short marriages.
(He knocks on wood of sofa and laughs)

MARGARET

You think that's funny, huh?

LEON

As a matter of fact, my first marriage was so short, it ended before the honeymoon ended.
(He laughs again)

MARGARET

I don't think that's funny. I think that's sick, real sick. Oh, you're a sly one, you are. Coming on so strong, so sweet, so lovey-dovey. Maybe you can pull that stuff on some dumb sixteen-year-old kid, but not on me, mister!
(She rises; pulls him up)
Get on your feet! On your feet! Move it! Move it!
(She pushes him to front door. He is totally confused)

LEON

Wha' wha'...Margie, wha' wha'...

MARGARET

Get your hands behind your back!
(She takes out nightstick)
Spread your legs.
(She hits floor with stick)
Wider! Wider!
(He does so)
I heard about you actors and what you do for kicks. I know all about it.
(She frisks him, going up the left leg)
Now where did you hide the stash? Where do you keep it? Huh? Huh?
(She runs her hands into his privates. He reacts)

LEON
(Jumps)

Ooooops!

MARGARET

Stand still! Stand still!
(She presses him to wall and frisks his right leg)
You got it on you somewhere, I'd bet anything on it.
(She hits his privates again, and again he jumps)

LEON

Ooooops! Ooooops!

MARGARET
(Pulls him away from wall by nape of neck)
I got a whiff of something the minute I walked in. What is it? Pot? Grass? You were smoking a joint, weren't you?

248

LEON

No, no. Chicken. I mean I have a pot of chicken curry simmering on the gas range. It's for my dinner.

MARGARET
(Moving to kitchen)
Oh yeah? We'll see about that!
(She enters kitchen)

LEON

Margaret, what got into you? We were having such a pleasant conversation. Why are you . . . ?

MARGARET
(Re-entering)
Three short marriages, huh? You think that's funny? Let me tell you about two short marriages, mister, that weren't so funny. Let me tell you how I've been used and abused by men like you for as long as I can remember. When I think of how dumb I was, how innocent, how trusting. . . . I get so damn angry I just wanna plug holes into every slimy, deceiving, two-legged male in this city.

LEON
(Sitting in chair)
Let's be calm now, Margie. Your record's clean. You don't want to spoil your record.

MARGARET

I didn't start out dreaming of being a cop. That wasn't my dream. My dream was to share my life with somebody, but it was no dice. You men put me into this uniform; you put this gun on my hip and you showed me what to do with it, so don't get smart with me, Leon, I'm warning you.

LEON

No, no. I wouldn't.

MARGARET

I've got more damn anger in me than I can handle. To get this job I hadda lift and carry a seventy-five pound dummy up and down a couple of flights of stairs; I hadda take courses in boxing and wrestling; I hadda learn how to swing a nightstick and put away six-foot apes!
(She hits hassock with stick)
But for the sake of my kids, I try my damndest to control the anger.

LEON

You sound like a wonderful mother.

MARGARET

I am a wonderful mother. That's all I have is being a wonderful mother. I met their father when I was sixteen; sixteen, what did I know. He was a tall, strong, handsome Irishman with a smile that was pure blarney.

LEON

I don't recall if I told you, Margie, but I'm not Irish. I'm not.

MARGARET

Short marriages, huh? He'd come in and out of the apartment as if it were a Chinese laundry, to drop off and pick up his shirts. That's when we had sex, when he was changing his shirts. He probably figured he was half undressed anyways, what did he have to lose. By the time the second kid was born, he was gone, out the door, leaving me with a drawerful of bills and two kids to support. What could I do? I had no trade, no experience. For months I looked for a job until at last I got one as a raccoon . . .

LEON

A raccoon?

MARGARET

Yeah, didn't you ever hear of the raccoons?

LEON

I heard of them but I didn't know they could get jobs in the city.

MARGARET

Raccoons are cocktail waitresses, rip-offs of Playboy Bunnies at a club that used to be in Greenwich Village. I wore long, black stockings, a mini-skirt and a low-cut blouse down to here.
(She indicates her belly button)
You know, very sharp. I wore a cap with furry raccoon ears and a furry raccoon tail.
(She demonstrates)

LEON

You must have been one terrific-looking raccoon.

MARGARET

Not bad, if I say so myself. I liked working there. I had an opportunity for advancement. I could have been Head Raccoon. What happened was the manager started hassling me. Using his hands. I hadda quit. That's when I met the other slimy skunk.

LEON

Heinz?

MARGARET

Transit officer, Henry Heinz. Soon after we were married, he decided he wanted to be a lawyer. Would sweetie-pie give him a hand until he finished law school? Eventually I found out he wasn't going to law school. He was using my money to pay rent for another apartment and he was keeping his hooker there. Can you believe it? Taking the food from the mouths of my kids to support his hooker? Did I tell you he died?

LEON

Yes, you did. I recall . . .

MARGARET

He didn't die but to me he's dead. Just like the other one. Just like all men are dead to me. Dead! Dead! Dead! And that, Mr. Rose, is the story of two short marriages that were not so funny!

LEON
(Rising)

Margie, all men aren't the same. Some men . . .

MARGARET

Are good and some are bad, is that what you were gonna say, Leon?

LEON

I was. I was also going to say that there are some men who are decent and trustworthy and generous.

MARGARET

Oh, yeah? Where are they?

LEON

Who?

MARGARET

These men you're talking about.

LEON

They're around. If you look, you'll find them.

MARGARET

They wouldn't be in this room, would they?

LEON

It's possible.

MARGARET

Okay, Leon. I'll give you a chance to prove it. Let's hear about your three marriages. Go ahead. Let's see how decent and trustworthy you were with your three wives.

LEON
(Incredulously)

This is silly. What are we having here, a trial?

MARGARET

That's the best suggestion you had tonight.
(She picks up Duncan Fife table)
That's what we're gonna do, neighbor.
(She moves to below the sofa, sets down table, takes off hat, puts stick and summons book on sofa)

251

LEON

You can forget it, Margaret.
(He starts to leave room)
I'm not participating in. . . .

MARGARET
(Picks up summons book and rises)
I noticed you piled boxes and cartons in front of the fire exit in the hall. I really don't want to give you another summons, Leon.

LEON
(Stopping at kitchen door)
How did I get into this? I didn't leave my apartment today and already it's costing me two hundred dollars.

MARGARET
Court is now in session. The question is: Did Leon Rose use and abuse his wives? Did he act in a manner detrimental to the health and welfare of women? Is he a slimy skunk like all the rest of them?
(She sits on sofa)
You can begin with your first wife.

LEON
I object.

MARGARET
What's your objection?

LEON
I object on the grounds of the First Amendment.

MARGARET
Objection overruled.

LEON
I appeal.

MARGARET
Appeal denied!

LEON
I ask for a recess.

MARGARET
On what grounds?

LEON
On the grounds that I have to go make a peepee.
(He starts to leave)

MARGARET

Peepee denied!

(He stops, returns)

LEON

This is incredible. This is really incredible.

MARGARET

I'm waiting, Mr. Rose. Your first wife. Or do you want me to write out the two summonses charged against you?

LEON

All right! All right! I'll do it. I'll do it. But there are going to be repercussions, I promise you.

(He gathers his thoughts)

My first wife. She . . . she was a young girl. We were both still in college. Her name was . . .

(He forgets. A blank look comes over him. Then he remembers)

Glenda Fogelman, that's her! I need no defense for that marriage, none whatsoever. There was a physical problem that destroyed it. On our honeymoon, I tried to, you know, consummate the relationship. But I couldn't do it. I couldn't. There was something. . . . I don't like to go into intimate detail, but it seemed to me her privates were built peculiarly.

MARGARET

Her privates were built peculiarly?

LEON

That's right. There was something. . . . How shall I express it discreetly without offending anyone's sensibilities? In my opinion, there was something, let us say, anatomically screwed up down there.

(He sits on box, right of sofa)

MARGARET

Are you saying, Mr. Rose, that the marriage wasn't consummated?

LEON

That's precisely what I'm saying. Try as I might, and try I did, day and night, night and day, I could not achieve what was required of me.

MARGARET

But you were kind to her?

LEON

No man could have been kinder. And I'm compelled to confess that I never worked so hard in my life with such poor results.

MARGARET

Go ahead, Mr. Rose.

LEON

It was dreadful; the worst honeymoon I ever had. The truth is we were both virgins.
I woke up one morning and she was gone.

MARGARET

She left you?

LEON

That's right.
(He rises)
She went and had the marriage annulled.

MARGARET

And your second wife? How were her privates?

LEON

Not bad, not bad. But she was a sick woman. Mentally. She was a very sick woman.

MARGARET

How long was that marriage?

LEON

Seventeen months. We had a son. He teaches now at Berkeley. I don't see him as
much as I'd like to.... That's how it is.

MARGARET

Did you, at any time, strike your wife?

LEON

Strike her?

MARGARET

Yeah, you know, hit her, punch her, knock her to the ground.

LEON

I am appalled; appalled and astonished that such an accusation could be made here.
I have always fought against brutality and injustice, whether it was described as
fascism, nazism, racism...

MARGARET

Just answer the question, Mr. Rose.

LEON

No. I never laid a hand on her. Never. Oh, on occasion, a light pat on the buttocks.
(He demonstrates)
But only done in the most playful manner. Barbara, that was her name. She was an
actress; a terribly ambitious and competitive woman. While my career was growing,
hers was shrinking. She couldn't tolerate my being more successful than she was. She
turned into a mean and bitter woman, and she started drinking heavily.

MARGARET

How heavily?

LEON

Well, let me put it this way: she was the only wife I had who knew how to make a vodka salad dressing. And I heard from a very reliable source that in 1962, she was voted Miss Jack Daniels by a chapter of Alcoholics Anonymous.

MARGARET

Stop exaggerating and stick to the evidence. You did nothing to cause her to drink? You didn't cheat on her? You didn't go out with other women?

LEON

I did not. I worked. I paid the bills. I gave her a home. I didn't fool around. What did I do? You tell me what I did!

MARGARET

Your third wife?

LEON

I don't like this, Margie. I'm not finding it amusing or. . . .

MARGARET

Your third wife!

LEON

I had it with college girls and ambitious actresses. I said to myself, if I ever marry again, it would be to a simple, devoted, uncomplicated woman. My third wife was an American Indian.

MARGARET

From a reservation?

LEON

No, from East Hampton. She was a Shinnecock. Evidently I don't have good judgment when it comes to women. Nothing I did could satisfy her. I wasn't rich enough, famous enough, sexy enough. One day she withdrew all our savings and ran off with a real estate salesman. Afterwards, I dated for a few years but I don't remember enjoying any of it. Listen, I learned a thing or two myself. Relationships are too painful. I make no pretense about it. I don't need women. I can do very well without them.

MARGARET
(Reacting strongly)

You can! I get up every morning and I get down on my knees and I thank sweet Jesus for giving me the strength to live a life without men. Do you know what it's like to feel clean and decent and free of you and your kind?

LEON

Not nearly as exhilarating as being free of you and your kind. You don't make love

255

to a woman anymore. That's over. That's in the past. Nowadays you have to service her. You have to engage in foreplay, titillation, excitation, lubrication. After a while you don't know if you're a man in bed with a woman or a mechanic working under an old station wagon.

MARGARET

If you can't stand the heat, mister, stay out of the kitchen!

LEON

Listen, lady, I don't need the heat and I don't need the kitchen. It so happens that I personally don't believe there is such a thing as a woman's orgasm. How do you like that?

MARGARET

If a woman were dumb enough to go to bed with you, she wouldn't believe there's such a thing as a woman's orgasm either.

LEON

Funny. Funny. I think it's the biggest fraud ever perpetrated against civilization. Vaginal orgasm, clitoral orgasm, multiple orgasm; multiple, multiple, multiple, orgasm! A man has to take a college course in gynecology just to know what all the screaming's about.

MARGARET

Screaming? Women scream when they're in bed with you? What do you do, tie them in chains and pretend you're the meow-meow man on the Pussy Grub commercial?

LEON

Don't push me too far, Officer Heinz. I'll let you go so far but beyond a point you're not going so far, I can guarantee you that.

MARGARET

I have a feeling, Mr. Rose, that you can't deliver the cookies. You're not afraid of being impotent, are you?

LEON

Afraid? That's been my secret wish since I was eighteen years old. Fortunately, I am mature enough so that I have control over my libido. If it's of any interest to you, I haven't had sex in thirteen months and I'm in the best physical condition I've ever been in.

MARGARET
(Boasting)

You think that's a big deal? I haven't had sex in nineteen months and last April I ran twenty-six miles in the Boston Marathon!

LEON

But you didn't win, did you?

MARGARET

No, I didn't win. But I had to jump over the bodies of fifty men who were in the same best physical shape you're in.

LEON
(Picking up Duncan Fife table and setting it down up right)
You think you're in better physical condition than I'm in?

MARGARET

I know I am.

LEON
(Returning to her)
All right. You said before you picked up a seventy-five pound dummy. Let's see you pick me up.

MARGARET
(Extending her hand)
Give me your hand.
(He does. She takes it)
I'll lift you in the fireman's carry.
(She reaches between his legs and starts to lift)

LEON
(Breaking away)
Let go! Let go of me! What's wrong with you?
(He turns upstage and pulls at his crotch)
I'm not asking you to lift me in a fireman's carry. I'm asking if you can pick me straight up.

MARGARET

You're . . . you're too heavy for me.

LEON

You're not too heavy for me. Do I have your permission to pick you up?

MARGARET

Where do you have to hold me? To pick me up?

LEON

Under your armpits.

MARGARET

You have my permission.
(He moves to her. Puts his hands under her armpits and lifts her straight up)

LEON

You feel light and comfortable. I can hold you like this all . . .
(He slowly lowers her to floor. They hold each other at arm's length)

257

LEON
Margie?

MARGARET
(Weakly)

Yes, Leon?
(They kiss, passionately. After a couple of beats, she pulls away and moves left, shaken)
You shouldn't have done that. You shouldn't . . .

LEON
I couldn't help myself.

MARGARET
Especially when I'm in uniform.
(She retreats to rear; he follows)

LEON
I didn't mean to offend your uniform. Would you like to get out of your uniform?

MARGARET
I already told you. . . . I haven't had sex in nineteen months. Didn't I tell you that?
(She crosses to ironing board, picks up spray bottle and sprays her face, to cool off)

LEON
Yes, you did. And I told you I didn't have sex in thirteen months but don't you think it's time for a change?
(He moves to her. She turns and sprays him in the face. He backs off)

MARGARET
Stop it, Leon! Stop it!
(She returns bottle to ironing board)
In my eight years on the force no perpetrator has ever kissed me. That's a criminal offense: harassing a police officer. So for your own good, stop it!
(She has picked up bandana and wipes her face; moves away)

LEON
Margie, listen, I know we've had our ups and downs. But something incredible is happening between us tonight. Don't you feel it?

MARGARET
I feel it. I do feel it. But we can't let it happen.

LEON
But why? I find you an extremely attractive and desirable woman.

MARGARET
Is that another line of yours?

LEON
(Protesting)

How can you ...

MARGARET

You're not still trying to get out of the summons?

LEON

I resent that! I'm a very successful actor. Do you have any idea how much I earned in 1958?

MARGARET

Why did you move from the East Side to this building, if you're so successful?

LEON

In the theater it ... it goes in cycles. You work day and night for a few years and then there's a period when there aren't any parts for you or ... I don't want to talk about it.
(He moves away)

MARGARET

I'm sorry. I shouldn't have asked you.

LEON

No, no, it's good for me to talk about it. Things are a little slow now, but that's the business.

MARGARET

Maybe you'll get the job you're practicing for, the opera singer.

LEON

It's a commercial. For a non-fattening pizza pie.

MARGARET

Doesn't it pay a lot of money?

LEON
(Moving to her)

If you get it. Anyway, who cares? I only do commercials when I have nothing else going for me, professionally. Last year, I ...
(Almost bawling, he can't go on. He sits on hassock, his back to her)
Once in a while I do get to feel insecure.

MARGARET
(Sitting in chair)

I ... I know what that's like. I must be the most insecure person in the world.

LEON

You? Insecure?

MARGARET
(Almost bawling)

I am. I am.

LEON

I never would have guessed that.

MARGARET

I am. I really am. If I read they're cutting the city budget or laying off civil service workers, I get so panicky. . . . I wonder where the money's coming from to pay the rent and the bills and . . .

LEON

You don't have to worry about your job, Margie.

MARGARET

Weekends I take a course on how to operate a computer, just in case.

LEON
(Taking her hand)

You see, you are special. Not one of my wives would have had the foresight to plan for an emergency.

MARGARET

Well, if you met my kids, you'd know why I do it. They're special.

LEON

I'm sure they are. I don't want you to worry, Margie. They'll never discharge you. You're a terrific police officer.

MARGARET
(Pulling back her hand)

And you're a terrific actor.

LEON

How do you know?

MARGARET

The way you talk to that cat on television. It's outstanding.

LEON

Are you paying me a compliment?

MARGARET

Leon, you deserve credit for achieving what you've achieved.

LEON

I am guilty of putting myself down. That's one of my bad habits. Margie, do you think I need a hairpiece?

MARGARET

What for? You're an attractive man.

LEON

You think so?

MARGARET

Of course.

LEON

Do you know that not one of my wives was a redhead? I have to say it, I find it
very . . .
(He reaches his hand to touch her hair)

MARGARET

I . . . I better go.
(She rises, crosses to sofa and picks up hat, stick and summons book)

LEON

Margie, don't go. Not yet. Let's talk.
(He rises)
You know when you live alone, sometimes you'd like to talk to someone and when
there's no one living with you, it becomes a little difficult.

MARGARET

I know what that's like but it gets scary for me.

LEON

What does?

MARGARET

Trusting somebody again.

LEON

Does it have to be that way?

MARGARET

Leon, let me tell you a secret.
(She sits on sofa)
I think God made a mistake in creating only a man and a woman. It's too hard for
us. A man and a woman are too opposite in their natures. I think, wouldn't it be
marvelous if there was a third something that a man and a woman could talk to and
have a relationship with besides each other.

LEON

What do you mean a third something?

MARGARET

It's something; someone. It would be like we had another choice; another chance.

261

LEON

You mean a third species with intelligence and sex like we have?

MARGARET

That's it. A different kind of human being or a vegetable even.

LEON

A vegetable. Maybe through evolution it could come from the same family as say carrots or brussels sprouts.

MARGARET

Maybe. That's not what I had in mind, but we don't know everything that could happen.

LEON

We don't. We definitely don't.

MARGARET

Then a man and a woman would have something else to turn to. They wouldn't have to put up with each other all the time. There wouldn't have to be so much pain.

LEON

Another species introduced into human society. A superior brussels sprout.

MARGARET

At least it would make life bearable. And the marvelous thing is that they'd automatically love you. Just for yourself. You wouldn't have to do anything and they'd love you.

LEON

And even if you did a dumb thing, they'd still love you.

MARGARET

That's it! That's it!

LEON

Now I'm going to tell you a secret. I think I saw them.

MARGARET

Who?

LEON

The superior brussels sprouts.

MARGARET

You saw them?

LEON

In the IRT subway; last Thursday. There were five or six of them. They got on the

262

train at 34th Street and they marched off together in a single file at the Washington Square Station. They were all wearing green sweaters and green hats.

MARGARET
(Laughing)
Oh, you're a great kidder, you are.

LEON
I don't think God made a mistake. He made only a man and a woman and we have to make the best of it.

MARGARET
It's too hard.

LEON
We have no choice. There is no third something.
(He touches her arm)
Margie, will you have dinner with me? I'd enjoy having your company.

MARGARET
I'd like to, I would ... but ... it isn't wise.
(She gathers her things together)
Besides, I'm really tired.
(She rises, puts her hat on, the nightstick in the ring)
Thanks for the hospitality.
(She starts toward front door)

LEON
(Rises)
Margie, didn't you forget something?

MARGARET
(Stopping, turns to him)
What?

LEON
The summons.

MARGARET
I ... I don't know where my head is tonight. Leon, I hate to. . . .
(She reluctantly gives him summons)

LEON
(Taking summons)
It's all right. You do your job. That's important.

MARGARET
And you'll keep the volume down on your phonograph.

LEON

You won't hear a sound from this apartment. Not a sound.

MARGARET

Thanks.

(She moves to door again, on platform right)

LEON

Why don't you stay just for a little while. As friends. It doesn't have to be more than that.

MARGARET
(Stopping)

Didn't you yourself say relationships are too painful?

LEON

I guess I did, but don't we have to keep trying?

MARGARET

No, Leon. I'm finished with trying. I can't anymore. I can't.
(She exits. After a beat, LEON crosses to front door and locks it. He slowly crosses to phonograph, putting summons in his pocket. He picks up sheet music from audio speaker and steps to turn on phonograph. He remembers, and turns down volume very low. He puts on needle and we can barely hear it. He starts to follow along with the music, stops, looks at door. He sighs and continues singing softly with record and crosses to sofa. He lies back, gesturing, and looks up at ceiling. An idea comes to him; he looks at phonograph, looks at ceiling again, rises and crosses to phonograph. He turns up volume to full; he sets down music sheet and picks up hat, singing boisterously and crosses to hassock, putting his foot on it and gesturing with the hat at ceiling. The doorbell rings. He stops singing)

LEON
(Excitedly)

I'm coming! I'm coming!
(He crosses to phonograph, turns down volume very low and moves quickly to door, straightening clothes, hat in hand. He unlocks door and opens it a crack, sees who it is and slowly opens it widely. MARGARET enters. She has taken off her tie, hat, belt and has rolled up her sleeves. She looks at him and she slowly crosses to sofa. LEON closes door. MARGARET turns and sits as LEON moves off platform right. He stops as lights fade with specials on them.)

CURTAIN

A Need for Less Expertise

I don't have more than a few themes that interest me: the "accredited" expert telling others how to live is one of them.

I am a dramatist rather than a novelist because I can't write prose that is disembodied. I must have a firm grip on the physicality of the speaker. The spatial sense of theater is important to me. I have no tolerance for a play that is primarily conversational. I must connect in a significant way the spoken word with the actor's being. Consequently, I value movement (theatricality?) as much as I do language.

The use of a tape commanding the actors into activity is what makes this play work for me.

"You must explain something."

"Yes?"

"Don't you write farces and light comedies?"

"No. I never have."

"But isn't that what your reputation is based on?"

"Perhaps. It's a convenient way to categorize what I do. But if you really want to know what I'm about, I'll tell you, borrowing a phrase of Wilhelm Reich: 'A person like me comes along once every thousand years.'"

—M.S.
March 9, 1983

TWICE AROUND THE PARK *was produced by Peter Witt, Margo Korda and Warner Theatre Productions in association with the John F. Kennedy Center for the Performing Arts, and opened at the Cort Theatre, November 4, 1982.* A NEED FOR LESS EXPERTISE *was first presented at Syracuse Stage, in Syracuse, New York.*

EDIE FRAZIER	*Anne Jackson*
GUS FRAZIER	*Eli Wallach*
VOICE OF DR. OLIOVSKY	*Paulson Mathews*

Directed by ARTHUR STORCH
Set design by JAMES TILTON
Costumes by RUTH MORLEY
Lighting design by JUDY RASMUSON
Sound by DAVID S. SCHNIRMAN

The high-rise co-op on the East Side of G U S *and* E D I E F R A Z I E R.

Fall; morning.

We hear a tape of Strauss's "Colonel Radetsky's March."

As the curtain rises, we see E D I E *and* G U S *jogging in the center of the room, side by side, in tempo to the music. They are obedient to the commands of a taped voice, which is that of a "professional educator." This is the first time they've heard the tape so their responses are a bit delayed, uncertain.* E D I E *wears snug-fitting peach-colored athletic shorts, a pink-striped, v-neck shirt and beige, heeled shoes.* G U S *wears green velour designer sweatpants and sweatshirt, gold chains and two-tone green sneakers.*

They jog to the music which builds to a finale and ends. They sigh with relief.

> DR. OLIOVSKY
> *(Taped voice)*

And stop.
> *(They do)*
You will now march in tempo around the room.
> *(The march is heard again)*
The wife precedes the husband. Here we go. Together now.
> (G U S *and* E D I E *march around the room, in tempo; over music)*
Posture upright. Shoulders back. Your spinal column is in line with the center of the earth and the highest reaches of heavens.
> *(Slight pause)*
Arms at sides. Fingers wiggle, fingers wiggle, fingers wiggle.
> *(Slight pause)*
Arms out front. Fingers wiggle, fingers wiggle, fingers wiggle.
> *(Slight pause)*
Arms stretching toward the ceiling. Fingers wiggle, fingers wiggle, fingers wiggle.
> *(Slight pause)*
Arms at sides. And stop.
> *(Music ends abruptly.* G U S *starts to sit on bar stool)*
Return to your original positions.
> *(They move to center again)*
Relax.
> (E D I E *flops over, at the waist)*
Up on your toes. Breathe in. Down on your heels. Breathe out. Relax.
> (E D I E *flops over again)*
The Hindu discipline of Tantra acquaints us with all the myriad facets of selfhood, and through exercise, control and awareness, selfhood itself is transformed into a bright diamond that is offered as a gift to the loved one . . .
> *(Slight pause)*
I now ask the wife to get the two towels.
> (E D I E *crosses to left table and picks up two towels)*

The wife will give one towel to the husband.
(EDIE returns center, gives one towel to GUS)
At my command, the husband, with his towel, will wipe the wife's perspiring brow, her flushed red cheeks, the beads of dew on her moist tremulous lips. He will say to her: thou art that half of my being which maketh me complete. Now.

GUS
(Mumbles)
Thou art ... half ...

EDIE
Of my being ...

GUS
Of my being ... uh ...

EDIE
Which maketh me ...

GUS
(Angrily)
Will you shut up and let me do it myself!
(She backs away. He walks up to cassette player)
She makes me complete. Smart ass!
(He snaps towel at player and returns center)

DR. OLIOVSKY
Now the wife, with her towel, will reciprocate the actions of the husband. At my command, she will wipe the husband's rugged, robust features.
(GUS straightens up)
She will say to him: thou art that half of my being which maketh me complete. Now.
(She wipes GUS' face; feelingly)

EDIE
Thou art that half of my being which maketh me complete.

DR. OLIOVSKY
Discard the towels, please.
(EDIE takes GUS' towel and returns them to table)
Standing face to face, the wife and the husband will now stare into the luminous depths of each others eyes, finding in them the love and solicitude that each feels for the other.

GUS
Edie ...

EDIE
Shhh ...

DR. OLIOVSKY
Relax. Enjoy the presence, the nearness of each other. You will notice that as a consequence of your strenuous exercises, you are both exuding a distinctly strong, pungent odor.
(GUS lifts his arm up and sniffs)
Take unto thine own body the essences of your lover's body. Breathe deeply. Breathe deeply. Breathe deeply.
(EDIE takes deep breaths and sniffs GUS)

GUS
What if somebody walks in and sees us?

EDIE
Gus, if you don't . . .

GUS
They could take us away to the booby hatch!

EDIE
Shhh! Pay attention to Dr. Oliovsky.

DR. OLIOVSKY
I now ask the wife and husband to sit, face to face, on a mat or covering of a similar kind.
(Pause as they do so)
I ask the wife to place her feet in the lap of the husband.
(She does so, GUS tightens)
I now ask the husband to remove the outer footwear from the wife's feet.

GUS
That's it. That's it for me. Don't tell anybody, Edie, but that guy's a whacko, a first class whacko!

DR. OLIOVSKY
The husband will now rotate each of the wife's toes, gently.

GUS
Listen to him. Jus' listen to him! He's got me rotatin' your toes now. The next thing you know he'll be askin' me to rinse out your pantyhose.
(EDIE doesn't move)

DR. OLIOVSKY
After the husband massages the wife's feet, the wife will reciprocate and massage the husband's feet.
(GUS rises and quickly turns off the cassette player)

GUS
Al must have been putting me on when he gave me that stupid tape. He said it was supposed to. . . .

EDIE

You promised. You promised you'd do all of Dr. Oliovsky's exercises when you came back from Cincinnati.

GUS

It wasn't what I . . .

EDIE

You promised. You swore on my mother's life you'd do it.

GUS

Can I talk? Can I get a word in here?

EDIE
(Rises)

I didn't know you had become such an accomplished liar.

GUS

Edie, it wasn't what I expected. I didn't expect the guy on that thing to be another one of those whacko marriage counselors. I thought. . . .
(E D I E starts to exit. G U S blocks her path)
Where are you going?
(E D I E waves her hand for him to let her pass)
What is this, the silent treatment? Are you givin' me the silent treatment? I told you a million times there's gonna be no more silent treatment in this house!
(She waves her hand again)
No, I'm not movin'. If you got any complaints, you make 'em like a mature, grown-up person!
(E D I E looks up, points to the ceiling. As G U S looks up, she slips by him and runs off)

GUS

Edie! Edie!
(He growls to himself, then crosses to telephone on bar. He puts on eyeglasses and dials. After a pause, into phone)
Francine? Gus. Let me talk to Al.
(Slight pause)
Francine, I have nothin' to talk to you about. Let me talk to Al!
(Slight pause)
Okay. Good morning. Now let me talk to Al.
(Slight pause)
Al? What the hell did you give me that stupid tape for? I thought it was supposed to turn us on.
(Slight pause)
You know what we've been doin' all morning? We've been wiggling our fingers and sniffin' at each other.
(Slight pause)
You call that dirty and sexy? I call it sick. That's what I call it.
(Slight pause)

Al, my marriage is in enough trouble. You don't have to give me more trouble. I'm not interested in . . .

(E D I E enters, left, wearing knee-length white kimono with pastel flowers; a grim expression on her face)

I can't talk now.

(G U S hangs up phone, returns it to bar and sits on right sofa, hands clasped behind his head and legs up on table)

E D I E
(With great effort)

One question. I have one question to ask you and then I'm never speaking to you again for the rest of my life!

G U S

That has to be some question. What a question that has to be.

E D I E

Are you going to give me an honest answer?

G U S

What's the question?

E D I E

Before I ask the question, I want an answer to the question I just asked you.

G U S

There are two questions?

E D I E

Do I get an answer?

G U S

To which question?

E D I E

To the last question I asked you.

G U S

Now we're up to three questions?

E D I E

I want an answer to my question, Gus.

G U S

I'll answer your question. I'll answer it. As soon as I can figure out what the hell your question is, I'll answer it!

E D I E

Do you have to raise your voice? Do you have to tell the entire neighborhood that you're the man of the house and I am merely the domestic?

271

GUS

I don't want to hear that again. Edie.
(He rises)
You happen to have your own checking account and your own credit cards. I don't give a checking account and credit cards to my domestics.

EDIE

Are you answering the question or not?

GUS

Yes. I'll answer the question.

EDIE

All right. This is the question. Are my feet sooo ugly . . .
(GUS growls and moves away from her. She follows him)
. . . so unattractive and sooo obnoxious that when you were asked to massage them a minute ago, you couldn't find it in your heart to do so?
(He sits on left sofa)
It occurred to me, suddenly and painfully, that in the twenty-six years of our marriage, you have never, not once, massaged my feet.
(GUS trying to control his anger, hits his hand on sofa)
Am I lying? Am I making it up?
(GUS can't answer)
Of course, since I gave you the silent treatment, you have to give me the silent treatment. It's tit for tat, tat for tit, is that it?

GUS
(With great effort)
I am doing my best, Edie, not to lose my temper. I am doing what for me is my best. You know I have a thing about people's feet. You know from the past that I can't stand feet. It's not your feet alone I can't stand, it's everybody's feet and you know it!

EDIE

Your wife's feet are not everybody's feet! They are your wife's feet. After twenty-six years of marriage, they should be very, very precious to you!
(GUS growls, rises, throws towel down on table and storms off into bedroom. He slams door. EDIE moves to telephone, puts on eyeglasses and dials. After a pause, into phone)
Francine? Edie. It's no use. He won't do the exercises. No, no, he didn't suspect anything. He couldn't care less. I don't know what I'm going to do now. I was hoping . . .
(Slight pause)
I am fighting for my marriage, Francine! My God, that's all I've been doing for the last two years. But he refuses to get expert help. After one visit to Dr. Spina, he won't go to another therapist. Do you know I'm the only woman in the Save-Your-Marriage Clinic who sits there without a husband? I'm also the only one who the instructor advises to get a divorce. He even says he's willing to go halfies on the lawyer's fee.

(Slight pause)
He's not joking. The man has no humor. He says. . . .
(G U S enters, moving quickly, wearing a trenchcoat and hat, carrying an umbrella.
He moves to front door)
Francine, I'll call you back. There could be an emergency here.
(E D I E hangs up phone; G U S turns to her)

GUS

I don't know what the hell's goin' on. Every week you find a reason to start a fight.
If it's not one thing, it's somethin' else. I have one lousy day off. Do you have to make
such a big stink about feet!

E D I E

You wish I was dead, don't you?

GUS

What are you . . . ?

E D I E

You wish I disappeared, that I was out of your life once and for all, don't you?

GUS

Edie, if you don't stop . . .

E D I E

Go ahead, get rid of me. Buy yourself a bottle of Fantastik. It works miracles on the
walls. For the bathroom you buy Magic Blue. What do you need me for? There are
no diapers to change. There are no children to raise. I'm useless to you. Go ahead,
Gus, get rid of me! Jump on me! Kick me! Strangle me!
(She lies supine on the floor, center, arms outspread)
Go ahead, what are you waiting for?
(She cries)

GUS

Will you . . . will you cut it out? Why do you have to start . . .
(He reaches down to help her up)

E D I E

No! Don't touch me! Don't . . . !
(She kicks her feet at him)

GUS

You keep this up. You just keep this up and I swear I'm walking out and I'm staying
out and that's gonna be the end of our marriage!

E D I E

Don't make me laugh. It hurts too much. It is the end of our marriage. I can't fight
anymore. I don't have the strength.
(G U S moves away. E D I E crawls on knees to left table)

273

I pleaded with you, on my hands and knees I pleaded with you for us to get expert help but oh, no, you wouldn't . . .

(She wipes herself with towel)

GUS

I wouldn't? Didn't I go with you to that cockeyed doctor . . . Doctor Spina on Madison Avenue? Didn't I go to his office with you?

EDIE

You did. Yes, you did. Once. But you didn't give him a chance.

GUS

I gave him plenty of a chance. Where did he get off asking me if I masturbated, huh? Where the hell did he get off askin' me a personal question like that?

EDIE

He asked you if you played with yourself, not if you masturbated.

GUS

What the hell difference does it make? Doesn't it come out the same? Doesn't it?

EDIE

You still could have answered. . . . The man's a scientist.

GUS

No, I couldn't answer. I'm not answering any pervert who asks me a personal question like that. I shoulda punched him out, that's what I shoulda done.

(He crosses up to right bar stool, takes off hat, sets down umbrella and starts to take off coat)

EDIE

All right, forget him. But you promised me, you swore to me that you'd do the exercises on Dr. Oliovsky's tape, didn't you?

GUS

Look, Edie. I told you a million times I'm not havin' anything to do with those whacko doctors.

(He takes off coat, sets it on bar stool, picks up water glass and pitcher)

EDIE

Dr. Oliovsky, for your information, is a world-famous nutritionist, psychiatrist and Oriental philosopher.

GUS

(Pouring water)

That's where he should go, to the Orient. I'd like to see how many suckers he gets there.

(GUS returns pitcher. EDIE picks up pitcher and glass and pours herself a drink)

274

EDIE

He has written, for your further information, seven best-selling books. He's an expert in his field. And he is trying to show us how to do things together, as a team, as a husband and wife.

(She returns pitcher to bar)

GUS

I'll tell you what I think of your so-called experts. I think they're a bunch of crooks and phonies, that's what.

(EDIE, frustrated, moves to left sofa, sits with drink)

Listen, I had a fellow workin' for me. He was built like a Mack truck. It so happens he had a problem. He couldn't fall asleep. That was his only problem. He goes to one of those so-called experts of yours. Just to get some sleep, that's all. For five years he goes. Five years. You know what happened? Today that man is in a coma. Today that man does nothing but sleep twenty-four hours a day.

EDIE
(Rises with towel)

Then it's over.

GUS

What's over?

EDIE
(Throws towel at GUS' feet)

Our marriage.

GUS

There's nothing wrong with our marriage, Edie.

EDIE

I don't believe this. I don't believe what I'm hearing.

GUS

If we have any problems we can discuss 'em like mature, grown-up people. We don't need . . .

EDIE

We do need. We definitely need. We don't have a marriage. It's a joke. It's a laugh riot. Whether you admit it or not, we're like strangers. We became like strangers, Gus, like strangers in the night.

GUS

After supporting you for twenty-six years, I became like a stranger in the night?

EDIE

That's right.

GUS

I'm not your husband? I'm not the father of your two rotten kids? I'm . . .

EDIE
(Moving to him)
A stranger in the night, yes. Sometimes when you come home from work and sit at the table without speaking, without looking at me, I say to myself, "Who is this man? What is he doing in my kitchen?"

GUS

You don't know it's me who just came home from work?

EDIE
(Shaking her head)
I don't. I honestly don't.

GUS

My face doesn't look familiar to you?

EDIE

A little. But I can't place it.

GUS

Who do you think is sitting at the table waiting for his dinner?

EDIE

A stranger. A complete stranger.

GUS
(Moving to right sofa)
That explains why I've been getting franks and beans six times a week.
(He throws towel on table and sits on right sofa)

EDIE

Six times a week? You haven't been home for dinner six times in the last six months! I don't know how you have the nerve to say we don't need help. There's nothing we share anymore. No dinners, no feelings, no affection. . . . Do you know what Dr. Hegelshin said?

GUS

Who's Dr. Hegelshin?

EDIE

A therapist I've been seeing. By myself. I do everything by myself or haven't you noticed.

GUS

How long has this been going on?

276

EDIE

Twice a week for eighteen months.

GUS

Thanks for mentioning it. Where did you get the money to pay for that?

EDIE

I sold my life insurance policy.

GUS

So if God forbid something happens to you, I'm left without a penny, is that it?

EDIE

You'll get more than a penny. I left you my Tiffany pearl necklace to go with your Gucci gold chains.

GUS

That's very generous of you. I break my back to make a living and you piss it away on those quacks.

EDIE

Dr. Hegelshin taught me more about myself than any man I ever met. He says it's unfortunate but I was born between a generation of domestics and a generation of women's independence. He says my generation was caught in between. We're the misfits, he says.

GUS
(Rises; moves to platform)

I can't stand this. I can't stand listening to this! Can't you stay away from those lunatics? What do those guys have to do with our lives?

EDIE

You see, we can't even have a quiet conversation without you starting a fight . . .
(She heads for bedroom)

GUS
(Following)

Who starts the fights? Who? Not me, sweetheart.
(E D I E stops, turns)
The truth is that as soon as the boys moved out of this house—that's over two years ago—you're the one who starts the fights and causes all the trouble, that's the truth!

EDIE

It could be you have something to do with it!

GUS

Me?

EDIE

Yes, you.
(She moves to him)
After the boys moved, you had to work six days, not five. Suddenly you put gold chains on your neck. Used my Oil of Olay without asking my permission. Suddenly you had to travel to Cincinnati and Chicago and who knows where to do who knows what! When was the last time you took me out, Gus? When?

GUS

Are you serious? Didn't I ask you to go down with me the other night to Mulberry Street for sausages and peppers? Didn't I?

EDIE

Sausage and peppers?

GUS

Yeah, sausage and peppers.

EDIE

Sausage and peppers?

GUS

Yeah, sausage and peppers.
(He moves to left sofa)
You got somethin' against sausage and peppers?

EDIE

You call that going out?

GUS

No, I don't call that going out. I call that ring-around-the-rosy, a pocketful of posy.
(He sits left sofa)

EDIE

That's not what I call going out. I call going out, going out to an expensive French restaurant, having a leisurely meal with French pastry and then going to a Broadway show that nobody can get tickets to.
(She moves to bar)
That's what I call going out.
(She picks up four shot glasses from behind bar and sets them on bar, next to each other. She opens scotch bottle and starts to pour four shots)

GUS

I have a business to run, Edie, I can't . . .
(He turns to see her pouring)
What are you doing?

EDIE

What does it look like I'm doing?

278

GUS

Since when do you start drinking ten o'clock Sunday morning?

EDIE
(Returning cap to bottle)
Since I realized I have a husband who's never at home and children who forgot where I live. Since I realized that I belong to a generation of misfit women who have nothing left to do with their misfit lives. It's over, Gus. Don't you know it's over?
(She picks up two shot glasses; speaks lines slowly, very dramatically, mournfully)
Pack up all your cares and woe,
Here we go, swinging low,
Bye bye, blackbird.
(E D I E tosses contents of one shot glass over her shoulder and downs the second one. She bangs glasses down on bar)

GUS
(Rises)
Edie. We gotta talk.
(He moves to left bar stool)
We have to sit down, just the two of us . . .
(He sits on left bar stool)

EDIE
I'm the one who's been the sucker, Gus, that's the conclusion I came to. If you remember, when we first met, I wanted to be a Radio City Rockette. Do you remember? Everyone said I had talent. I'm not making that up. I remember when you'd come to my house on Jamaica Avenue, I'd be practicing my dance routines. I was so busy . . . I had so many plans for the future. You'd get mad waiting for me. You used to wait for me, Gus, isn't that something? I was so busy with my career, with my . . . So . . . so what's the outcome? I get married, I have children. Twenty-six years later my husband has a life, my boys have a life, and I'm left with zilch, absolute zilch. It's over. You know it's over.
(E D I E picks up the other two shot glasses, recites three random lines from a song. She again empties one shot glass over her shoulder and downs the other. She returns the empty glasses to bar and reaches for bottle. G U S grabs bottle away from her)

GUS
Be fair now, Edie. You have to be fair, too. Didn't I tell you to get a job?
(She straightens and turns to him, glaring)
Didn't I say that no woman can stay in the house all day without going bananas? Didn't I tell you that?

EDIE
(Moving down to right sofa)
Oh, ·sure, thanks a lot. What job do you think I could get after being married for twenty-six years? Scrubbing floors at the YMCA? Selling shishkabob at the United Nations?
(She sits, right sofa)

279

GUS

You got a short memory, that's your trouble.

(He sets down bottle on bar and rises)

You forgot what it was like when I was on the streets, pushing a hack, before I built up my own fleet of cabs and started making money. You forgot the hard times we had. Now that you're living in a fancy co-op on the East Side and you got a closetful of mink coats, you have to find reasons to make yourself miserable.

EDIE

You're not going to have to worry about yours truly anymore.

GUS

Is that supposed to be a threat?

EDIE

You'll know soon enough. What gets me, though, what makes me so mad, is that I'm such a sucker. I'm still trying to save our marriage. I'm mad at me, that's who I'm mad at. Did you ask yourself why Al gave you Dr. Oliovsky's tape? He gave it to you because I told Francine to tell him to give it to you.

GUS

You're serious?

EDIE

I'm serious. I knew you wouldn't do it if you found out it came from me. That tape, for your information, saved Al and Francine from getting a divorce.

GUS

Who told you that?

EDIE

Francine, who else?

GUS

Al didn't say anything to me about it.

EDIE

She was filing the papers already. She said she had enough of Al and his sleeping with other women.

GUS

Al doesn't sleep with other women. That's gossip.

EDIE

Are you serious?

GUS

It's malicious gossip, spread by certain people in the used car business, for reasons I can't go into at the present time.

EDIE

Gus, she caught him in bed with an eighteen-year-old beautician.

GUS

Al explained that to me.

EDIE

What did he explain, that he was getting a shampoo and a blow-dry?

GUS

Can I talk? Can I get a word in?

EDIE

Talk. You can talk yourself blue in the face and it's not gonna change the fact that Al got into that beautician's pants.

GUS

Edie, Al swore on his life to me that the whole thing was a complete misunderstanding.

EDIE
(Rises)

He swore on his life?

GUS

That's what he . . .

EDIE
(Moves to phone, picks it up and crosses to GUS*)*
I think you ought to call him. He could be dead by now.
(She holds receiver at his face)

GUS

You got that out of your system?
(He moves to sofa, left, sits. She returns phone to bar, moves down to center, begins)

EDIE

Whether you know it or not, your friend Al did all the exercises with Francine. Every night. She said for the first time since she knew him, he looked at her as if she were a virgin goddess.

GUS

Edie, if you expect me to look at you . . .

EDIE

Gus, be honest with me.
(She sits next to him)
Do you want a divorce? Is that what you want?

GUS

Did I say I want a divorce? Don't go putting words in my mouth.

EDIE
(Testing him)

Let's face it, these aren't the good old days. A marriage doesn't work, you don't stick together and torture one another. You go out and get a divorce.

GUS

That's true. That happens to be true. Over ninety-three percent of my drivers are divorced or hiding from their wives.

EDIE

Do you know my Aunt Ellie is getting a divorce?

GUS
(Genuinely shocked)

You're kidding?

EDIE

I'm not kidding. Forty-seven years of marriage. She's leaving my Uncle Joe.

GUS

For somebody else?

EDIE

No, for a career in public relations.

GUS

George and Betsy are getting a divorce, too.

EDIE

As of when?

GUS

As of yesterday. George told me last night.

EDIE

You see, everybody's getting divorced these days. It's getting so that if you tell someone you've been married for twenty-six years to the same person, they look at you as if you're demented.

GUS

I noticed that myself. Between the two of us, I stopped telling people I'm married to the same person for twenty-six years.

EDIE

What do you tell them?

GUS

I . . . I usually say you're my second wife.

EDIE

That's your fantasy, isn't it? To have a second wife. You're still living with your first wife and already dreaming of your second wife!
(She cries)

GUS
(Rises, moves to center)

Edie, that's not . . .

EDIE

Why are we playing these games? What's the sense of it? We both know I'm a misfit. We both know I was born too early to be independent and too late to be a domestic!
(She rises, crosses to him)
Why don't you get rid of me so you can get a second wife? Go ahead, jump on me! Kick me! Do your dirty work, Gus!
(She lies on floor in fetal position)

GUS

Okay. Okay. You did it this time!
(He moves to right bar stool and puts on coat, hat and picks up umbrella)

EDIE

It's over. The party's over. The piper has to be paid. I don't know what I'm waiting for. I don't know why I don't have the courage . . .
(GUS moves to front door; she speaks in deeper voice, on her knees, arm outstretched)
Gus . . . don't . . . don't go . . . please . . . there's something I have to tell you.

GUS

You ought to be ashamed of yourself, carryin' on like this. . . . What is it?

EDIE

Yesterday . . . yesterday I felt so alone, so depressed . . . I . . . went to see . . . the regional president of . . . of Suicides Anonymous.

GUS

The regional president of . . . ?

EDIE
(On her knees)

Suicides Anonymous. Mr. Marsh He's an insurance agent. He lives in Scarsdale, on two acres of land. You should have seen him, Gus. The man tried to kill himself nineteen times. He had scars on his wrists; he had rope burns on his neck, and there was a hole, a large, empty hole . . .
(Jabs finger at her temple)
right here in his head.

You wasn't . . . ?

EDIE
(Moving on her knees to right sofa)
Oh, wasn't I? I was. I was. But he talked me out of it.

GUS
How'd he do that?

EDIE
He took me to a French restaurant for lunch.

GUS
He what?
(He moves behind sofa to left of Edie)

EDIE
I had rack of lamb, sautéed cauliflower and French pastry for dessert. I was in seventh heaven.

GUS
Edie, if I ever find you went out with him again, I'm gonna break every bone in your body. Is that clear?
(GUS moves to center)

EDIE
Yes. It's clear. But I can't go on like this anymore, Gus. If I could make it on my own, I would have left you years ago. I would have walked out, but I don't know how. Dr. Hegelshin said it. Women of my generation don't know how to walk.
(She moves to him on her knees)
We're not ambulatory!
(She kisses his hand; sobbing)

GUS
Come on, cut it out, will you? You don't have to cry.
(She kisses his sneaker)
Edie! Cut it out! Okay. Okay. If doin' the exercises on that stupid tape'll make you feel any better . . .
(She jumps up)

EDIE
You'll do Dr. Oliovsky's tape with me?

GUS
I'll do it. It's no big deal.

EDIE
You're not gonna change your mind; you're not . . .

GUS
(Growling)

I said I'll do it and I'll do it!
(Moving to right bar stool)
Don't make me lose my temper, Edie.
(He takes off coat and hat and sets them with umbrella on stool)

EDIE
(Taking off robe)

I won't. No more.
(She puts robe on left stool)
Gus, we have to do everything, without exceptions. Francine says that's the only way it works.

GUS

Okay.

EDIE

Promise?

GUS

Promise.
(E D I E turns on cassette player and moves to left table; she wipes her face)

DR. OLIOVSKY

To your original positions, please.
(They move to their places, stand side by side, facing foward)
I now ask the wife and husband to stand side by side. Place your hands flatly on your heads.
(They do so)
Tantra teaches us how to free our bodies of inhibition and repression. Toward that goal, we will now do the free-form pelvic rotation exercise with control and awareness. Refrain from intimacy.
(E D I E steps away from G U S)
Both the husband and wife will now bend the knees slightly forward. In tempo, throw the pelvic area to the left, to the rear, to the right, and as far forward as possible. Now face each other.
(March music begins. They follow instructions)
Here we go. Together now. Pelvis left, rear, to the right, and forward. To the left, rear, to the right, and forward. To the left, rear, to the right, and forward. And stop.
(Music stops)
Hands at sides. To accommodate the modern western couple, I have adapted the Tantric rituals to suit our own life style and culture. The essence, however, remains the same. The wife should now seat herself comfortably.
(E D I E sits on rug, center)
I now ask that the husband dance for the wife, in any manner he desires, delighting in the movement and freedom of his body, displaying his physical self for the wife's pleasure.

(We hear a Hawaiian drum: a chant begins. G U S *turns in disbelief when he hears the chant, then, as the drum begins, he starts to dance, very erratically, having a hard time keeping tempo. He gets into it and swings his arms and moves his legs.*
He breaks into shadow-boxing and this carries him down right. He skips and breaks into rope skipping. He moves back center, flailing his arms and breaks into jumping jacks. He continues swinging his arms around until he throws one last swing up in the air, facing upstage, and wrenches his back. He grabs the base of his back and leans on right sofa. He does one stretch on the sofa and then crosses to right table, picks up glass and towel; he sits)
And stop.

(Music stops)
The husband should now seat himself comfortably.

(G U S shrugs)
The wife will now dance for the husband . . .

(E D I E rises)
. . . in any manner she desires, delighting in the movement and freedom of her body, displaying her physical self for the husband's pleasure.

(We hear the same music again. E D I E *moves her hands slowly as the chanting begins. As the music breaks into drums, she jumps and wiggles her rear end in tempo to the music, moving toward* G U S *who is attentively watching. She moves next to him and shakes her arms and leans into him, facing upstage. She turns and wiggles her legs at him, then facing front. Slowly, in tempo, she moves away from him doing some kind of strange belly dance. She breaks into a shuffle, tap step and taps across to down right of* G U S. *She then shuffles off to Buffalo and then breaks into a time step, and then into "wings." Ending with knee slaps, hip slaps, and toe slaps and finishing with one arm out front and the other on her hip.)*
And stop.

(The music stops)
I now ask the husband to sit on the floor, legs spread in the shape of an open nutcracker.

(G U S has risen and stops when he hears "Nutcracker"; stunned. He looks at
E D I E. *She looks at him. Finally he puts down towel and crosses to center where he does as instructed)*
I now ask the wife to sit within the defined area between the husband's outspread legs . . .

(E D I E does so)
. . . and that the spinal column of both husband and wife be in line with the center of the earth and the highest reaches of the heavens.

(We hear "March of the Sugar Plum Fairies" begin to play softly under)
Enjoy the presence, the nearness of each other. I now ask the husband to place the fingers of his left hand on the left side of the wife's forehead. Stroke gently. Gently. Now place the fingers of the right hand on the right side beneath the wife's chin. Stroke gently. Gently. The husband will now remove the left hand from the wife's forehead and press it to the wife's left breast.

(G U S, who has been following the instructions perfectly, does so, wiggling his fingers under her chin. E D I E *reacts uncomfortably)*
Through the tips of your fingers become aware of the pleasurable sensations that lie dormant in the texture and protuberances of the wife's body. Now place your right hand on the wife's right breast . . .

(He does so, E D I E *is very uncomfortable)*
... and allow your left hand to slide over the stomach and up and down the wife's thighs ...
(This is more than E D I E *can stand. She barks a scream, jumps up and runs to turn off the tape)*

E D I E

You're right, Gus. He's a whacko; he's a first class whacko! I should have listened to you. If we could talk out our problems ...

G U S

I'm not talkin' out any problems! You put me through the wringer before to get me to do what's on there. Now you're tellin' me you don't want to do it?

E D I E

I was wrong. Can't I be wrong?

G U S

You could be wrong, but you're not making an idiot out of me!
(He rises and heads for door)

E D I E

Gus, don't. I'm not the type of woman who can ... do things like that. I have to feel there's something ...

G U S
(Stopping)
Okay. You brought the subject up. It's time you heard what's been botherin' me for more years than I can remember and that's your sexual attitude.

E D I E

What's wrong with my sexual attitude?

G U S

Plenty's wrong. You don't know how to enjoy yourself in bed. It should be fun, but with you ... it gets too serious.

E D I E

How does it get too serious?

G U S

Did you ever see yourself when you have sex? Did you?

E D I E

I try to look in the mirror you put on the ceiling, but your head always gets in the way.

G U S

You don't know how to relax, how to let yourself go. You don't make noises, you don't talk ...

EDIE
(Moving to right sofa, sits)
You know what my upbringing was. You know I was raised very strictly. The truth is, until recently, I didn't know you were allowed to talk during sex. I didn't even know you were allowed to keep a light on.

GUS
(Moving to center)
I tried to teach you, but you didn't wanna listen.

EDIE
You always made it impersonal, like I'm anyone, not me. That's why I couldn't do the exercises on the tape. I always think of sex as a solemn occasion, like a wedding or a funeral.

GUS
It's been like a funeral, that much I can tell you.
(Slight pause)
It doesn't have to be that, Edie. It can be fun. You can talk, you can bounce on the mattress, you can laugh . . .

EDIE
You can also laugh when you have sex?

GUS
That's . . .

EDIE
Out loud?

GUS
I'm tellin' you people laugh when they have sex. Take my word for it.
(He moves around sofa)

EDIE
What type of laugh is it? Is it a silly laugh like . . .
(She offers a silly laugh)
Or like this?
(She offers another laugh)

GUS
It's a laugh. Any laugh. It could even be a belly laugh.
(He offers a belly laugh)

EDIE
I don't know if I can do that one.

GUS
You don't have to do that one. I said you can do any . . .

288

EDIE

What else, Gus? This is helpful. In case we decide to have sex in the future.

GUS

Okay. We can talk about it. We're mature, grown-up people. Why don't you ever get undressed in the bedroom when I'm in the bedroom?

EDIE

I don't . . . ?

GUS

No, you don't. Why do you have to go into the bathroom . . .
(He moves onto platform)
to get undressed and then, when I'm not looking, sneak . . .
(He imitates her sneaking)
back into the bedroom, get into bed, pick up a magazine, and make believe you've been sitting in bed all day?

EDIE

I . . . ? Me . . . ?

GUS

Yeah, you.
(He moves around sofa)
I'll tell you something else. If they took me down to the police station and a hundred naked women were standing in a line-up with their faces covered with black hoods, I couldn't identify your body.

EDIE

I admit I'm a little shy about exposing myself . . .

GUS

Edie, to a stranger in the night you expose yourself, but to a husband of twenty-six years, all you can do is get undressed and hope for the best.

EDIE

Now that's helpful. That I find very helpful.
(She rises, moves to right of him)
Gus, it's no big deal. I can do it. I can. I can do everything you're suggesting so long as I feel there's affection, that it's me. That I know you know it's me. I can get undressed in the bedroom and I can laugh during sex.
(She laughs, then stops abruptly)
Is that it?

GUS

If you moved around a little when you laugh, it would also be helpful.

EDIE

No big deal. I can do it. I can . . .

289

(She imitates the earlier pelvic rotation exercise, hands on head, laughing wildly)

GUS

That's it! That's exciting! Edie, what I'm getting at is that we don't give up on Dr. Oliovsky yet. I've come to the conclusion that man's brilliant. Brilliant.

EDIE

Gus, that man's off the wall. How can he expect people to make love by the numbers?

GUS

Look, he's got us talkin' about certain things that've been botherin' us and he's showing us different exercises to bring us together.

EDIE

His voice is creepy.... We're not machines.

GUS

I'll be affectionate. I'll know it's you I'm with. Will you try?

EDIE
(Taking his hand)

I'll try.

GUS

We have to do everything he says. Promise?

EDIE

I promise.

GUS
(Moving to tape player)

Thanks. I appreciate it.

(He turns on player)

DR. OLIOVSKY

Now I ask the husband and wife to prepare themselves for sexual union. With control and awareness to guide you, you will soon join in a lover's embrace and the sweet juices of passion will flow from one to the other in a gushing, endless Niagara.

(GUS and EDIE look at player)

The husband will now entwine his left arm around his wife's waist.

(EDIE steps down and GUS does so)

The wife will lean her cheek on his brawny shoulder.

(She leans her head on GUS)

Clasp hands.

(They do so as we hear the Peer Gynt Suite*)*

Stroll arm in arm into the magical forest of each other's desire.

(They move awkwardly, left)

Smell the scented fragrance of desire.

(They turn, walking right, sniffing)

Listen to the birds of desire singing in the treetops.
(We hear birds over the music. Walking upstage, G U S *moves his hand down*
E D I E's *back to her rear)*
Control.
(G U S quickly moves his hand)
Control. Do not be impatient.
(They continue walking around the right sofa)
Return to your original position.
(They do so)
I now ask both wife and husband to kneel side by side at the altar of love. Hands on thighs, please.
(They kneel. G U S *puts his hand on* E D I E's *thigh. She removes it)*
The wife and husband seeking to practice the discipline of Tantra in order to achieve everlasting and ever-increasing sexual ecstasy must be one in spirit and body . . .
(G U S, during the above, leans back on his knees and leers at E D I E. *She looks straight ahead and does not notice)*
Between wife and husband there can be no secret, no betrayal, no hidden remorse to prevent complete union.
(G U S, getting tired, starts closing his eyes)
I now ask that wife and husband unburden themselves of all guilt and deception. If one or the other has had sexual relations outside the bonds of matrimony . . .
(G U S's eyes pop open)
. . . a brief indiscretion, a tryst, an affair, an adulterous liaison, now is the time to free oneself of remorse and communicate openly to the loved one. Tear down all barriers that separate the two halves! Rip asunder the fabric of lies and hypocrisy! Let there be. . . .
(During the above, G U S *has quickly moved backwards on his knees to the player and turns it off. He stands, right of the player)*

GUS

You got his number, honey. That man's not in his right mind. Hey, I got it! Why don't we get dressed, get in the car, and drive up to Connecticut?
(She doesn't respond)
Okay. Cancel it. I know this expensive French restaurant on East Fifty-second Street. They got a great Sunday brunch. We can . . .
(During the above G U S *has crossed to above the bar, put on the eyeglasses, picked up a telephone book and begins leafing through it)*

E D I E

You must think I'm the biggest nincompoop in the world.

GUS

Now what are you talkin' about?

E D I E

I am not a dope, Gus. Contrary to your opinon of me, I am not a dope.

GUS

Where do you find these things to argue about? Will you cut it out?

EDIE

Four times I called your hotel when you were on one of your famous business trips. And four times there was no one in your room at three o'clock in the morning. What do you have to say about that, smart ass?
(He takes off eyeglasses)

GUS

Edie, you know I'm a deep sleeper.

EDIE

I let the phone ring for twenty minutes!

GUS

I didn't hear it, I swear.
(He moves around bar with phone book)
Don't you remember the night there was a fire in the kitchen and the fire department came and I didn't hear anything?

EDIE

You were in Chicago the night we had the fire in the kitchen.

GUS
(Behind sofa, left)
That's what I'm saying, I didn't hear anything. But when you called, I was in my hotel room, wasn't I?

EDIE
(Rises)
If you're going to lie, let's put an end to this masquerade. Dr. Tobias suggested we . . .

GUS

Dr. Tobias?

EDIE

He's a psychologist I go to when Dr. Hegelshin is on vacation. He suggested that in view of your habitual lying we should try living in separate parts of the apartment, divide it . . .

GUS

Okay. Okay. You don't have to go dividing up the apartment.
(He moves behind the bar; puts down the phone book)
If you have to know. . . . I got myself mixed up with some Mafia poker players. We meet in different hotel rooms.
(He moves to below bar)
That's where I am when you phone me at night; playing poker with the Mafia and doin' my best not to win too much money.

292

EDIE
(At down right of bar)
Do you want me to walk out? Is that what you want?

GUS
I don't know what you want. Whatever I say . . .

EDIE
I want to know how many women you . . . you've been with.

GUS
Edie, for cryin' out loud, there were no women.
(She crosses past him moving to bedroom)
I had no reason to . . .
(She doesn't stop)
One!
(She stops, turns)
Only one. She was a Lufthansa reservation clerk.
(Pause)
In Chicago. That's the truth.
(She starts off again)
Two!
(She stops, turns. Pause)
Only two. She was the sister of the Lufthansa reservation clerk. In Cincinnati.
(EDIE stares at him)
Look, Edie, before the boys moved, I didn't . . . not even once, I swear. But after. . . .
I was miserable, too. You were so busy with your psychologists and therapists
and . . .

EDIE
How many, Gus?

GUS
Guess. Go ahead and guess. You might be pleasantly surprised.

EDIE
I'm in no mood for your . . .

GUS
A baker's dozen.

EDIE
Thirteen?

GUS
A baker's dozen is only thirteen?

EDIE
How many did you think a baker's dozen was?

GUS

Uhh . . .

EDIE

Are you answering me or not?

GUS

What difference does the number make? I was wrong. If it's any use, I'm sorry. I am. Edie, I stopped. I did.
(He moves away from her)
I couldn't live like that.
(He sits on right table)

EDIE
(Moving to him)
I suspected it. I suspected it all along.

GUS

I'm glad I told you. I am. The truth is it wasn't as much fun as you might suspect.

EDIE

Awww. It was painful for you? The whole baker's dozen?

GUS

One thing I found out is that any woman who goes to bed with a married man has serious mental problems.

EDIE

You told them you were married?

GUS

I didn't lie. Everyone of 'em knew you were my wife and I was devoted to you.

EDIE

You should have asked them to phone me. It would have been nice hearing that from someone.

GUS

Why don't you let me make it up to you?

EDIE

How? By buying me another fur coat?

GUS

No. By goin' to work five, not six days; by comin' home early every night; by bein' with you more and takin' you out more.
(He rises, moves to her)

EDIE

It seems so easy for you. Don't you know what you did?

GUS

What I did, everybody's doin'. Everybody's gettin' more. For an intelligent woman, you sure don't know what the hell's goin' on!

EDIE

Are you disappointed in me, Gus? Did I let you down by not sleeping with other men?

GUS

I learned from what I did. I learned to appreciate what it is to have a family and a home. We can have a better marriage now. I promise you.

EDIE

I don't know what to do. I don't.
(She moves, sits on sofa)
I don't even know what I'm feeling. I never expected this. Never.

GUS

Edie, let's go for a walk, huh? Let's get some fresh air. We've been in all morning.

EDIE

No, you go. I have to think. I have to be by myself and think about this, all of this, very, very carefully. Go, you go.

GUS

Edie . . .

EDIE

Go! Leave me alone!

GUS

Okay, okay. I'll leave you alone. I'll bring us back some delicatessen. We'll have a nifty lunch. We'll enjoy ourselves. We'll have fun.
(During the above, GUS crosses to left bar stool and puts on coat, hat and picks up umbrella and moves to front door. He stops, turns; emotionally)
I begged you not to play that stupid tape. Didn't I beg you?
(He exits. After a few beats, EDIE rises, crosses up to cassette player and turns it on. She returns to left sofa, sits)

DR. OLIOVSKY

. . . forgiveness and compassion. I now ask the husband to slowly disrobe the wife.
(Pause)
I now ask the wife to slowly disrobe the husband.
(Pause. GUS storms back in, slams door and crosses to right of right sofa. He stops, realizes the tape is on)

I now ask the wife and husband to lie down on the couch or bed and delight in each other's nakedness. And thus we conclude the first lesson of "Dr. Oliovsky's Long Playing Tantric Guide and Exercise Book for Married Lovers."

(During the above, GUS moves up to left bar stool, sets down hat and umbrella; he moves to cassette player and turns it off, probably at "and thus we conclude . . .," and takes out tape. He tries to break it but can't. he throws it to the floor and stamps on it a few times. He moves to sofa and sits next to EDIE. She looks away, chin cradled in hand. He looks at her, then looks down at her feet. He gets an idea. Looks at her again, then the feet. He reaches down and pulls her right foot onto his lap; he removes her shoe, takes a deep breath and starts to massage her foot. She clasps her hands behind her head and stretches out her body triumphantly. We hear march music and the curtain falls.)

Luv

I got lucky with this one. Lucky with the casting; lucky in the directing; and lucky in the day and month and year of its New York opening.

When it was produced in London it flopped.

In New York, during previews, theater-party ladies left at the end of each performance arguing with each other: "Why did you get tickets for this show? Can you please explain that to me?" "I'll kill Gert. I swear I'll kill her."

But professional people encouraged us.

And actors, director and writer were of one mind: we were all doing the same play.

So it worked out well.

I wrote the play in Ibiza, Spain, where I had rented a house for twenty-five dollars a month and drank cognac at four cents a glass. My wife cooked on a wood-burning stove. We walked into town every day and sat in the sun in front of the Montesol Hotel. We were running out of money when a telegram arrived from London saying an English company wanted to buy the film rights to Ducks and Lovers *for three thousand dollars. We danced on top of a table and filled everyone's glass with the bright yellow afternoon sun.*

The play was in my head, all of it. I sketched an outline: A meets B who is about to commit suicide. B broods over the emptiness of life. A tries to convince B that there is love in the world, a reason to live, etcetera, etcetera.

Hollywood bought the film rights. I turned down an offer to write the screenplay, feeling that I wanted to continue writing for the theater. My Los Angeles agent wooed and wined me and I finally agreed that I would do a screenplay in the near future. I never heard from him again; that is, not until Tootsie *opened, nineteen years later. Then I received a telephone call from him: "Hey, how are you, fella? You're not gonna believe this, but I finally got a screenplay for you!"*

—M. S.
March 9, 1983

LUV *had its world premiere at the Booth Theatre New York City, on November 12, 1964, and was presented by Claire Nichtern.*

HARRY BERLIN	*Alan Arkin*
MILT MANVILLE	*Eli Wallach*
ELLEN MANVILLE	*Anne Jackson*

Directed by MIKE NICHOLS

Set Design by OLIVER SMITH

Costumes by THEONI V. ALDREDGE

Lighting Design by JEAN ROSENTHAL

Music for Song by IRVING JOSEPH

ACT ONE

Evening.

*A bridge. The railing of the bridge crosses, rear, at an angle: it is inter-
rupted on the left by a small boxlike alcove, then continues, swooping
above and disappearing out of sight. On the right is a thick red coil from
which cables descend at regular intervals and connect to the railing. Two
wooden slab-boarded benches, placed back to back, one facing downstage,
the other upstage, are at the right, also at an angle. Farther on the right
is an old iron-cast lamppost. which is lit. On the left, forward, is a nondescript unmarked sandbox, no larger in size than three orange crates
lying side by side. Farther left, forward, is a public wire-mesh trash basket. A curbstone cuts across the front at an angle and the entire stage is
raked.*

*The faint sounds of a foghorn, a motor churning in the water, a buoy bell,
etc.*

H A R R Y   B E R L I N *(tall, flabby, with a bristly mustache, in ill-fitting
rumpled clothes: a threadbare dark-green corduroy jacket, an open-
necked faded blue work shirt, no tie, very large khaki pants tied to his
waist by a string, dirty white tennis sneakers) leans on the railing in the
alcove, rear, facing upstage, and stares at the river below.* M I L T
M A N V I L L E *(thin, erect, of less than average height, in a sharply tai-
lored "continental" brown suit, pink shirt with rolled collar, bright yellow
tie and pocket handkerchief, large cuff links, and brown suede shoes)
enters, left, paces up and down, looks at his watch anxiously; his eye soon
falls on the trash basket; he is drawn irresistibly toward it; he bends over
and examines a worn discarded velvet-collared gray herringbone
overcoat.*

H A R R Y *turns.* M I L T *notices him, stares forward, trying to recall where
he has seen him before.* H A R R Y *takes pad, pencil from pocket, writes a
note, slaps it on railing; he drops his jacket to ground and climbs up on
railing.*

> ### MILT
> *(With a sense of recognition, moving up to him)*

Is it . . .
> *(H A R R Y turns, stares down at him)*

No, Harry Berlin! I thought so! I just caught a glimpse of you and I said to myself,
"I bet that's Harry Berlin. I just bet that's Harry Berlin." And sure enough, it's old
Harry Berlin himself.
> *(Taking H A R R Y's hand; shaking it)*

How have you been doing, Harry? What's been happening?
> *(H A R R Y squats and slowly comes down from railing)*

It must be . . . why, at least fifteen years since I saw you last. We had that party after graduation, I said, "Keep in touch," you said, "I'll call you in a few days," and that's the last I heard of you. Fifteen years.

HARRY
(Feigning recognition)

Is it fifteen years?

MILT

Fifteen years.

HARRY

Hard to believe.

MILT

Fifteen years next month as a matter of fact.

HARRY

Time sure flies.

MILT

It sure does.

HARRY

Fifteen years next month.

MILT

Fifteen years.

HARRY
(Slight pause)

Who are you?

MILT

Milt! Milt Manville! Your old classmate at Polyarts U.

HARRY
(Grabbing his hand)

That's right! Milt! Milt Manville!
(They embrace; laugh joyfully. HARRY *puts on jacket, then crumples note, throws it over railing as* MILT *speaks)*

MILT

Say, Harry, I've been doing wonderful for myself; terrific. Got into the brokerage business during the day: stocks, bonds, securities, you know. The money's just pouring in; doing fabulous. Got into secondhand bric-a-brac and personal accessories at night: on my own, great racket, easy buck. And, say, I got myself married. Oh yeah, I went and did it, finally did it. Ellen. A wonderful, wonderful girl. Do anything for her. A home in the suburbs, no kidding, thirty-five thousand, and that's not counting the trees, big tremendous trees; you should see them. Hey. Look at this watch. Solid gold. Twenty-two carats.

(Opening his jacket to reveal garish yellow lining)
Notice the label?
(Unbuttons shirt)
Silk underwear. Imported. Isn't that something?
(Lifts arm)
Hey, smell this, go ahead, smell it.
(H A R R Y is reluctant to come too close; M I L T presses his head to his armpit; laughing)
Not bad, huh?
(Solemnly)
Well, how's it been going, Harry? Let's hear.

HARRY
(Mournfully)
Awful, Milt; awful. It couldn't be worse. I'm at the end of the line. Everything's falling apart.

MILT
(Perplexed)
I don't get it.

HARRY
The world, Milt. People. Life. Death. The old questions. I'm choked with them.

MILT
(Still perplexed)
Oh.

HARRY
(Arm around him, leads him forward)
I must have been out of school for only a couple of weeks when . . . it happened. Out of the blue. Disillusionment. Despair. Debilitation. The works. It hit me all at once.

MILT
Oh. Ohhhh.
(H A R R Y sits on curbstone. M I L T puts down white handkerchief, sits beside him)

HARRY
I remember . . . I was sitting in the park. It was Sunday, a hot lazy Sunday. The sun was burning on the back of my neck. An open book was on my lap and I was kind of daydreaming, thinking of the future, my plans, my prospects . . . Then . . . Suddenly . . . Suddenly I looked up and I saw, standing there in front of me . . . How can I put it in words? It was a dog, Milt. A fox terrier. I'd swear it was a fox terrier. But who knows, I . . .

MILT
(Interrupting)
Let's just say it was a dog, Harry.

301

It was a dog. Right.

A dog. Go ahead.

And ... And he was there, right in front of me, standing on his hind legs and ..
He looked almost like a little old man with a little white beard and a little wrinkled
face. The thing is ... Milt, he was laughing. He was laughing as loudly and as
clearly as I'm talking to you now. I sat there. I couldn't move. I couldn't believe what
was happening. And then, he came up to me, now he was walking on all fours and
... When he got up to me ... When he got up to me, he raised his leg and ...

No.

(Nodding, with twisted expression)
All over my gabardine pants. And they were wet, through and through. I could swear
to that! Then he turned right around and walked off. The whole thing was ... It
was all so unreal, all so damn senseless. My mind ... I thought ...
(Emotionally)
Why me? Out of everyone in that park, out of hundreds, thousands of people, why
me?
(MILT looks about bewilderedly)
What did it mean? How do you explain it?
(In control of himself)
That started it; right there was the beginning. From that minute on, it changed,
everything changed for me. It was as if I was dragged to the edge of the cliff and
forced to look down. How can I make you understand? What words do I use? I was
nauseous, Milt. Sick to my soul. I became aware ... aware of the whole rotten senseless stinking deal. Nothing mattered to me after that. Nothing.

Your plans to go to medical school?

I couldn't.

The book you were writing?

(Throwing up his hands)
No use.

Your Greek studies?

I couldn't. I couldn't go on.
(Rises; moves to sandbox, paces around it; M I L T *also rises)*
No roots. No *modus vivendi*. I had to find some answers first. A reason. I traveled, went everywhere, looked everyplace. I studied with a Brahmin in Calcutta, with a Buddhist in Nagoya, with a rabbi in Los Angeles. Nothing. I could find nothing. I didn't know where to turn, what to do with myself. I began drinking, gambling, living in whorehouses, smoking marijuana, taking guitar lessons . . . Nothing. Still nothing. Tonight . . . Milt, tonight I was going to end it all, make one last stupid gesture of disgust and . . . that would be it!

MILT
(Glances at railing)
You don't mean . . .

HARRY
That's right.

MILT
(Going to him)
How terrible. How terrible, Harry. I'm ashamed of you at this minute. I'm ashamed to have been your classmate at Polyarts U.

HARRY
Ask me what I believe in, Milt.

MILT
What do you believe in, Harry?

HARRY
I believe in nothing, Milt.

MILT
Nothing? That's terrible. How can someone go on living without believing in anything?

HARRY
That's the problem I'm faced with. And there's no answer to it, none, except down there!
(He points to railing, moving to bench)

MILT
(Turns H A R R Y *toward him)*
Now let's not lose our heads. Let's control ourselves. Keep calm. Keep calm. Now listen to me. I can understand. I can understand everything you said, but, Harry . . . Don't you think it's more than unusual, just a little more than unusual, that I happened to be passing at the very minute, the precise exact minute, that you were contemplating this . . . this horrible thing?

HARRY
(Pointing upward)
You don't mean . . . ?

MILT
(Throwing both hands up defensively)
I'm not saying it! I didn't say it!
(Wagging finger)
But just remember, science doesn't have all the answers!

HARRY
Talking about it only makes it worse, Milt. You don't know what agony I've been
through. It's gotten so bad that sometimes, sometimes, in the middle of the day or
night, without a warning of any kind, my whole body becomes paralyzed, I can't
move a muscle and . . .
*(In mid-speech his body stiffens like a board and he topples forward. MILT catches
him at the last moment, shouts and shakes him frantically)*

MILT
Harry! What is it? Harry, for God's sake . . .
*(He runs around in a complete circle, holding HARRY whose stiff body revolves
like the hand of a clock)*
Help! Help! Help, here! Help! Help!
(To HARRY)
Look at me! Speak to me, Harry!

HARRY
(Calmly)
That's the way it happens.

MILT
(Sitting on sandbox)
You scared the life out of me. That's terrible. Why don't you see a doctor, a specialist,
someone . . .

HARRY
I don't have to see anyone. I know what it is, Milt. The will to live drops out of me,
plops right out of me. Why move? I say to myself. Why do anything? But that's not
all of it. Sometimes, sometimes, I can't see, I lose the power of sight completely and
I grope about . . .
*(Throws up his hands, feigns blindness and moves dangerously close to the edge of
the stage)*
Milt . . . Milt . . . Where are you? Are you still here, Milt?

MILT
(Jumps up, grabs him in the nick of time)
Right here, Harry. I'm right here.

HARRY
(Clawing behind him at MILT's *face)*
Help me, Milt. Help me get to the bench.

MILT
(Pushing him forward)
Of course. This way, Harry. That's it. Watch your step. Here, here it is.
(They're seated on bench)

HARRY
(Calmly)
Thank you, Milt.

MILT
Is there . . . anything else I can do?

HARRY
No. I'm all right now. That's the way it happens.

MILT
I would never have believed it.

HARRY
Why see? I say to myself. Why be a witness to it?
(Grabbing MILT's *lapels)*
Why, Milt? Why?

MILT
I don't know, Harry. I don't know.
(Pulling himself free; straightens tie, etc)

HARRY
So I go blind and I don't see. The whole thing becomes completely automatic. I have
no control over it.

MILT
But there must be something you can do.

HARRY
(Cupping hand to ear, feigns deafness; loudly)
What did you say, Milt?

MILT
I said, "There must be something you can do to correct . . ."

HARRY
I can't hear you, Milt. Speak slowly and I'll try to read your lips.

305

MILT
(Speaking slowly, loudly, drawing out words)
I said, "There must be something you can do to . . ."

HARRY
(Abruptly; calmly)
I hear you now, Milt. That's another one of my . . . my fits. Sound becomes so damn painful to me . . . Why listen? I say to myself. Why listen?

MILT
Incredible. I wouldn't have believed it was possible.

HARRY
Well, it is. Look at me. I'm a living example of it. Now you can . . .
(He feigns muteness, his mouth opening wide and closing without uttering a sound; gesturing)

MILT
(Becoming increasingly distraught)
Harry? Are you speaking to me, Harry? Harry, I can't hear you. Can you speak . . .
(HARRY removes pad and pencil from jacket pocket, jots something on pad)
Oh, God, not that, too.
(Glances at HARRY's note)
I understand, Harry. I . . . Give me that.
(Takes pencil and pad from HARRY; he starts writing)
"Dear Harry, What we have to keep in mind, no matter what . . ."
(HARRY pulls pencil out of MILT's hand. MILT pulls it away from HARRY)

MILT
(Angrily)
The least you can do is let me finish!
(Starts writing again)

HARRY
I can hear you, Milt.

MILT
You can?

HARRY
I can't speak when that happens, but I hear all right. Why speak? I say to myself. Words have no meaning; not anymore. They're like pebbles bouncing in an empty tin can.

MILT
(Pockets pad, pencil)
I don't know what to say, Harry.

HARRY

What can you say? It's no good, Milt; no good. For cryin' out loud, let me get it over
with!
*(Removes rope with noose from jacket pocket as he speaks, puts noose over his head
and after throwing rope over crossbar on lamppost, tries to hang himself by pulling
on end of rope)*

MILT
(Rises)

No, no! Harry! Harry, will you listen to me?
(Slapping at his hands)
Let go! Let go of it!
(HARRY slumps to foot of lamppost where he sits dejectedly)
There's plenty of time for that!
*(He takes rope from lamppost and at the same time releases pin from crossbar so
that it can swing)*
Did it ever occur to you that you're in the state you're in because you've never known
the feeling that comes with money, with power, with influence?

HARRY
(Removes noose from his neck; disparagingly)

Ahhh, Milt . . .

MILT
(Rolling rope together)

Now don't brush it aside. Look at me, Harry, and ask yourself, "Why did he go up
so high and I go down so low?" Ask yourself that.
(Moves to trash basket)
We both started out on the same foot; as a matter of fact you started out ahead of
me, you had the money your folks left you. I had nothing but my two hands and a
quick eye. When other people slept, I worked. When other people said it couldn't be
done, I went out and did it.
*(He lifts worn velvet-collared herringbone overcoat out of basket—it is buttoned; he
ties collar with rope, making a bag of it)*
And through diligence, self-confidence, perseverance, I've made something of myself!

HARRY
(Rises)

My folks left me a few stinking thousands, that's true, but don't you forget I never
lived with them, I was brought up by my grandparents, and it was hell, believe me,
it was hell.

MILT
(Drops overcoat to ground)

Ha! You should have lived with my folks for a couple of weeks, then you would have
known what hell is really like. Those two were like a pair of cats at each other's
throat. And the poverty, the lousy humiliating poverty. I didn't start school until I
was eight years old because I didn't have a pair of shoes to wear. Oh, yeah. Lucky

for me the kid downstairs was hit by an ice-cream truck and I got his shoes. Even then they were so tight on me I couldn't walk. I was put in a special class for disabled children.

HARRY

You think that was bad? My grandparents used to lock me out of the house. They couldn't stand the sight of me because I reminded them of my father. I remember one day I came home from school during a blinding snowstorm and the door was locked. I knocked and yelled and beat my poor little frozen fists on the door . . . They laughed at me. They laughed! Picture that for yourself. A tall skinny kid standing out there in the snowstorm, wearing nothing but a thin torn jacket and a paper bag for a hat, knocking and yelling, "Let me in. Please, let me in!"

MILT

Paradise.

(Slight pause)

It was paradise compared to my childhood. Picture this. It's late at night. The wind's blowing outside. A small undernourished boy sits by the cold kerosene stove, feeding his toy wooden horse a bit of bread that he stole during dinner. The parents are quarreling. "If you don't like it here, get the hell out," the father shouts. "You're telling me to get out," the mother shouts back, and with savage hysterical fury she picks up the boy's toy wooden horse and throws it at the father. He ducks and it smashes against the wall. The boy drops down beside his broken toy horse, the only thing he ever loved, and he cries quietly.

HARRY
(Moves right, then whirls back to MILT; *pugnaciously)*
Did you ever get beaten?

MILT
(Emphatically)
I did.

HARRY
With what?

MILT
A strap, a stick, a radiator cover.

HARRY
A chain?

MILT
How thick?

HARRY
As thick as my wrist.

MILT
(Foiled; moves away, turns)
What did you get for breakfast?

308

At home?

MILT
At home.

HARRY
A glass filled with two-thirds water and one-third milk.

MILT
Coffee grounds, that's what I got.

HARRY
With sugar?

MILT
Not on your life. I ate it straight, like oatmeal.

HARRY
(Foiled; moves away, suddenly turns)
Did your mother ever kiss you?

MILT
Once. When I stuck my head between her lips and a picture of Clark Gable.

HARRY
Well, that's better than I did.

MILT
(Foiled; moves about)
What presents did you get for Christmas?

HARRY
Presents? When I was five my grandparents bought a box of doughnuts and every Christmas until I was seventeen I got a doughnut.

MILT
You were a lucky kid and you didn't know it.

HARRY
(Bawling)
They were cinnamon doughnuts!

MILT
Harry, you're missing the whole point. Even if we started out on the same foot, I went ahead and became a success, I pulled myself up to a position of responsibility, of respect, of importance. And don't think it was easy. It was dog-eat-dog all the way.
(Picks up overcoat, puts wine bottle, magazine into it)
But I stuck with it, gave it all I had, worked at two jobs, stocks, bonds, securities during the day, secondhand bric-a-brac and personal accessories at night.

(Takes naked doll from trash basket, waves it in air before inserting it into overcoat)

Rain or shine, sick or well, seven days a week, fifty-two weeks a year. I never let up, not even after I had achieved what I had set out to do. Right to the top. On my own. Every inch of the way.

(Removes baby's chamber pot from trash basket, turns it in his hand before dropping it into overcoat)

And let me tell you, Harry, nothing, nothing succeeds like success.

(He ties bottom of overcoat with rope)

HARRY

You know I'm not interested in any of that, Milt. I need something else to go on. A *Weltanschauung*. A reason for living. That isn't easy to come by, either.

(He moves to curbstone, right)

Everything I taste turns sour in my mouth. Everything I touch becomes dust in my hands. It's as if I was standing at the bottom of the world and all I'd have to do is sit down to be dead.

(He sits down on curbstone)

MILT
(Leaving overcoat on ground, moves to him)

Stop talking like that. How could you have changed so much? I still can't believe it. At school you were one of the boys, full of life, ready for a laugh and a good time at the drop of a hat.

(Squatting behind him, holding his shoulder and pointing out into the distance)

Remember, Harry, remember our marching down the football field in our red and gold uniforms, you leading the Polyarts All-Girl Band on the right, with me leading them on the left, our batons twirling in the air . . .

(He rises, struts up and down the bridge, singing, twirling an imaginary baton—he throws it up, catches it, kicks it with the heel of his shoe, catches it, performs tricks of this sort)

Alma mater, alma mater,
Forward to the fray;
We will win our victory,
And move right on our wa-a-a-a-ay.

(HARRY nods, mumbles, "Yes, yes, I remember, yes, yes . . .")

Alma mater, alma mater,
Lift your light up high;
We will win our victory,
And come back by and by.

Da, da, da, da, da, da, da . . .

HARRY
(Rises, breaking spell of past with an anguished shout)

It's no use, Milt. Cut it out. It only makes it worse!

(MILT slumps on bench, panting heavily. Pacing)

You're right, though. At school everything was different. I was different. I expected so much ... From myself. From the world. From the stars, the sun ... Do you remember what they used to call me at school?

MILT
(Humbly)

Dostoyevski.

HARRY

That's right. Dostoyevski. What ambition I had. What energy. My medical career, my writings, my Greek studies ... Always had my nose in a book, always scribbling things down, projects, plans, new ideas, new fields to investigate, to explore ...
(His voice dwindles to a wail; he suddenly pulls off jacket, throws it to ground)
Let me do it now and be done with it!
(He climbs onto railing)

MILT
(Runs after him)

Harry! Harry!
(HARRY covers his face with his hands, screams and jumps off the railing, landing to his stunned surprise on the bridge; he turns and rushes back to railing. MILT grabs him, throws him down to ground)

MILT

Listen to me a minute. This is terrible, terrible. That you should treat life so cheaply ... It's a sin! There.
(He boots him in the backside)
I said it and I'm glad!
(Contemptuously)
Look at you. At your age, worn out, defeated, wrecked in body and soul. It takes guts to go on living, Harry. It takes guts to make something of your life.
(From behind he holds HARRY under his arms and lifts him to a sitting position; softer tone)
Harry, listen to me. Love ...

HARRY

Love?

MILT
(Taking chin in his hand)
Yes, Harry. Love, human love, the love of a small boy for his toy wooden horse, the love of an old classmate, the love of a man for a woman. Doesn't that mean anything to you?

HARRY

What do you think's been keeping me going this long?
(He rises, moves left, forward)

MILT
(Rises)

Well?

HARRY

I don't know if I can love, Milt.

MILT

That's what everyone says until they meet the right woman. And then . . .

HARRY

What?

MILT

You don't know?

HARRY

How could I?

MILT

You don't mean . . . ?

HARRY
(Shaking his head; mournfully)

Not once.

MILT

Oh, Harry. Harry, to have lived and not have loved . . . Do you call that living?
(Stepping on sandbox)
You don't know what life is, how can you destroy it?

HARRY
(Moving right to lamppost. Picks up jacket on way)

Love. We read about it, all right; we hear a lot about it. But where is it, Milt?
Where? I haven't seen it and I've been through the mill and around the world twice.
(Puts jacket on bench)

MILT
(Moving to him)

It's because your eyes are closed, Harry; your eyes are closed. Do you think I could
go on, working day after day, giving my youth, my health, my life itself, for a handful
of shekels, for a few clammy coins, if there wasn't some compensation for it, something that made it all worthwhile?

HARRY

You do understand.

MILT

Of course I understand. Ask me what I believe in, Harry.

HARRY

What do you believe in, Milt?

312

MILT

I believe in love, Harry.

HARRY

Love?

MILT

Love!

HARRY

If I thought there was a chance . . .

MILT

Of course there's a chance. Being alive gives you that chance. And now that we've met . . . I'll help you, Harry; introduce you to people, show you around. You'll meet some woman and, boy, let me tell you, one day you'll get down on your knees and thank me. What do you say?

HARRY

I don't know how I'm going . . . You have to understand . . .
                    (Turns away from him)
It's not easy . . . Life . . . The stars . . . The sun . . . I . . .
    (He suddenly stiffens and falls backward like a pole; MILT *catches him, prevents
                    him from falling to ground)*

MILT

Harry! Harry! Don't start that again!
                    *(*MILT *sits on bench, holding* HARRY*'s stiff body)*
For God's sake. Harry . . . Love.
                    (Shouts in his ear)
Love!

HARRY
    (His body relaxing, he slides between MILT*'s legs)*
It . . . It did it, Milt. It worked. I swear.
                    (Rises)
As soon as you said the word love, I felt my whole body begin to melt and I . . . I
suddenly felt . . .

MILT
                    (Rises)
You see? What did I tell you? Give it a chance.

HARRY
                    (Enthusiastically)
Give love a chance.

MILT

Why not?

HARRY

I have nothing to lose.

MILT

What can you lose?

HARRY
(Pointing to rail)
I can ... always end things if I want.

MILT
(Repeating his gesture)
Of course you can.

HARRY

All right, Milt.

MILT
(Retrieves jacket, puts it on HARRY, buttons it)
That's my old school buddy. Now you promise ...

HARRY

You have my word on it.

MILT

No more of this foolishness.

HARRY
(Sits on bench)
No more.

MILT

Wonderful. Wonderful.
(Sits beside him)
There's nothing in the world like it, Harry. It's like getting a new lease on life; it changes everything; one minute you're down in the gutter, the next you're up in the clouds. Do you know I'm more in love today than on the day I married.

HARRY

You don't mean ... ?

MILT

That's right. But my wife won't give me a divorce.
(Rises)
She's a wonderful woman, Harry; don't get me wrong. I'd do anything for her. But once love goes, what's left? There's no thrill to it, no excitement, no surprises ... Look, here's her picture.
(Takes out wallet photograph)

HARRY

Your wife?

MILT

No, no, the girl I want to marry. Linda. Isn't she beautiful? Everything she does has grace and charm, a fascinating Oriental quality. Look at her eyes, Harry, her mouth, her young virgin voluptuousness. Oh, God, you don't know how much I love this woman, Harry. I can't bear being away from her. Not even for a minute. It's sheer torture.

HARRY

Why don't you get a divorce?

MILT

All I have to do is ask Ellen and . . . You don't know women, Harry. Say no, they'll say yes. Say yes, they'll say no. It can't be done that way. Never. Look at me, Harry. I look happy, don't I? I look as if I have everything in the world to live for. Well, I don't. I'm miserable; positively miserable.
(Moves left, talking to photograph)
Linda, my sweetheart, what's going to happen to us?

HARRY
(Crosses to MILT, puts arm about his shoulder)
Come on, Milt; get a hold of yourself.

MILT
(Moves right, with HARRY's arm still about his shoulder)
That's easy for you to say, Harry. You don't know what torture it is. We work in the same office; we can't speak to one another, we can't look at one another . . .
(Both move left, with HARRY now stroking MILT's neck)
We have to meet in back alleys and bus terminals and crowded, noisy saloons. Do you know what that's like? Any other woman would have given up on me long ago. But she . . . That woman . . . I tell you, I'll go out of my mind!
(Buries his head on HARRY's shoulder)

HARRY
(Consoling him)
It couldn't be that hopeless, Milt. Why don't you . . .

MILT
(Pulls back)
I've tried everything, everything! She won't give me a divorce. I know she won't. I wouldn't even bother asking her. I've been over this a thousand times, Harry. Linda and I do nothing else but talk about it.
(Turns away from HARRY in his misery)
There's only one answer and that's if she wants a divorce herself, if she meets someone and . . . meets someone and . . .
(Turns to HARRY)

315

(HARRY puts his hand up in a gesture of refusal and moves to the bench and sits.
MILT follows him to bench, puts arm around his shoulder and grabs his hand)
Harry, Harry, buddy, buddy, old classmate of mine.
(Pulling HARRY's hand back and forth)
Alma mater, alma mater, forward to the fray; we will . . .

HARRY
(Freeing his hand and stopping MILT)
Oh, no. Definitely not. Don't ask.

MILT
Is this what I get for saving your life? Talk about gratitude! Harry, all I want you
to do is meet her, just meet her.

HARRY
I said no.

MILT
(Humbly)
Dostoyevski.

HARRY
That's not going to help. So let's drop it.

MILT
Okay. Okay. That's your privilege.
*(Removes jacket, folds it and places it on the bench. Runs to railing left of alcove
and jumps up on it)*

HARRY
(Running after him; holds on to his knees)
Milt! Cut it out! Milt!

MILT
Let go of me!

HARRY
Don't be a fool!

MILT
How long do you think I can go on like this, living with one woman, loving another?
I can't sleep, I can't eat, I can't work . . . What do you think I'm made of?

HARRY
You couldn't be serious.

MILT
Couldn't I? Look. Look at this.

316

*(He removes a large wicked-looking knife from a leather sheath on his belt.
HARRY dances away fearfully)*

Did you ask yourself why I came here tonight, Harry? Did you ask yourself what
I'm doing in this godforsaken place?

HARRY

You don't mean . . .

MILT
(Jumps down from railing)

Ellen should be here any minute. Draw your own conclusions.
(He returns knife to sheath)

HARRY

No. I don't believe it. That's the ugliest, the most cowardly and revolting . . . You
were actually going to . . .

MILT

Yes! Yes! It's her or me. One or the other. I can't go on like this anymore, Harry.
Now will you let me . . .
(He dashes to railing. HARRY grabs him. They struggle)

HARRY

No, Milt! Milt! What are you doing?
(He throws MILT to ground; surprised tone)

This isn't like you.
(Sits on MILT's backside)

You were always so levelheaded, always so damn anxious to make something of yourself and get ahead in the world. You're not going to throw it all away now, are you?

MILT
(In despair)

I've had as much as I can take of this misery.

HARRY

Always working, from the first day of school, thinking about business, finance, invest-
ments, Wall Street . . .

MILT
(Looking up at HARRY)

What's the good of bringing all that up? Don't you see, Harry? I've had it.
(Clutching throat)

Up to here, I've had it!

HARRY

But love, Milt; what about love?

MILT

Love?

317

HARRY

Love. The thing you were talking about only a minute ago.
(They rise to their feet)

MILT

Linda . . .

HARRY

Linda. Exactly.

MILT

Harry, meet her; just meet her.

HARRY

Linda?

MILT

No, no, Ellen. Meet Ellen.

HARRY

Will you promise to stop this nonsense?

MILT

I promise. Yes.

HARRY

And the . . .
(Points to knife)

MILT

No more. I promise.

HARRY

Let me have it.
(HARRY takes the knife from him. Suddenly, unexpectedly, he turns, throws knife at sandbox; it sticks, vibrates rapidly. HARRY falls back into MILT, amazed by his own expertness)

MILT
(Staring at knife in sandbox, with admiration)
Just meet her, Harry. I know you two will hit it off. She reads, Harry, book after book after book. And she paints, and she plays guitar . . .

HARRY
(Puts jacket on MILT, buttons it)
Classical or flamenco?

MILT

What's that?

318

HARRY

The guitar. Does she play classical or flamenco?

MILT

I don't really . . .

HARRY

I play flamenco.

MILT

She's good at it; very good at it, whatever it is. And she reads, Harry. That woman reads continuously, books I never heard of . . . with hard covers, too!

HARRY

All right. I'll meet her. But that's all I'll do.

MILT

That's all I want you to do.

HARRY

Don't forget your promise.

MILT

I won't. You have my word on it.
(ELLEN's footsteps are heard off right)
Did you hear . . . That's her. She's coming.
(Leads HARRY to alcove, left)
Wait here, Harry. I'll bring her over. Wait right here. Don't move.
(MILT hurries to right where he meets ELLEN as she enters. She wears a mink coat, skirt, blouse of same color, alligator bag and shoes, a black kerchief on her head, a pair of dark sunglasses; she carries a rolled graph, about three feet long—a window shade in a wooden casing. HARRY tactfully leans over the railing and stares at the river below)

MILT

Ellen, where were you? I was getting worried.
(He removes her kerchief and sunglasses, puts them on bench)
You'll never guess what happened. I ran into an old friend of mine. Harry Berlin. Remember me telling you about Harry Berlin?
(He unbuttons her coat, straightens blouse; on his knees he puts his hand under her dress and pulls her slip down)
We roomed together at Polyarts U. I want you to meet him, El. He's a wonderful guy. You two are going to love one another.
(He takes comb from his breast pocket, starts combing and "teasing" her hair extravagantly with the finicky adroitness of a couturier. He goes on for a while before he speaks)
I want Harry to see what a lucky guy I am. There that does it.
(He hums contentedly; when he is done he takes compact from her pocketbook: moves her to lamppost for better light, tilts her head back; puts lipstick on her

319

*mouth; blots her lips with Kleenex and rouges her cheeks with a long rouge brush
he takes from his breast pocket)*

It was the funniest thing. I came up here to meet you and there he was, like he is now, leaning over the rail. I recognized him at once. But he's changed, El. You're going to have to be nice to him. He's been through hell, the poor guy. Don't you remember me telling you about him? Top man at Polyarts U. The fellows used to call him Dostoyevski. What a guy. Plays a terrific guitar. He's sick now. Needs encouragement. Love. A reason for living. Don't get frightened if he has a fit. He comes right out of them. Poor guy.

*(He holds compact under her mouth; she spits uninhibitedly on cake mascara;
M I L T stands behind her, energetically rubbing brush on mascara; tilting her head
forward, he applies it to her eyes)*

We have to darken these. Does wonders for your eyes. Gives them a deep almost Oriental look. There, there, that's better.

(Returns compact to her pocketbook, takes out atomizer, sprays her)

Let me see. You look positively ravishing, El; beautiful.

(Returns atomizer; takes her hand)

Now come, I want . . .

ELLEN
(Pulling free; restrained anger)

No, Milt.

MILT

Why not? He's waiting . . .

ELLEN

He can wait. I want to talk to you.

*(Returns kerchief and sunglasses to her pocketbook; places pocketbook beside
bench)*

MILT
(Annoyed)

El . . .

ELLEN

What I have to say will only take a few minutes. There may not be many more of them. You didn't come home until after one last night.

MILT

I told you what happened, hon. I was stuck in the office. These clients came and the boss was there and I couldn't . . .

ELLEN
(Sharply)

Milt.

MILT

It's the truth, El!

320

ELLEN

It wouldn't give me any satisfaction to prove you're lying, so we'll let it stay like that. I have something to show you. I made this while you were out last night.
(She hooks graph to lamppost)
Let me explain it to you.
(She pulls graph down to its full length; points with finger)
These black vertical lines divide our five years of marriage into months; these blue vertical lines divide the months into weeks. Now. Each time this red horizontal line running across the top of the graph hits the blue vertical line, that indicates the number of sexual experiences over a seven-day period.

MILT
(Covers graph with his body)
Ellen, for God's sake . . .
(Looks about in embarrassment)
We can talk about this later.

ELLEN

You're always saying later. That's a favorite play of yours. No, Milt. Not tonight. These things must be said while they still can be said.
(Mumbling under his breath MILT crosses to bench, sits)
I'd like to continue if you don't mind. Now. You'll notice on this graph how at the beginning of our marriage the red horizontal line touches the blue vertical line at a point of . . . fourteen, fifteen times a week, and how, gradually, the number of contacts become less and less until eighteen months ago, when we have an abrupt break-off, the last time being July twenty-third, the night of your sister's wedding, and after that date the red horizontal line doesn't touch the blue vertical line once, not once! I have nothing further to say, Milt.
(She tugs down on graph so that it snaps up cleanly and disappears in the wooden casing; pause)
When something like this is allowed to happen to a marriage, you can't go on pretending.
(Removes graph from lamppost)
You want to pretend. Oh, the temptation is great to overlook, to find excuses, to rationalize.
(Waving graph)
But here, Milt, here are the facts. Our relationship has deteriorated to such an extent that I don't feel responsible anymore for my own behavior.

MILT
(Rises, arms held out, smiling)
Hon, you're mad at me.

ELLEN
(Still angry)
It isn't a question of being mad at you. We've gone a long ways from that.

MILT

I see.

(Takes graph from her)
Just the same I'd like to ask you something, El.

ELLEN

Speak. I can't stop you.

MILT

Do you think our marriage is a failure?

ELLEN

I do.

MILT
(Triumphantly)
I thought so. I thought that was behind it. Well, before I give you a divorce . . .

ELLEN

There isn't going to be a divorce.

MILT

There isn't?

ELLEN

We've made a mistake, but we've got to make the best of it.

MILT

We'll act like civilized human beings.

ELLEN

I have no intention of doing otherwise.

MILT

Good.
(Formally)
Ellen, I'd like you to meet a friend of mine whom I accidentally bumped into a little
while before you came and who is now waiting over there for us.

ELLEN
(Stiffly)
I know what my duties are.

MILT

Then let me remind you that since he is a friend of mine that you treat him with
every courtesy and that any kindness extended to him is considered a kindness by
extension to me.

ELLEN

I understand fully.

322

Good. Do you have anything more to say?

ELLEN

Nothing.

MILT

Very good. So long as we understand one another.
> *(Puts graph down on seat of bench and goes to* HARRY*)*

Harry. Harry. Sorry to keep you waiting.
> *(Arm about* HARRY, *brings him down to where* ELLEN *waits)*

Well, here she is. Harry Berlin. Ellen Manville.
> *(They stare blankly at one another)*

Ellen Manville. Harry Berlin.
(Still no reaction from them; he stands between them, arms around their shoulders)
My two best friends.
> *(Turns head quickly from one to the other; hugs them)*

My best classmate . . . My best wife . . . I've looked forward to this for years. I . . .
> *(Turns head. They don't budge)*

I'll tell you what. I'm going to leave you two alone to . . . to get to know one another.
> *(Slides out from between them and begins to move left)*

I'll be back. Don't go 'way.
> *(Stops, takes* HARRY *by his arm and pulls him off, left)*

Huh . . . Harry. I did a silly thing. Left the house without taking any money. Could you loan me five bucks until later?

HARRY
> *(Takes out some crumpled bills and gives him one)*

Is it enough?

MILT

Sure, sure, just till later . . .
> *(Puts money in pocket)*

Harry, she's a wonderful girl. But she's had a terribly rough time of it. Try to understand her.
> *(Moves left; loudly)*

See you both soon. You'll love one another, I know you will.
(Picks up coat and exits. In a second he pops back in, grabs the basket in one jerk and exits)
(There is a long uncomfortable pause. ELLEN *takes out a cigarette from a package in her coat pocket, lights it, and leans against the lamppost, front.* HARRY *buttons his shirt, takes a ready-made tie from his jacket pocket, and hooks it onto his collar. He carefully buttons his jacket and brushes his pants. After preparing himself, he crosses to* ELLEN's *right and grabs the lamppost with one hand)*

HARRY

Classical or flamenco?

Flamenco.

HARRY
Me, too.
*(Sings a few bars of a flamenco melody. There is no response. A slight pause
HARRY points out over audience)*
That's the Empire State Building over there.

ELLEN
(Without looking; wrapped in her own suffering)
I know.

HARRY
I'd like to go there sometime.

ELLEN
I wouldn't.

HARRY
You wouldn't?

ELLEN
I wouldn't.

HARRY
You're probably right.
*(Takes off tie and puts it back into his pocket, unbuttons collar and jacket, moves
back to the bench and sits left. A pause. HARRY looks up)*
A star . . . First one. You can hardly see it, it's so weak. "Starlight, starbright, first
star I see tonight, wish I may, wish I might . . ."
(To ELLEN)
Make a wish.

ELLEN
I wish . . . I wish I was a lesbian.

HARRY
(Slowly turns and looks at her)
You don't mean that.

ELLEN
(Throws down cigarette and grinds it under her shoe)
I do. I certainly do. Then I wouldn't have all these demeaning problems.
(Again leans against lamppost)

HARRY
You'd have other problems.

ELLEN

Like what?

HARRY

Like picking up girls, for one.

ELLEN
(Bitterly)

That would be simple. All I'd have to do is learn how to be a liar and a hypocrite.

HARRY

There's a lot more to it than that. Do you know what you have to pay for a haircut these days?

ELLEN

I'd pay for it. Gladly. Anything but this heartache; anything.
(Puts her hand up and grabs lamppost)

HARRY

Look, you don't have to stay if you don't want to. I can tell Milt . . .

ELLEN

I have nothing else to do.

HARRY

The same here.
(Pause. ELLEN *leans against the lamppost, stares up at the sky, one hand clutching the post and one foot pressed to it. She starts to sing in a deep lugubrious voice, softly at first, almost to herself, but with obvious feeling. She is indifferent to* HARRY *who shifts about on the bench nervously)*

ELLEN
(Sings)

Love cast its shadow over my heart.
Love changed my life right from the start.

HARRY
(Uncomfortably)

I know, Milt told me everything.

ELLEN
(Sings)

I cried it couldn't be,
Then Love laughed back at me.

HARRY

It'll work out all right.

ELLEN
(Sings)

Why did you come?
Why did you stay?

HARRY

You have to be patient with him.

ELLEN
(Sings, opening her coat)

Why did you take me,
Only to play?
Oh, Love. Love. Love. Love.
Look what you've done to me.

HARRY
(Shrugging, with a sigh)

Well . . . Sometimes it happens that way.

ELLEN
(Wipes a tear from her eye)

I am sorry. I'm afraid I'm not myself tonight.

HARRY

Don't apologize.

ELLEN
(Leaves post and looks about)

It is nice out.

HARRY

Probably rain soon.

ELLEN
(Moves downstage and looks out over audience)

How far down do you think it is?

HARRY

Far enough.

ELLEN

You know, I'm afraid of water. I can't swim a stroke. But tonight . . . with the moon
shining on it, it looks quite beautiful and . . . and almost inviting.

HARRY

You shouldn't talk like that.

ELLEN

Shouldn't I? Harry, what do you think I did with my life? What do you think made
me the way I am? You don't have to answer that. When I look back . . .

326

(Looks out once more)

It couldn't have worked out very differently. My childhood was impossible, absolutely impossible. My parents separated when I was three. I spent six months with one, six months with the other; they passed me back and forth like an old sack.

HARRY

That was a lot better than I did.
(Rises; moves left)
My folks left me with my grandparents. I saw them maybe once every four or five years. It was hell, Ellen; believe me, it was hell.

ELLEN

Not as bad as what I went through, Harry. Oh, no.

HARRY

Worse than what you went through, Ellen; lots worse.

ELLEN

You ever live with an alcoholic?

HARRY

My grandfather drank . . .

ELLEN

Enough to have delirium tremens?

HARRY
(Wagging his hand)
He used to shake a little . . .

ELLEN

Well, it's not the same thing, oh, no, Harry, it's not the same thing.

HARRY
(Foiled)
Anyone ever call you a bastard?

ELLEN

A relative or a stranger?

HARRY

A relative.
(No answer)
Well, they called me one.

ELLEN

I never had a birthday party.

HARRY

I didn't know when my birthday was until I got a notice from my draft board.

ELLEN

Did anyone ever try to rape you?

HARRY
(Thoughtfully)

Ahh . . .

ELLEN

I said, "Did anyone ever try to rape you?" When I was fifteen, Harry, only fifteen. Two boys . . . If I hadn't kicked and screamed . . .

HARRY

Where was it?

ELLEN

Where was what?

HARRY

That the two boys grabbed you.

ELLEN
(Holding head in hands; traumatically)

In Queens. On Parsons Boulevard. When I was walking home from the bus stop.

HARRY
(Vehemently)

I've never been to Parsons Boulevard. Never. I don't even know where the hell Parsons Boulevard is!

(ELLEN crosses to HARRY)

ELLEN

I was lonely, Harry; I was always lonely.
(HARRY moves upstage and begins to walk along rail to the right. ELLEN follows him, pulling at his sleeve)
There was no one for me to talk with, or share things with. I couldn't make friends because I never stayed in one place long enough. I went deeper and deeper inside of myself. I read and fantasized and was far too bright for my age. And before I knew it I had grown up, life was for real.
(They continue offstage and with ELLEN talking incessantly, turn and come back on, moving to the left of the alcove)
On the one hand, I possessed a cold calculating mind; it was sharp as a razor, incisive, penetrating. Men were afraid of me. They were afraid of my mind, my power of analysis, my photographic memory. They wouldn't discuss things with me. They became resentful and standoffish and avoided me because I was a threat to their feelings of masculine superiority.
(ELLEN stops HARRY and both turn downstage)
Ask me a question, Harry.

HARRY
How many states did Al Smith win in the election of 1928?

ELLEN
In the election of 1928 the presidential candidate Alfred E. Smith won eight states: they were the states of Arkansas, Alabama, Georgia, Louisiana, Massachusetts, Mississippi, Rhode Island and South Carolina.

HARRY
(Nodding, shakes ELLEN*'s hand)*
It's been very nice speaking to you, Ellen. But I really have to go. Tell Milt . . .

ELLEN
Please, Harry. Stay. Don't go yet.
(Stops him, and again begins to move right along the railing with him)
You see, on the other hand, on the other hand, Harry, I was a woman, a woman who wanted to be loved, who wanted to have children, who wanted all the common dreary horrible middle-class things . . .
*(*HARRY *turns back and wearily moves left, leaning on the railing.* ELLEN, *not noticing, continues off right)*
things that every other woman takes for granted. I willingly . . .
*(*ELLEN *realizes he is no longer with her, and turns and runs left after him.*
Catching up with him, she continues)
I willingly succumbed to biological and sociological necessity. I willingly confessed my womanhood. But how do I bridge the gap? I didn't ask for universal education. Why was I educated, Harry, if I'm compelled to live this fractured existence?

HARRY
(Angrily; moves to sandbox and sits)
Nobody thinks of these things until it's too damn late!

ELLEN
(Moves right to bench, sits)
Now there's so little to believe in, so little to keep me going.

HARRY
Love?

ELLEN
Love?

HARRY
Love. What about love?

ELLEN
Oh, I don't know. Once. Yes. Once.

HARRY
Once is enough. It's more than most people had.

329

ELLEN

You know nothing about women, Harry. For a woman to have never known love isn't tragic. The dream is still there. The dream . . . She needs that more than she does the reality. But to have love become a shabby cynical emotion . . . To watch it change into pettiness and hate . . . That's what destroys her. She loses her dream and . . .

(Through clenched teeth)

It makes an animal of her, a vicious little creature who only thinks of scratching and biting and getting revenge. Look, Harry, look!

(She pulls a large unsheathed bread knife from inside her coat; rises. HARRY looks from the knife in her hand to the one beside him sticking into the sandbox)

Do you know what I was going to do with this?

HARRY

You don't mean . . . ?

ELLEN

(Moves to left, stabbing air viciously)

Yes. Milt Manville! Milt Manville! I was going to use it on him.

(HARRY gets up and moves upstage to ELLEN's right. She turns to him)

I can't go on like this anymore, Harry. I know he's lying to me. I know he's seeing another woman.

(ELLEN again turns left and slashes the air)

I won't have it! I won't let him!

HARRY

Ellen, don't, he's not worth . . .

(Moves toward her)

ELLEN

(Suddenly turning with knife so that HARRY has to jump back to avoid being slashed)

What's left for me? I don't make friends easily. I can't start again. Don't you see, there's only one thing . . . Only . . .

(Grabs knife in both hands and raises it over her head)

Yes! Yes!

(HARRY grabs her wrists with both hands and struggles with her to prevent her from plunging the knife into her chest)

HARRY

Give it to me. Give it . . .

ELLEN

Leave me, Harry. Please . . .

HARRY

A smart girl like you . . .

ELLEN

I want it this way. Please . . . Please . . .

(The knife turns in her hand and is now pointed at HARRY'*s Adam's apple. He leans over backward to prevent being stabbed until he is lying supine on the ground, with* ELLEN, *in a state of hysteria, bent over him and trying, without knowing it, to plunge the knife into him)*

HARRY

No, no, Ellen . . .

ELLEN

I won't have it. I won't!

HARRY

What are you . . .

ELLEN

Good-bye, Harry!

HARRY

For cryin' out loud . . .

ELLEN

Good-bye, everyone!

HARRY

You crazy bitch, will you cut it out!

*(*HARRY *finally manages to turn the knife aside. The knife drops to the ground. She stands erect, steps over* HARRY, *and moves to the bench; she weeps quietly into her hands.* HARRY, *after several attempts, manages to get up. He crosses up to the rail and leans over it; retches hollowly. He then picks up the knife and moves to* ELLEN, *offering her his handkerchief)*

ELLEN
(Taking handkerchief)

Thank you.

HARRY
(Now offers knife)

Do you want this?

(She shakes her head)

Are you sure?

(She nods and he puts knife into his jacket pocket)

You're not going to be this dumb again, are you?

ELLEN

No, Harry. I am sorry.

HARRY
(Buttons her coat)

You promise?

ELLEN

I promise.

HARRY

All right. Let's forget it.
(And suddenly, unexpectedly, HARRY *takes the knife from his pocket, whirls to the left and hurls the knife at the sandbox; a second knife appears downstage of the first, vibrating rapidly.* HARRY *moves away with a slight swagger and sits down at the right of the bench)*

ELLEN
(Sits next to him and returns handkerchief to him, placing her head on his shoulder)
I've been a great deal of trouble to you.

HARRY

Forget it.
(Gets up and moves downstage, sitting on the curb)

ELLEN
(Moves downstage and sits to the right of HARRY *)*
I don't often meet people who take kindness for granted.

HARRY
(Moves away)

Forget it.

ELLEN
(She moves to him)

I have to tell you . . .

HARRY
(Turning, shouting)
I said forget it! Forget it!
(Rises and moves left away from her)
What's wrong with you? You're giving me a headache!
(Wailing)
Have a little pity for the next guy.
(Sits down on sandbox)

ELLEN
(Pause)

I am sorry, Harry.

332

HARRY
(Without turning)

That's all right.

ELLEN

Milt has spoken about you. Frequently.

HARRY

It's fifteen years since I saw him.

ELLEN

He has nothing but good things to say.

HARRY

I changed. I changed a lot.

ELLEN

You were something of a father figure to him.

HARRY
(Turning to her)

He never told me that.

ELLEN

You know how he is.
(Gets up and moves left)

HARRY

He should have told me. I could have helped him with his homework.

ELLEN

Harry, isn't there anything . . .

HARRY

Nothing. For me . . . there's nothing.

ELLEN

You can't mean that.

HARRY

I can't. Ha, ha!

ELLEN

You've never been in love, have you?

HARRY

Love?

Love. It's there. In all of us.

But I thought . . .

It's hard to kill a dream, Harry.
          (Sings romantically, directing the song to HARRY)
Love cast its shadow over my heart,
Love changed my life right at the start,
I cried it couldn't be,
                    (Moves to HARRY *and unbuttons coat)*
Then Love laughed back at me.
Oh, why did you come?
Why did you stay?
                    (Touches his face with her hand)
Why did you take me,
                    (Lifts his hand and brings it slowly, steadily upward)
Only to play?
Oh, Love. Love. Love. Love.
Look what you've done to me.
          (Places his hand on her breast and closes the coat over it)

          (As she sings, shifts about agitatedly)
Ellen, stop it; that's enough . . . Why don't you sit down? I want to speak to you, tell
you something about myself. I . . . You don't know me, Ellen. I'm a dead man. Dead
inside. Dead to everyone and . . . everything. Ellen, will you stop that damn singing!
I'm trying to explain. I'm not the kind of man you think. I can't change.
                    (In despair)
What's the good? The jig's up. The chips are down. No way out.
                    (Softly)
Ellen . . . Ellen . . .
(As she places his hand on her breast, HARRY *bolts upright, his eyes widen, and*
                    he begins to sing with a great fervor)
Love cast its shadow over my heart,
Love changed my life right from the start.
Da, da, da, dum, de, dum . . .
*(*HARRY *gets up and taking* ELLEN *in his arms, with great style and grace and*
          with a formal dip, begins to waltz her about the stage)

                    (Exultantly)
Dance with me, Harry; dance.

It's been years . . .

Turn me! Turn me!

HARRY

It's fun. I'm having fun!

ELLEN

Let yourself go. Harry!

HARRY

I feel like singing at the top of my lungs!

ELLEN

Then sing, Harry, sing!
(Holding hands and carried by the momentum of their emotions, they both sing the following lines superbly as though an aria)

HARRY
(Singing)

Oh, Ellen, I think I'm in love with you.

ELLEN
(Singing)

Oh, Harry, can it possibly be?

HARRY
(Singing)

I never felt this way before.

ELLEN
(Singing)

My heart is beating like a banging door.

HARRY
(Singing)

Oh, how good it feels to be in love with someone like you.
(They kiss, sink slowly to their knees, ELLEN ending cradled in HARRY's arms)

ELLEN
(Looking up at him)

Dostoyevski.

HARRY

Ellen Manville.

ELLEN
(Rises to her knees)
I didn't really think it could happen to me again.

HARRY

I feel like a kid, all weak and sticky inside. Is that . . .

ELLEN

That's part of it. Say it, Harry.

HARRY

Say what?

ELLEN

Just say it!

HARRY

You don't mean . . . ?

ELLEN

Yes, yes, say it!

HARRY

I . . . Ellen, it isn't easy. I never . . .

ELLEN

Say it! Say it!

HARRY
(With great difficulty; voice distorted unnaturally and only after several attempts)
I la . . . I la . . . I . . . I . . . I lo-o-o-o-ve . . . ye . . . ye . . . you.

ELLEN

Oh, Harry.
(They kiss and then rise)
Harry, do you still feel that there's nothing . . .

HARRY

Don't say it. No. Life . . . Life is a mystery.

ELLEN
(Turns downstage)
Do you hear the birds singing?

HARRY
(Behind her, with his arms around her)
Yes, yes.
(Gesturing)
Here, birdies; here, birdies . . .

ELLEN

Do you see the sun?

HARRY

It's a beautiful sun.

ELLEN

It's our sun, Harry.

HARRY

Sun, I love you!

ELLEN

It's all happening so quickly. I'm dizzy.

HARRY

Me, too. Ellen ... You say it.

ELLEN

You want me to say it?

HARRY

Yes, Say it. Please.

ELLEN

Harry ...
(Inhaling deeply)
Harry ... I like you very much.

HARRY

Like me?

ELLEN
(Turns to HARRY *)*
I think you're one of the nicest and most thoughtful people I ever met.

HARRY

What're you talking about?

ELLEN

Isn't that what you wanted me to say?

HARRY
(Angrily)
No. No. Not on your life! You say what I say. I said it. Now you say it. Fair is fair!

ELLEN
(Sits down on the bench)
But, Harry, I don't know. Really. I've been hurt once and ... it's just that I have to be sure. I'm confused. I wasn't prepared for anything like this ... I ...
(Turns left to HARRY *)*
Harry, *how much* do you love me?

HARRY
(Moves to the bench; outburst)

A lot! An awful lot!

ELLEN

But *how much?*

HARRY
(Slight pause; begins to answer; gives it up)

I see what you mean.

ELLEN

It's a problem. Love isn't a commodity that you can measure. And yet there are different degrees of it. We have to know what we can expect from one another. Am I the first woman you ever loved, Harry? The truth, now.

HARRY

I swear, Ellen. That's the truth. Before I came on this bridge tonight, I never looked twice at any woman.

ELLEN

But you did sleep with other women, didn't you, Harry?

HARRY

And you? What about you?

ELLEN
(Rises. Gets graph from upstage bench, and hands it to him)

Here. Read this. It contains the whole story. But remember, he was my husband, it had nothing to do with personal likes or dislikes. How many, Harry? I'd like to know.

HARRY

Ellen, I don't remember, I couldn't ...

ELLEN

An approximate figure will do. I just ...

HARRY

Twenty-eight!

ELLEN
(Slight pause)

Twenty-eight different women or one woman twenty-eight times?

HARRY

Six women once and one woman twenty-two times.

ELLEN

Who was she, Harry?

I ... Ellen, I ...

ELLEN
(Firmly)
I want to know who she was, Harry.

HARRY
(In exasperation)
Gussie Gooler! Gussie Gooler! But it wasn't love, Ellen. We were kids. Dumb foolish stupid kids. Her brother was my best friend!

ELLEN
Thank you for being honest.

HARRY
Is Milt the only one?

ELLEN
The only one.

HARRY
(Waves graph before setting it down to the right of the sandbox)
I'll read this tonight.

ELLEN
(Softly)
Harry.

(They embrace)

HARRY
You do love me, don't you?

ELLEN
You know I do.

HARRY
How much, Ellen? Tell me.

ELLEN
That's the very problem we're faced with.

HARRY
You're right. That's the problem.
(HARRY suddenly stumps on ELLEN's upstage foot; she howls, hops on the other to the right of the bench)

ELLEN
Owwwww! What did you do that for?

(Grinning sheepishly)

Do you still love me?

ELLEN
(Slight pause)

Yes ...

(Limps to him)

Yes, I do.

HARRY

There, there, that proves it! If you could love me after I did something like that to you, there isn't any ...

(ELLEN *pulls back her arm and punches* HARRY *savagely in the stomach.* HARRY *doubles over in pain, gasps for breath)*

ELLEN
(Bending over him)

Has your love for me changed, Harry?

*(*HARRY *is unable to answer)*

Has it, Harry?

HARRY

No. No. It's ... It's all right.

(Forces himself erect)

ELLEN

Now I know I didn't make a mistake!

*(*HARRY *embraces her, with his arms around her, from behind)*

And I will be a good wife to you. I have no qualms about getting a job, working, anything, until you get back on your feet. I've learned a good deal being married to Milt and this time, I know, I ...

(HARRY, *as she talks, grabs the top of her blouse and rips the front of it down)*

HARRY

Well?

ELLEN
(Gulping down her anger, staring at torn blouse)

I love you, Harry.

HARRY

The same as before?

ELLEN

The same.

HARRY
(Takes her in his arms)

Harry Berlin is happy! For the first time in fifteen years Harry Berlin is actually happy!

(In his exuberance leaves her and steps up on sandbox)
I'm not going to disappoint you, Ellen. I'll come out of it.
(ELLEN reaches into her coat pocket and takes out a pair of scissors. She quietly crosses to HARRY, as he talks, and cuts the piece of rope holding up his pants. They fall about his ankles and she puts the scissors back in her pocket)
I'll make good. I know I will. I don't need anything but what I got. I . . .
(HARRY stops, looks down at his pants. He closes his jacket about himself, modestly)

ELLEN
Have your feelings for me decreased in any way, Harry?
(Slight pause)
Have they, Harry?

HARRY
(Arms crossed)
It's cold.

ELLEN
I asked you a question, Harry.

HARRY
I love you, Ellen.

ELLEN
Despite everything.

HARRY
Despite everything.

ELLEN
Oh, Harry . . .
(She gets up on sandbox and embraces him. During the embrace he reaches down, pulls up his pants and fastens them)

HARRY
(In curt, businesslike tone)
Ellen . . .

ELLEN
Yes, Harry.

HARRY
Do you love me, Ellen?

ELLEN
I love you.

341

HARRY

Please turn around.

ELLEN

Harry . . .

HARRY

Do what I told you.

ELLEN
(Gets down from sandbox)

I love you, Harry.

HARRY

I love you. Now do what I told you.
*(*ELLEN *turns around.* HARRY *quickly rips the mink coat off her and in a single gesture hurls it over the railing)*

ELLEN
(Running to railing)

My coat! My coat!
(After looking over railing she turns and doubles over in a fit of soundless hysteria.
HARRY *takes her in his arms and leads her, writhing and floundering about, to the bench. He finally gets her to sit down)*

HARRY

Do you still love me?

ELLEN
(Shouting)

I bought it with my own money!

HARRY

Yes or no? Do you love me or don't you?

ELLEN
(Sobbing)

I love you.

HARRY
(Embraces her)

I love you, too, Ellen. I can't believe it.
(Rises)
Everything's clearing up for me. I have the feeling I can start writing poetry again.
I wrote tons of it at school.
(Reciting)
"Under the starlit window, two lovers lie in bed; naked up to their shoulders, for
neither has a head. One lover touches the other, the other . . ."

ELLEN
(Coolly; rising)

Harry.

HARRY
(Going to her)

Yes, Ellen ... Darling.

ELLEN

May I have your jacket?

HARRY

My jacket?

ELLEN

Please give it to me.

HARRY

Ellen ...

ELLEN

I said, please give it to me.
(He gives her his jacket)
Harry, I love you.

HARRY

I love you, Ellen.

ELLEN

I know you do.
(Slight pause)
Harry ...
*(*ELLEN *gestures upstage.* HARRY *follows her glance to river)*
Good-bye.

HARRY

You don't mean ... ?

ELLEN
(Turning downstage; emotionally, burying her face in his coat)
I can't watch! I can't!

HARRY
(Nodding; resignedly)

Good-bye, Ellen.

(Moves to railing)

343

ELLEN
(Sobbing into hands)
Good-bye, my dearest; good-bye.

HARRY
(Moves downstage)
I ... I love you.

ELLEN
I love you! I love you!
(HARRY climbs up on the railing right of the alcove; he is about to throw himself into the river when MILT comes in down left. MILT, seeing HARRY, drops the overcoat he is carrying which is now of enormous size, and running to rail grabs HARRY about the legs. He attempts to pull him down but HARRY holds on tightly to the cable)

MILT
Harry! Harry! For God's sake!

HARRY
Get away ...

MILT
Listen to me.
(Trying to pull him down)

HARRY
Let go!
(Kicking at MILT)

MILT
Love, Harry, love!

HARRY
That's what it is, you damn ass! Now will you let ...

ELLEN
(After putting on HARRY's jacket runs to him)
No, Harry. Don't. You don't have to. It's true. It's really, really true!

HARRY
Ellen!
(HARRY slides down the cable to the ground, and embraces ELLEN. They kiss. MILT stands nearby, viewing them critically)

MILT
(Slight pause)
What's going on here?

344

ELLEN
(Breaking the embrace)

You tell him.

HARRY

No, you better tell him.

ELLEN

I think it wiser if you told him.

HARRY

Do you think so?

ELLEN

I do, Harry.

HARRY

Okay.
(Kisses her hand, crosses to MILT *)*
Milt, it worked out all right. We're in love and we'd like . . .
(Turns to ELLEN *)*
We'd like to get married.
*(*ELLEN *comes to* HARRY *and they embrace,* MILT *quietly watches)*

MILT

I see. Leave my best friend with my wife alone and this is what happens. You ought to be ashamed of yourself. The both of you!
*(*MILT *moves down left.* ELLEN *follows down after him and* HARRY *comes to her right and puts his arms about her)*

ELLEN

Milt, I want a divorce. And the sooner you give it to me the easier it'll be for all of us.

MILT

A divorce. I see. Five years of marriage and you come up to me and say, "Milt, I want a divorce," and I'm supposed to take it all, say nothing and go right along with this preposterous and morally contemptible idea!

HARRY

Come on, Milt. Cut it out. You know . . .

MILT
(Sharply)

Never mind what I know, Harry. This is between my wife and myself. It has nothing to do with you. Not yet, at any rate.

ELLEN

Milt, we haven't been happy together. It's obvious that our marriage has failed.

345

MILT

Not completely, El. We've had some good times. Hon, remember when we first moved into our place and the painter locked himself in the bathroom and couldn't get out?

(He breaks into uncontrollable laughter, which she joins)

ELLEN

He was banging and screaming . . .

MILT

And the people next door . . .
(Takes ELLEN *in his arms and moves her away from* HARRY, *to his left)*

ELLEN

The people next . . .

MILT

They thought . . .

ELLEN

They thought . . .

MILT

He was your father . . .
*(*HARRY *attempts to separate* MILT *and* ELLEN*)*

ELLEN

That he came to take me back and you two were . . .

MILT

We two . . .

ELLEN

Were fighting . . .
*(*HARRY, *having failed to separate or get between them, grabs the bottom of* ELLEN's *jacket and tries to pull her back)*

MILT
(Rubbing tears from his eyes)

What a time.

HARRY

Ellen.

ELLEN
(Ignoring him)

That was really something.

HARRY
(Louder)

Ellen!

MILT
(Suddenly grim; holding E L L E N *from* H A R R Y *)*
She's still my wife, Harry, and so long as she's my wife I have the right to talk to
her without your interrupting!

ELLEN
(Conciliatory, takes M I L T *right to bench)*
Milt, we have to reach a decision.

MILT
I only want what's best for you, hon.
(E L L E N *sits on bench)*

HARRY
Does she get a divorce or doesn't she?

MILT
(Turns back to H A R R Y *)*
Do you think you know this woman well enough so that you can talk of marriage?
What do you know about her? You met her twenty minutes ago, Harry; only twenty
minutes ago. Do you know that her mother was an alcoholic? That she can't see
without glasses? That she shaves her legs and never cleans the razor?

ELLEN
(Protestingly)
Milt . . .

HARRY
I love her, Milt.

MILT
Love. That's a fancy word. Well, before I give my consent to this marriage, Harry,
I'm going to make sure that you kids know what you're doing. I'm not having this
woman go through the same lousy deal she had with me, twice! Oh, no. I'm not going
to let it happen.
(Turning to E L L E N; *quietly)*
Hon, do you know that he's a sick man, that he has fits?

ELLEN
I know, Milt . . .

MILT
Are you sure . . .

ELLEN
I love him.

MILT
He doesn't have a job.

347

HARRY

I'm getting a job.

MILT
(To HARRY, *snapping)*

What kind of job?

ELLEN
(Pleadingly)

Milt.

MILT
(To ELLEN*)*

All right. All right. If that's what you want . . .
(Moves down left with his back to bench)
I'll give you a divorce, hon.
*(*HARRY *crosses to bench, sits and embraces* ELLEN*)*
But don't depend on me for anything. You're both old enough to know your own
minds.
(Moves up right and kneels on upstage bench between them)
Don't come to me asking for help, money, alimony, legal fees, or anything like that
because you won't get it. You make it on your own or you don't make it.
(Behind them, hands on their shoulders; as a blessing)
Love one another, live moderately, work together toward a common goal, show
patience and consideration for each other's needs and desires, respect each other as
individuals during the good times and the bad, and you'll make a go of it. El . . .
(He kisses her on cheek)
Every happiness. Harry . . .
(Shaking his hand)
You're getting a wonderful girl. Nobody knows that better than I do. Take care of
her.
*(*MILT *moves left,* HARRY *follows him)*

HARRY

Thanks. Ahhh . . .
(Holding MILT*'s arm; whispering)*
Say, Milt, that five bucks . . .
*(*ELLEN *takes comb out of bag and fixes hair)*

MILT

She's a wonderful girl, Harry. You're a lucky guy.

HARRY

I know. But that five . . .

MILT

You speaking to me, Harry?

HARRY

Who do you think I'm speaking to?

MILT

That's funny. I can't hear a word you're saying.
(Cheerfully)
Something's wrong. Speak slowly, Harry, I'll try to read your lips.
(ELLEN comes up to them)

HARRY
(Drawing out words)
That five bucks you took from me, I . . .
(He glances down to see ELLEN staring up at him)

ELLEN

What is it, Harry?

HARRY
(Not wanting her to know)
I . . . I just . . .

ELLEN

You can tell me. I want to help you. That's why I'm here. Only to help you and be with you.

HARRY
(Softly)
Ellen . . .

ELLEN

My Harry . . .

HARRY

Empire State Building?

ELLEN

Yes. Yes. The Empire State Building.
(Hand in hand, they run off right, laughing happily)

MILT
(Watches them go, then cries out in ecstasy)
Linda! Oh, my Linda!
(He runs right, jumps on the bench and springs to the crossbar of the lamppost, around which he revolves, singing joyfully, his knees curled under him)
Love cast its shadow over my heart, etc.

CURTAIN

ACT TWO

Several months later: early evening.

The same as Act One.

E L L E N *is seated on the right of the downstage bench, in a black leather coat, black high-neck sweater and skirt. She is wearing black tights and low-cut black boots, with a large copper necklace and large hanging copper earrings. Her hair is now in a ponytail, and she is reading a paperback copy of* The Second Sex.

Riding a small Valmobile motor scooter, staring straight ahead, M I L T *crosses the bridge, right to left above the bench, and exits. He immediately re-enters and crosses to above bench, where he stops. He is now wearing a bright brown and yellow flecked sports jacket with a yellow shirt and olive tie, brown slacks, and brown shoes. A brown visored cap completes his outfit. Both he and* E L L E N *speak with exaggerated cheerfulness.*

MILT
(As he stops the scooter)

El? Ellen? Is that you?

ELLEN
(As if trying to recall who he is)

Milt. Milt Manville.

MILT

This is incredible.

ELLEN

Isn't it? You're the last ...

MILT

How are you, El?

(Gets off scooter)

ELLEN

Fine. Fine. You?

MILT
(Parks scooter and shuts off motor)

Fine. Fine.

ELLEN

Linda?

MILT

Couldn't be better.

(Puts cap aside)

Harry?

350

ELLEN
(With inarticulate admiration)

Ahhh, he's . . .

MILT

Happy, huh?

ELLEN

Very very happy, Milt. At times it's frightening. Do I merely thank you or . . . or what?

MILT
(Sits down left ELLEN)
I knew you were right for each other. Didn't I tell you?

ELLEN

It's more than that. Much more. It's . . .
(Glances at wristwatch)
In an hour or so we're going to the museum.

MILT

Is it open at night?

ELLEN

Open . . .?
(Breaks out in deprecating laughter)
Oh, Milt, Milt. Milt Manville. I am sorry. So many memories come back. Yes, Milt. The Modern Museum is open every Thursday evening.
*(*MILT *"ahhh's," and "ohhh's" and "ahummmm's, ahummmm's" all through* ELLEN's *lines, to mitigate if not destroy the sting of her remarks. When* MILT *speaks,* ELLEN *does likewise, laughing artificially, murmuring and by her approval making his remarks innocuous)*
Harry and I go to museums together and we borrow books from the public library and we play flamenco duets and it's an entirely different life than what we had. Different, richer, more rewarding . . . I . . . I don't want to hurt your feelings, Milt. Let's . . .

MILT

No, no. No, you're not. I'm glad. El. It's worked out perfectly. For both of us. Linda . . .
(Smiles)
My Linda . . .
(He laughs aloud at thought her name evokes)
That woman . . . She . . . She has this dance she does before we go to bed. It's . . .
(Laughs. ELLEN *murmurs and nods agreeably)*
Some sort of Arabian belly dance. She puts a lampshade on her head, you know, and . . . She's fantastic. I don't know where she learned it but . . .

351

ELLEN

That's why I have the greatest and deepest respect for Harry Berlin. I learn from him. Constantly.

MILT

The same with Linda. Every day it's something else.

ELLEN

The experiences he's had, just being with him is a lesson in itself.

MILT

If I told you the things I learned from Linda . . .

ELLEN

Do you find you laugh more. Milt?

MILT

You hit it, El. That's it. That's the big difference.
(Laughing)
We get up in the morning and we start in laughing . . .

ELLEN
(Laughing)

With Harry, too . . .

MILT
(Laughing)

She carries on . . .

ELLEN
(Laughing)

The tricks and jokes, he's . . .

MILT
(Laughing)
I say, "Linda, Linda, I can't laugh more, no, I'll bust, I'll . . ."
(Suddenly overcome by misery)
Oh, God, oh, God!

ELLEN

What is it, Milt?

MILT

I can't lie to you. Not to you, El.

ELLEN

Lie to me? About what?

MILT

She left me. Walked out.

ELLEN

When was that?

MILT

Two, three days ago. I heard from her lawyer this morning. El, I don't want to be a
two-time loser. What's wrong with me? What do people have against me? Tell me.
It's driving me out of my mind.

ELLEN

Perhaps you ought to go see her, speak to her, see if you can't get her to reconsider.

MILT

See who?

ELLEN

See Linda.

MILT
(Rises and paces left)

That lazy bitch! Who wants her? She can rot in hell for all I care!

ELLEN

That's not nice, Milt.

MILT
(Pacing)

I know it's not nice. I had to live with her!

ELLEN

You're exaggerating. She couldn't be that bad.

MILT

That's what you say.

ELLEN

You always complained that there were no surprises in our marriage. Didn't she
have any surprises for you?

MILT

She had surprises. Boy, did she have surprises! As soon as we were married . . . It
wasn't the same person. She was different. Physically. All over.
(Shudders)

She even started growing a mustache. No kidding. I mean it. I couldn't recognize
her. I used to come home and think I was in the wrong apartment.

ELLEN

It's not an uncommon affliction among certain women. You should have given her sympathy, not criticism.

MILT

I should have given her shaving cream, that's what I should have given her.

ELLEN

I won't listen to you, Milt. You're being cruel and unkind. She must have had some assets for you to marry her.

MILT
(Moves to bench, sits left of ELLEN *)*
El, I don't make accusations lightly, you know that, you know it's not like me; but I'm willing to bet you anything that that woman had me under the influence of drugs or . . .
(Leaning toward her; ominously)
narcotics.

ELLEN

How could she have done that?

MILT

By intravenous injections. While I was sleeping.
(Rolls up sleeve, shows his forearm; solemnly)
Look at this.

ELLEN
(Examines arm)
Milt, you've had those freckles ever since I've known you.

MILT
(Shrilly)
Purple ones? Did I ever have purple freckles?
(Gets up, paces left)
I know I'm right, El. A human being couldn't change as much as she did. Overnight. Even her voice, it started coming out through her nose.
(Holds fingers to nose, mimicking)
"Hey, whatta you mean by comin' in here an' leavin' the door open." That's how she sounded. It was incredible.

ELLEN

Did she at least keep the apartment clean?

MILT

Keep it clean?
(Crosses down right, to the front of the bench. Turns back to ELLEN *)*
El, hit me there.

(Points to back)
Go ahead. Hit me.
(She hits him on back. A thick cloud of dust rises from his jacket. E L L E N *coughs,
waves dust away.* M I L T *points out the floating dust)*
Now am I exaggerating? Now am I making it all up?

ELLEN
(Contemptuously)
That's despicable. That is despicable.

MILT
She quit her job, didn't do a damn thing but lay in bed and eat bonbons all day.

ELLEN
That is ab-so-lutely despicable.
(Heatedly)
I'm sorry. There's just no excuse for it. None. What an obnoxious horrible foul-mouthed rat-faced lascivious woman she must have been.

MILT
She was, she . . .

ELLEN
How could you have lived with her four months? Didn't you have any pride, any sense of self-respect?

MILT
I wanted . . .

ELLEN
Would I let you leave the house in a jacket like that?

MILT
(Shaking head)
No. No.

ELLEN
Did I lie in bed and eat bonbons all day?

MILT
(Shaking head)
No. No.

ELLEN
Why didn't I?

MILT
Because you were good. Because you were unselfish.

355

ELLEN

Because I was a jerk, that's why.
(Wipes hand on Kleenex from coat pocket)
Because I didn't use sex instead of washing the dishes.

MILT

She did, El, she ...

ELLEN

You don't have to draw pictures for me. Rat-faced paranoiac women. All of them.
I'll become ill if I continue to talk about it. You should be happy to be rid of her.

MILT
(Pained expression)

Happy? How can I be happy?

ELLEN

Milt, there isn't someone ... ?
(MILT nods, lips in a pout, with the forlornness of an old man)
You are irresponsible. There's no other word for it.
(Impatiently; puts book in pocketbook)
I have to go. I have my own problems, Milt. I can't spend all night.

MILT

I couldn't help it, El. Honest. I couldn't. Do you think I want to throw away my life
like a lovesick schoolboy? But she ... This woman here ...
*(Takes out wallet photograph and looks at picture so as to arouse ELLEN's
curiosity)*
Beautiful. Too, too beautiful.
(Moves left to center; to photograph)
Sweetheart, if only I had the courage to speak to you ...

ELLEN
(Crossing to him, peering over his shoulder)
Perhaps you can arrange to ... Let me see that.
(Surprised)
Milt, this is my photograph!

MILT

Of course it's your photograph.

ELLEN

You took it at your sister's wedding, the same night ...

MILT

July twenty-third. Don't you think I know it?

ELLEN

You don't mean ... ?

356

MILT

Yes! Yes!
(M I L T crosses right to bench, sits. E L L E N moves left)
Oh, El . . . How stupid, how inexcusably stupid I was. I didn't realize . . . I didn't think . . . You were all I wanted. Ever, ever wanted. That first night with Linda it came to me, you, you, you, and since then I've been in such misery.

ELLEN
(Her back to M I L T)
I don't want to hear any more, Milt.

MILT

You have to, El. I've been living with this inside of me for months. It's been tearing me apart. I'm not here by accident. Harry phoned. He asked me to meet him, to collect some money I owe him. But that's not why I'm here. I came because I had to find out how you were doing, what you were doing, what chance I had . . .

ELLEN

Whatever you thought, Milt, is totally irrelevant. I'm Mrs. Harry Berlin now, and if you've made a mistake you have no one to blame but yourself.

MILT

That doesn't make it easier, El. It was my fault. Okay. I admit it. I was a stupid, selfish, hypocritical, egotistical, narrow-minded nitwit. Just like you always said. But, oh, El, hon . . .

ELLEN
(Moves left)
No. Let's stop it now. There's nothing I can do, Milt. It's too late. Besides other considerations, Harry needs me. He depends on me.
(Paces right to center)
In fact if I don't get home to feed him soon he won't have any dinner.

MILT

You feed him?

ELLEN

Two-thirds water and one-third milk. That's all he'll take. He . . . he's gotten worse, Milt. He's had a great many fits and . . . It hasn't been easy for me, either. But I know what my duties are. Marriage is more than the two people involved in it. That's something you would never acknowledge. Above everything else, despite my educational background, despite my academic achievements, I want to be a good wife and a good mother. But where is the man to whom I can be a good wife? Where are the children who cry for my arms and the milk in my breasts?

MILT
(Rises, arms outspread)
Here! Here I am!

357

ELLEN

You?

MILT

Yes, me.
(Moves to ELLEN *)*
Don't you see, El? I love you. I always loved you.
*(*ELLEN *moves away left)*
For God's sake, have pity. Don't close the door on me.

ELLEN

No, Milt. I may have the intelligence of a man . . .

MILT

Hey, listen, what was Sugar Ray Robinson's record from 1940 to 1944?

ELLEN

From 1940 to 1944 Sugar Ray Robinson had a record of fifty professional bouts. He won forty-nine, thirty-four by knockouts, fifteen by decision, and he lost only one in 1943 to a certain Jake LaMotta.

MILT
(To himself)
I knew that schmuck last night was wrong.
(Moves to ELLEN *)*
Oh, sweetheart, I missed you so much . . .

ELLEN
(Moving away from him)
The intelligence of a man, Milt, yes, but the emotions of a woman, the innate insecurity of a woman. I refuse to be passed back and forth like an old sack.

MILT

I'd never do that.

ELLEN

You did it once.

MILT

If you gave me another chance . . .

ELLEN

You keep forgetting I'm a married woman, Milt.

MILT
(Quacking words like a duck)
Ellie?

That's not going to help.

MILT
(Still quacking)

Won't you please reconsider?

ELLEN
(Moves down left to sandbox)

I'm in no mood for any of your games, Milt.

MILT

Okay, Okay. Listen. Just tell me you love Harry Berlin, that you're happy with him, and I'll walk away from here and, I promise, you'll never see me again.

ELLEN

Love Harry Berlin?

MILT

Just say those words and it's good-bye to Milt Manville and his silly stupid but sometimes lovable ways.

ELLEN

I . . . I can't. It's impossible. You talk about misery! Ha!
(M I L T crosses down to E L L E N)
That makes me laugh. Misery!
(M I L T holds his hands out to her)
You can't imagine how it's been.
(She takes his hands and both sit down on the sandbox)
He . . .
(Puzzled expression)
Who is he? What is he? Why didn't you shake me by the shoulders and slap my face and . . . do anything to stop me? He . . . He isn't human, Milt. That man . . . He lays in the corner of the living room, rocking on his back, wearing a paper bag on his head, yes, a paper bag, mumbling and groaning hour after hour . . . I have to feed him, wash him . . . I can't tell you everything. I'm too ashamed.

MILT

The filthy beast!

ELLEN

That's what my marriage to Harry Berlin has been like.

MILT

Then why? Tell me why?

ELLEN

Ask me what I believe in, Milt.

MILT

What do you believe in, Ellen?

ELLEN

I believe in marriage, Milt.
(Rises, moves left)
I believe in a man coming home at five o'clock with a newspaper rolled under his
arm and a silly grin on his face and shouting, "What's for dinner, hon?" I believe in
the smell of talcum powder and dirty diapers and getting up in the middle of the
night to warm the baby's bottle. I can't help it. I'm made that way.
(Paces up and down stage)
But why did they teach me trigonometry and biochemistry and paleontology? Why
did they so sharpen my intellect that I find it impossible to live with a man?
(To MILT)
I'll never forgive the Board of Education for that. Never.
(Crosses up right to center)

MILT
(Moves up to ELLEN's left)
If you'd listen to me . . .

ELLEN

I wouldn't have divorced you, Milt. You know that. But you brought it about, coldly
and deliberately. You forced me to marry Harry. And now I don't trust you. And
where there's no trust there can't be love.

MILT

Then . . .

ELLEN

It's over.

MILT

Nothing I do or say . . .

ELLEN
(Moves to left of bench)
The door is closed, Milt.
(MILT nods sadly. He sings in a heartbroken voice)

MILT
(Sings)
Love cast its shadow over my heart.

ELLEN
(Sits down on bench)
Don't, Milt; please, don't.

MILT
(Sings as he crosses to ELLEN, *left of bench and touches her hair)*
Love changed my life right from the start.
I cried it couldn't be.

ELLEN
(Shuddering from his touch)
We can't start all over again.

MILT
(Turns away in anguish)
Then love laughed back at me.
Oh, why did you come?

ELLEN
It's too late, Milt. No.
(Flings herself on seat of bench and puts legs up over back of bench)

MILT
(Sings)
Why did you stay?
Why did you take me . . .
(Turns, sees ELLEN, *stops in surprise. Rushing to bench, he sits and takes her in his arms)*
El . . .

ELLEN
Milt . . .
(As she throws her arms about him, another cloud of dust rises from his jacket)

MILT
Oh, my sweetheart.
(They kiss)

ELLEN
(Staring up at him)
Dostoyevski.

MILT
No, honey. Milt. Milt Manville.

ELLEN
(Sits up in MILT's *arms, with legs along bench)*
Milt. Yes. Milt. Oh, I always loved you, Milt.
(Kisses him)
I come here almost every night, hoping you'll show up. I didn't want to marry Harry.

MILT
(Kisses her)
You didn't want to marry Harry, did you?

ELLEN
(Returning kisses)
You know I didn't want to marry Harry.

MILT
I know. I know.

ELLEN
I was praying you wouldn't believe what I said before.

MILT
I didn't. Honest.

ELLEN
Harry wasn't taking me to the museum tonight; he doesn't take me anyplace, not
even to the movies.

MILT
I know. Now don't worry. It's all going to work out; you'll see. First thing I'm going
to do, hon . . . I'm giving up my secondhand bric-a-brac and personal accessories job.
I'm through working nights. I'm through scrounging in garbage pails.

ELLEN
But it means so much to you.

MILT
You mean more, much more. Our happiness means more. We're going to have to
make some sacrifices, learn to do with less, budget ourselves . . . It won't be easy.
(Rises and crosses left to trash basket)
But every day at five I'm opening that front door and . . .
(Picks newspaper out of trash basket)
With this newspaper under my arm and a silly grin on my face . . .
(Pantomimes kicking door open)
"What's for dinner, hon?"

ELLEN
Steak, French fries, catsup and mashed baby lima beans, everything you like!
(Runs to him and throws herself into his arms)

MILT
(Twirls her about and then puts her down)
Just the way I like it.

ELLEN
And I'm not contradicting you anymore, Milt. Never. Never.

362

MILT

One job's enough. I'm going to spend every single evening home with you.
(About to throw newspaper into basket, looks at it, has second thoughts and slips it
into his side pocket)

ELLEN

I'm not keeping any records and . . .
(Steps up on sandbox)
Ask me a question.

MILT

What countries formed the League of Nations in 1919?

ELLEN

I don't know.

MILT

You don't know?

ELLEN
(Steps down from sandbox)
I don't know and I don't care to know. I'm submerging my intelligence so that we
can be happy together.
(Embraces MILT)
That's all I want, Milt.

MILT

And all I want is you, sweetheart, and the opportunity to be incredibly rich someday.

ELLEN

You will be; you will. But . . . Harry Berlin. What about Harry Berlin?

MILT

You'll get a divorce.

ELLEN

He'll never give it to me, Milt.

MILT

We'll have him sent away.

ELLEN

It would take years, money . . .

MILT

I thought of that. El, listen. Harry should be here any minute.
(Looking about)
El, he's a man who's contemplated suicide.

363

If he should happen to lose his balance ...

ELLEN

What are you saying, Milt?

MILT

If he fell off the bridge and ...

ELLEN

No, no. Don't say any more.

MILT

But it's the only way.

ELLEN

I won't have it. No.

MILT
(Petulantly, moves up right to right of alcove at the rail)
Then you really don't love me.

ELLEN
(Crosses up to the left of MILT *)*
I do, Milt.

MILT

No, you don't

ELLEN

I do. I swear I do.

MILT

If you really loved me nothing would stand in our way. Nothing in the world!

ELLEN

Don't you understand, Milt? That's murder.

MILT

Murder? Who said anything about murder? Are you out of your mind? All I said ...

ELLEN

We'll get into trouble. I know we will. What if we get caught?

MILT
(Moves down right to front of bench)
You don't love me. I don't think you ever sincerely and truly loved me.

ELLEN
(Moves down to MILT*'s left)*

That isn't so.

(Puts out her hand to him)

MILT
(Pulls away from her)

Don't touch me.

ELLEN

Milt.

(Moves toward him)

MILT

I said don't touch me.

ELLEN

You're being childish.

MILT

Why? Because I'm asking you to show me your love, to do this one lousy thing for me!

ELLEN

What do you want me to do?

MILT

You know.

ELLEN

Harry Berlin?
(The sound of halting footsteps are heard off right)

MILT

Harry Berlin.

ELLEN

It's just that I don't think that's the answer. Can't you . . .
(Hears the footsteps)
Is that him coming?

MILT
(Looks right)

It's him. That's him.
*(*ELLEN *begins to move left)*
Come here!
(Excitedly as she comes to him)
Look, El, leave this to me. I'll take care of it.

365

(Begins to lead her off left)
You walk down here a little. I want to speak to Harry privately. Don't listen and
don't watch.

ELLEN
(Stops and begins to protest)
You're not ... Milt, you wouldn't ...

MILT
(Pushes her off left)
Just stand over ... look. Come here.
(They exit left. HARRY *enters, right. He is wearing the worn velvet-collared
herringbone coat which had been in the basket in the first act: unshaven, disheveled.
He uses a cane, his right leg is stiff, paralyzed. He moves along, dragging his right
leg, leaning on cane. He crosses between lamppost and bench and moves up left
above the bench)*

HARRY
Milt ...
(Notices the scooter)
Milt? Are you here, Milt? You cheap bastard, where's my five bucks?
(Moves left to center)
Ohhh ... Ohhh ... that dog. That crazy dog. On my leg. He did it on my leg. I can
still feel it, wet and smelly ... It's still there ... Away, get away from me. Away ...
*(Reversing the cane in his hand, he swings it at imaginary dog by his right leg.
Finally turns, and with cane reversed moved up into alcove. As he does,* MILT
slowly sneaks out from down left and moves toward him, sinisterly)
Ohhh, Ellen, my sweet, sweet, sweet Ellen. Where are you?
*(*HARRY *turns downstage, barely missing seeing* MILT *who scurries back off.*
HARRY *turns back to the alcove railing right)*
Ohhh, my Ellen, my sweet, sweet Ellen.
*(As he leans on the wrong end of the cane, it slips from beneath him and he falls to
the ground. As he puts the cane down,* MILT *rushes toward him to push him over
the railing. When* HARRY *falls,* MILT *is unable to stop himself and dives over the
right railing of the alcove.*
*There is the sound of a large splash, followed by a heavy spray of water which rises
above the railing and lands on* HARRY. HARRY *holds out his hand to check if it's
raining, looks up at the sky. Hooking one of the cables with his cane, he pulls himself
erect.* ELLEN *enters left)*

ELLEN
Milt?

HARRY
(Turning)
Ellen!

ELLEN
It's you. Where's Milt?

366

HARRY

Milt?

ELLEN

I thought I heard . . .
(Moves right, leans over railing; softly)
Milt? Milt? I can't see a thing down there.

HARRY
(Looking over railing in alcove)
Is he down there?

ELLEN

I don't know where he is. He was with me a minute ago. He asked . . .
(Looks at HARRY)
Are you sure he wasn't here?

HARRY

I was supposed to meet him. What are you . . .

ELLEN

Never mind me. Where did he go now?
(Moves to right of bench)

HARRY

He owes me five bucks. You can't trust anybody.

ELLEN

You are interested in money, aren't you, Harry?

HARRY
(Moves downstage)
Not for myself. I wanted to buy you something for your birthday.

ELLEN

That's very thoughtful of you. But my birthday isn't until next August.
(Sits down right of bench)

HARRY

I was saving for it. Don't start, Ellen. For cryin' out loud. I'm a sick man. Sick! My leg.
(Paces left, his limp very pronounced)
It's paralyzed. I can't move it.

ELLEN
(Irritably)
There isn't anything wrong with your leg.

HARRY
(Limps right)

There isn't? Then why doesn't it . . .
(Stops, trys to bend his right leg; to his surprise it bends easily and he can raise it)
You're right!
(Joyfully he flexes leg up and down; begins to run in circles about the stage, tossing his cane over the railing)
It's . . . moving! It moved! I can walk again! Look, look, I'm walking. I'm walking!

ELLEN

Harry . . . Harry, I have to speak to you. Please sit down.
(Gestures to bench)

HARRY
(Crosses to bench, lies supine on it, his head in ELLEN's lap)

What would I do without you? How would I live? My own sweet precious . . . Oh, Ellen, hold me, hold me, I need you so much . . .

ELLEN
(Resisting)

No, Harry. Not tonight. Sit up now.
(HARRY gets up and sits in her lap, facing left)
Sit up properly.

HARRY
(Tries to embrace her)

What is it my dear one, my darling, my . . .

ELLEN

Harry, stop it and pay attention. This is important. I've tried . . . I've tried to be a good wife to you. But despite all my efforts our marriage is a failure.

HARRY
(Dumbfounded, stops his attempts to embrace her)

Our marriage . . . a failure?

ELLEN

Yes, Harry; a failure.

HARRY
(Crosses his right leg over his left; there is a pause)

I . . . I don't know what to say, Ellen. This is a complete shock to me. Up until this minute I thought we were a happily married couple!

ELLEN

You thought . . .

HARRY

I had no idea.

ELLEN

How could you have thought that? Didn't you hear me walking the floors nights; didn't you hear me crying in the bathroom?

HARRY
(Shaking head)

No. No.

ELLEN

What did you think I was doing in the bathroom all night?

HARRY
(Slight pause; desperately)

Ellen, I love you!

ELLEN

I asked you a question, Harry.
(Bodily picks up HARRY, *and sets him on the bench to her left)*
What do you think I was doing in the bathroom all night?

HARRY
(Shaking his head dumbly)

I didn't want to think about it. I used to get up in the middle of the night and look at the ceiling and wonder to myself: "What could she be doing in the bathroom so long?" But I didn't want to change you, Ellen. I wanted you to be just the way you are. Is that a crime?

ELLEN

You should have made it your business to know what I was doing.

HARRY

I will. From now on . . .

ELLEN

Our marriage has been a failure from the first day. I don't have one memory worth keeping.

HARRY

Oh, no. No, Ellen. We had lots of good times. Remember . . .

ELLEN

Remember what?

HARRY
(Slight pause; angrily)

Where's my paper hat?

ELLEN

I don't have your paper hat and you know it. Our marriage was a mistake, Harry, and anything we can do to terminate it would be a step in the right direction.

HARRY
(Legs over ELLEN's *lap)*
I couldn't, Ellen. I'm responsible for you.

ELLEN
(Pushes them off)
Responsible for me? You must be joking. You haven't worked a day or given me a penny since we were married.

HARRY
I was hoping to surprise you.

ELLEN
You succeeded in that.

HARRY
(Rises; stands left of bench)
I haven't been wasting my time. I've been doing a lot of thinking, planning . . . I'm going to go back and do what I always wanted. What I should have stuck to. Go back and start right at the beginning. Ellen, in the fall I'm applying for medical school.

ELLEN
Harry, it won't do.

HARRY
All right. All right. I understand. Night calls, operations, blood all over my clothes . . . It's not all easy going. All right. Law school. In the fall I'm registering for the Bar.

ELLEN
No, Harry.

HARRY
(Shouting in frustration)
Why not?

ELLEN
Harry, I don't love you anymore. That's all there is to it.
(Rises and moves downstage)

HARRY
You don't . . .

ELLEN
I doubt if I ever loved you.

HARRY
(Moves to her, arms outstretched, fingers reaching)
Ellen, you don't know what you're saying. Love! Love!

ELLEN

What about love, Harry?

HARRY

It's ...

(Stops in confusion)

ELLEN

What is it? I'd like very much to hear your definition.

HARRY
(Raises his arms to the sky, fingers reaching)
The birds, the sun, our sun ...

ELLEN

I don't see any sun, do you?

HARRY

Where's my paper hat?

ELLEN

I don't have your paper hat.

HARRY
(Angrily)
Well, somebody's got my paper hat. It's not on my head, is it?

ELLEN
(Crosses left in front of him, moves left)
You pretend love means so much to you but it doesn't, Harry. You use it to justify your own indecisiveness.
(Turns back to him)
What makes me so angry is that you've been using me as well. I do your work, fulfill your obligations ... How can you say that's love? If anything, love is a giving and taking, an interchange of emotions, a gradual development based on physical attraction, complementary careers and simple social similarities.

HARRY
(Clasps the back of the bench with one hand, presses the other to his cheek;
indignantly)
So that's what you think!

ELLEN

That's precisely what I think!

HARRY

No romance, no tenderness, no subconscious ... Love is *ooonly* a gradual development based on physical attraction, complementary careers and simple social similarities. That's *aaaall* it is.

371

Yes. That's *aaaall* it is.

HARRY

And you're not ashamed to say that to me?

ELLEN

Why should I be ashamed?

HARRY

Love is a gradual development based on physical attraction, complementary careers and simple social similarities!

ELLEN

That's right.

HARRY
(Moves right to lamppost, turns back to ELLEN *)*

I can't get over it. My wife. My own wife. The woman who took the holy vows with me. You can stand there and look at me and say . . .

ELLEN
(Curtly)

Love is a gradual development based on physical attraction, complementary careers and simple social similarities!

HARRY

Ellen, do what you want with me, curse me, step on me, tear me to pieces, but I beg you, out of consideration for all the days and nights we lived as man and wife, *do not say* . . .

ELLEN
(Parrotlike)

Love is a gradual development based on physical attraction, complementary careers . . .

HARRY
(Moves back to lamppost and cries out)

Ahhhhhh!
*(*ELLEN *stops.* HARRY *moves left to front of bench)*
I do not believe that this is happening to us. Not to us. Not to Harry and Ellen Berlin.

ELLEN

It is happening to us. And you have to see it for what it is. It's not pleasant but there's no use pretending. There's something else you ought to know, then I'm done.
(Turns away from him)
Harry . . . I'm in love with Milt Manville; and he loves me.
*(*HARRY *freezes in absurd posture;* ELLEN *moves left, not noticing him)*
We both realize now that we acted too hastily. It's unfortunate that you came along

372

when you did. I have no doubt that Milt and I would have mended our differences . . .

(MILT *enters, right, wearing faded denim trousers which are too short and tight for him, a very large blue and white striped jersey that hangs over his trousers and a small black officer's jacket, without buttons or gold braid; his hair, which is still wet, lies flat on his scalp, and he has on a very small, white, sailor's cap. He is wearing sneakers without socks; he carries his clothes, still dripping, in a package tied by rope under his arm. Enraged, he storms by* HARRY *and paces back and forth center stage)*

Milt! What happened to you? Where were you?

MILT

Don't ask. Just don't ask. It was terrible.

ELLEN

But I . . .

MILT

I said don't ask!

ELLEN
(Moves to MILT*)*

Why are you angry with me?

MILT
(Glaring at HARRY, *puts his bundle down on upstage bench)*

He's at it again, huh? He tried to kill me, did you know that?

ELLEN

Harry?

MILT

Harry. Your husband. The one you were so worried about.

ELLEN

Oh, no.

MILT

Oh, yeah. He threw me off the bridge. Right over his shoulder. Lucky for me a barge was passing. They picked me up, gave me these clothes, a cup of coffee and a doughnut.

(Shouting)

It was a cinnamon doughnut.

ELLEN

My poor Milt. You don't know how glad I am you're safe.

MILT

No thanks to you.

373

Milt! How can you say that?

MILT

Well, whose fault is it? I told you there was only one way out of this. It's him or us. One or the other. Ellen, sweetheart, it's not what you think.
(Crosses down right to right of HARRY)
Look at him. He's no good to anyone, not even to himself.
*(*ELLEN *follows and stands left of* HARRY; *both lean their elbows on his shoulders and examine him)*
We'd be doing him a favor. When you get down to it ... What is it? Euthanasia. That's what it is. And remember what you said about euthanasia, hon?

ELLEN

They should be destroyed. Painlessly. By an impartial board of prominent citizens.

MILT

That's what you said. Well, isn't it the same as if we were on that board of prominent citizens? I mean, logically speaking.

ELLEN

There isn't much difference.

MILT

Of course not.

ELLEN

It's one of degree, not of kind.

MILT

Exactly.
(Slight pause)
I love you, El.
(As ELLEN *moves to* MILT, HARRY *slowly begins to fall left. They both catch him and hold him up)*

ELLEN

I love you, Milt.

MILT

For all eternity.

ELLEN

For ever and ever.

MILT

El.

ELLEN

I'm so nervous.

MILT
(Takes her hand)
Don't be. Just look at my eyes, at me, sweetheart. Don't look at him and don't think about what you're doing. Just look at my eyes and say I love you, Milt Manville.

ELLEN
I love you, Milt Manville.

MILT
(Facing HARRY, puts his arms around him, about his chest, and begins to pull him left)
I love you.

ELLEN
(As HARRY gets past her, she bends down and picks up one leg in each hand and standing between them, helps MILT carry him up left to the alcove)
My Milton.

MILT
Ellen sweetheart.
(They stare into each other's eyes)

ELLEN
How I do love you . . .

MILT
Soon we'll be together. Always together.

ELLEN
My darling husband-to-be.
(They carry HARRY to the right railing of the alcove, ELLEN having circled left, so that MILT is closest to the railing. MILT lays HARRY's still-rigid body on his stomach on the railing, while ELLEN puts his feet down on the ground)

MILT
(At railing)
Ellen, get him around . . .

ELLEN
(Butts against HARRY's backside with her head in an attempt to push him over)
I love you, Milt Manville.
(Repeats line again as she butts HARRY)

MILT
(In an effort to pull HARRY over, MILT puts one leg over railing straddling it, as he pulls at HARRY. However, ELLEN inadvertently pushes HARRY against MILT, throwing him off balance)
You're pushing me here . . .

ELLEN

I love you, Milt Manville. I love you, Milt Manville.

MILT

(In attempt to regain balance, pulls other leg over railing. But ELLEN *continues to push* HARRY *against him)*

Ellen ... For God's sake ... You're pushing me, Ellen ... Ellen ...

*(*MILT *slips off the railing, screaming, with hands clutching empty air. Again a splash, and then a spray of water, which hits* HARRY *as it breaks over the railing.* ELLEN *runs frantically to the railing right and peers over.* HARRY *suddenly comes to with a shudder of his head)*

ELLEN

Milt? Milt? Where are you? Are you there, Milt? Answer me! Oh, no, no, no ...

(Turning back from rail, begins to sob, wildly)

HARRY

(Now fully conscious, sees her, and goes to her)

Ellen, don't ... I'm all right now. It was nothing.

(Embraces her)

You do love me, I knew you loved me. The birds, the sun, our sun ...

ELLEN

Oh, stop it.

(Pulls away from him)

Milt. He fell over. He's down there!

HARRY

Milt?

ELLEN

He's drowning. Why don't you do something?

HARRY

(Runs to left)

Help. Somebody. Help us!

ELLEN

(Runs to right)

Help! Help!

(Runs to left)

HARRY

(Running right)

Help us! Somebody!

(Runs left to alcove and climbs up on railing right of alcove. Shouts)

Milt, hold on, hold on!

ELLEN
(Runs up right to railing left of HARRY *and looks down)*
Do you see him?

HARRY
There. That's him. He's getting into a rowboat. Where that light is.

ELLEN
(Waving)
Milt! Milt!

HARRY
(Shouting)
Hey, Milt! What the hell's wrong with you?

ELLEN
He can't hear us.

HARRY
(Still shouting)
You dumb bastard!

ELLEN
Thank God he's safe.
(Moves right, looks over railing)
How do I get down . . . No. I'll wait here for him. He knows I'll be here.
(Sits on bench)

HARRY
(Gets down from railing)
I never thought he'd do anything as stupid as that.

ELLEN
He didn't . . . Oh, forget it.

HARRY
(Goes to bench and lies down with head left and feet right in ELLEN's *lap)*
What a world. People trying to kill themselves, jumping off bridges, turning on gas, taking poison . . . They know; they feel it. The sky, look for yourself: it's been trying to rain all night but it can't do it, it can't, it's empty, like everything else, empty and dead. And soon . . .

ELLEN
(Sharply; pushing him off bench. HARRY *lands on hands and knees)*
That's enough of that, Harry. Don't pretend you didn't hear me before. I told you Milt and I . . .

377

HARRY
(Gets up, moves left)
You told me. All right. You told me. But why? What did I do wrong? Explain it to me. Give me a reason.

ELLEN
I've given you a dozen reasons. But if they won't do ...
(Takes a small, rolled paper graph from her bag which is on the ground, right of the bench)
Look. Look at this.
(HARRY sits left of her on bench, and she unrolls graph)
These black vertical lines divide our four months of marriage into days. Now each time the red horizontal line hits the black vertical line that indicates one sexual experience over a twenty-four-hour period.

HARRY
Where's the red horizontal line?

ELLEN
There is none.
(Rolls up graph)
Now do you understand?

HARRY
Why didn't you tell me? I'm trying to be a good husband, but if you don't tell me ... I was never married before, you were, don't forget that!

ELLEN
You're supposed to know some things yourself.

HARRY
I was giving you time. I wanted us to become friends first ... get to know one another, and then ...
(Gestures)
You should have told me. You definitely should have!

ELLEN
A lot of good that would have done.

HARRY
Why do you say that?

ELLEN
No normal man could have behaved the way you have these past four months. I'd rather not say any more.

HARRY
No, no, say it.
(Crosses legs and leans back on bench)

ELLEN

It'll be painful.

HARRY

Say it. Go ahead.

ELLEN

Very well. I'll say it. You think you know yourself, Harry, but you don't know your-self at all. You never loved me. You're incapable of that kind of love. You loved . . . All this time . . . You loved . . . Milt.

HARRY

I . . . What?

ELLEN

Yes, Milt. Milt Manville. You always loved him, I imagine. Even back at school. You married me as a substitute figure because you couldn't confront him and your own latent homosexuality.

HARRY

What are you saying?

ELLEN

I'm saying you're queer, Harry.

HARRY

No. No, it can't be, I . . .

ELLEN

It can be and it is. All this explains your attitude toward life, your fits and
(Holding up graph)
everything else. I am sorry but you asked for it.

HARRY
(Incredulously)

I love Milt Manville.

ELLEN

I'm afraid you do, Harry.

HARRY

It's ridiculous. I don't even like the guy!

ELLEN

Don't you, Harry? The way he has of laughing, the way his lips curl up when he smiles . . .

HARRY
(Open-faced)

His lips . . .

379

ELLEN

The way he carries himself, like a soldier, and when he's excited, his eyes, how they shine and sparkle . . .

HARRY

His eyes . . .

ELLEN

We both love him, Harry.

HARRY
(Half convinced)

Milt.

ELLEN
(Nodding)

Milt.

HARRY
(Regretfully)

I never sent him flowers.

ELLEN

It's not an easy thing for someone to acknowledge.
(Puts graph back into bag)

HARRY

His lips, his eyes . . . his legs . . .
(Grimaces, expels a sound of repulsion)
No, no, you're crazy, Ellen. It's you I love, you!
(ELLEN rises, moves away right)
I'll show you. I'll prove it to you.
(He throws her over his shoulder, runs about madly, indecisively, back and forth across bridge)

ELLEN
(Kicking, screaming)

Harry! Harry!

HARRY

I'll take you away. Someplace, anyplace. You'll be happy! happy! I'll make you happy!

ELLEN

Put me down!

HARRY

We'll be happy! happy! We're going to be happy! happy!

380

ELLEN

Harry, will you put me . . .

HARRY
(Lays her out on bench, smothers her with inept hugs)
Happy! Happy! Happy! Happy! You little honey-bunny, you . . . You mousy-wousy
hot little flousy . . .

ELLEN

Don't! Stop it!

HARRY
(Growling as he kisses and bites the nape of her neck)
Grrrr . . . Arrrr . . . Grrrrr . . .

ELLEN
(Stamping her feet on bench)
Harry, no more, stop it now!

HARRY
(Suddenly stops, gets up from her, and moves left)
What's wrong? I'm trying to do what you told me. For cryin' out loud! Is there no
satisfying a woman!

ELLEN
(Sitting up)
Don't talk to me anymore . . . Just leave me alone and don't talk to me.
*(MILT enters down right, crosses to left, where he paces back and forth, even more
enraged. He is wearing a very large pair of white bell-bottom trousers, a T-shirt,
and a very small, ripped black wool sweater, sneakers, and a yellow southwester
oilskin cap)*

ELLEN
(Rises and crosses to him)
Milt!

MILT
(Turning on her)
Don't talk to me.

ELLEN

What is . . .

MILT

I said don't talk to me!

HARRY
(Moves to ELLEN's right; to MILT)
It's about time you got here. I've been waiting . . .

381

MILT

Oh, shut up!

HARRY

Where's the five bucks . . .

MILT
(Crosses right, in front of HARRY; *sits center of bench)*
Did you hear me say shut up!

HARRY

Ellen, will you . . .

ELLEN

The same goes for me. Shut up!
(Crosses right to bench; sits right of MILT *)*
*(*HARRY *defiantly moves to bench, sits down left of* MILT. *The three of them are now seated on the bench, grimly, stiffly,* MILT *between the others, arms folded. A moment passes.* HARRY *takes out a pad and pencil, begins to write a note.* MILT *glances at him, and* HARRY *turns so that he cannot read the note; then hands pencil and pad to* ELLEN, *carefully sneaking it over so that* MILT *cannot read what he has written. She, without reading it, tears off note, crumples it and throws it over her shoulder, writes a brief note to* MILT, *passes pad and pencil to him. Without reading it, he throws entire pad over his shoulder. He is about to throw the pencil away as well, has second thoughts, and begins to put it under his cap.* HARRY *slaps his hand and pulls pencil away from him)*

ELLEN
(Quacking; not spoken)
Miltie? Miltie?

MILT

Don't bother me.
*(*HARRY *takes a small banana from his coat pocket and begins to peel it)*

ELLEN
(Quacking each word)
Don't be angry with me.

MILT

Will you stop that stupid quacking.

ELLEN

Why is it my fault?

MILT

I asked you to do a simple lousy thing . . .
*(*HARRY *begins to eat the banana)*

382

ELLEN

I tried.

MILT

Not very hard, did you?

ELLEN

I did. Have pity. You're absolutely all I have.

MILT
(Cynically)

I bet.

ELLEN

Would I be here otherwise, pleading with you like this?

MILT

You still could be lying.
(HARRY peels it down farther, and continues eating)

ELLEN
(Sticking her chin out)
Is this the face of a liar, Milt? Is it?

MILT
(He closely examines her face)
Why do I keep torturing myself! I'm not made of stone, El. You know me; you know how I am.

ELLEN

Oh, Milt.
(They kiss in a passionate embrace. HARRY watches; then takes final bite of banana, throws peel over his shoulder off the bridge, and pulls MILT away from ELLEN)

HARRY

Hey, cut it out! That's my wife you're kissing there, buster!

MILT

Harry . . . for God's sake. Give us a break, will you?
(Puts hand on HARRY's knee)

HARRY
(Draws back, glances from corner of eye at MILT's hand; meaningfully)
Don't try anything funny.

MILT

What's that?
(Puts his arm on top of bench around HARRY)

HARRY
(Draws back even farther)
Just don't try anything funny. I love her. Her! Not you! Get that into your thick head!
(Slight pause)
I can't help it.

MILT
(Removes his arm)
I love her, too, Harry. And I can't help it. Why don't we . . . let her choose between us.

ELLEN
That's fair, Harry.

MILT
It's democratic.

HARRY
(Hesitates, finally deciding, gets up. MILT gets up with him)
Ellen, my life, my . . .

ELLEN
(Rises; abruptly)
I choose Milt Manville.
(Taking her bag and MILT's hand, she begins to move up left around the bench)

MILT
(Going with her)
Sorry, Harry.

HARRY
(Moves up left above bench, grabs ELLEN and pulls her from MILT)
It's no good. I can't do it. I can't let you go. Don't ask.
(ELLEN ends up to the left of HARRY)

ELLEN
(Emphatically)
But, Harry, I don't love you.

HARRY
I don't give a damn whether you love me or not! I love you! I love you!
(Placatingly)
Ellen, you loved me once. You can love me again.

ELLEN
I'll never love you again, Harry. Now that I've lived with you I find you an utterly obnoxious person.

All right, that's a beginning; that's a start.

ELLEN
(Crosses right to upstage bench. Puts her bag down on bench)
What are we going to do, Milt?

MILT
(Moves left to HARRY *)*
Harry, listen to me. Listen. I'm married to a woman at this very minute who has more things in common with you . . .

HARRY
Forget it. I'm not interested.

MILT
She reads, Harry, and she . . .

HARRY
I don't care if she belches Beethoven! I'm satisfied with Ellen.

MILT
Are you going to be able to keep an eye on her twenty-four hours a day? Because you're going to have to, Harry. The first chance we get we're checking into a hotel and it's not going to be to watch television, you can take my word on that!

HARRY
(Moves right to ELLEN *)*
Ha! Ellen isn't the type to . . .

ELLEN
Don't count on that, Harry.

HARRY
You'd go with a man who's not your husband to some cheap sleazy hotel room that doesn't even have a television set!

ELLEN
(Crosses left to MILT *)*
It would have a television set, wouldn't it, Milt?
(No response)
Milt?

MILT
(Finally getting word out)
Of . . . of . . . of course!
(Forcefully)
It would be a first-class highly recommended A-1 hotel, with private bath, cocktail lounge, room service, breakfast in bed, everything!

ELLEN
(Turns to HARRY; *decisively)*
I certainly would go to a first-class hotel with a man who's not my husband. And under the circumstances I would not consider it immoral.

HARRY
It's all a nightmare. A nightmare. None of it is real. You don't understand. If I lose Ellen, if I stop believing in love, I have nothing, nothing!
(Runs to railing to the right of alcove and jumps up on it)
I might as well jump off the bridge right now!

MILT
(Runs to him, grabs his legs)
Harry . . . you wouldn't . . . ?

ELLEN
(Going to MILT; *pulls him away)*
He has no choice, Milt.

MILT
That's true.
(They both move downstage)

ELLEN
If only I could have loved him more.

HARRY
I said, I might as well jump off this bridge right now. Doesn't anybody listen to me?

MILT
You tried, hon. Don't blame yourself. You were wonderful to him. I'm to blame for this. He was my best friend and I let him down.

ELLEN
You didn't, Milt. Don't even think it.

HARRY
What's happening?
(Stares down at water below)

MILT
I did my best. God knows I did my best.

ELLEN
You did. No friend would have done as much. I don't believe it.

HARRY
Hey!

MILT

There's no helping each other, is there?

ELLEN

We're all locked up in ourselves, in little separate compartments.

HARRY

Alone. All alone. No love. No hope. Nothing. Nothing. Aww, the hell with it.
(Takes white, woman's bathing cap out of pocket, puts it on)
Let death come early. Yes. Yes. Let death come early.
(Holds nose; falls backward off bridge. There is a splash. As MILT *runs up to the railing to look over, a spray of water breaks over the railing and hits him. Soaking wet, he turns to* ELLEN, *and squirts out a mouthful of water)*

MILT
(Moving to her)

El!

ELLEN
(Embracing him)

Milt!

MILT

We're together.

ELLEN

At last. At long last.

MILT

My sweetheart.

(They kiss)

ELLEN

We will have a baby, won't we?

MILT

Of course we will.

ELLEN

And we'll name him after Harry Berlin?

MILT

Harry Manville?

ELLEN

Harry Manville. I'm so happy, Milt.

MILT

Harry must be happy, too.

387

He is. I know he is.

MILT

I love you, sweetheart.
(Kisses her and sweeps her up in his arms. Carries her to scooter as he hums the "Wedding March." She laughs, joins in. He puts her down, and goes to the scooter)

ELLEN

I love you, my darling first-and-only husband.

MILT
(Taking scooter off stand)

Not as much as I love you. Never. Never.

ELLEN

More than you love me.

MILT
(Turns to ELLEN *)*

You couldn't love me more than I love you.

ELLEN

Much, much, much more.

MILT
(Slight pause)

How much more?

(Starts the scooter, gets on)

ELLEN
(Apprehensively)

Milt . . .

MILT

That's a reasonable question.

ELLEN
(Gets on scooter behind MILT *)*

Don't start.

MILT

Just how much more?

ELLEN

Please, Milt.

MILT
(Beginning to drive off right)
No, no . . . never mind "please Milt." What about Harry?

ELLEN

What about Linda?

MILT

I never loved Linda.
(They are disappearing offstage)

ELLEN
But, you slept with Linda, didn't you? Didn't you? Didn't you . . .?
(As they exit, H A R R Y appears and begins to climb over the railing. He has lost his overcoat, is soaking wet, and is draped in seaweed. As he gets over the railing, he yells after M I L T)

HARRY
Milt! Milt! Where the hell are you going? Ellen, bring him back . . . Where's my five bucks, you cheap bastard!
(Suddenly a dog dashes onstage from off right. H A R R Y sees it, howls with terror, begins to run left. The dog catches him and begins to pull at his pants leg. H A R R Y runs about in a circle trying to dislodge him, and finally in desperation runs to the lamppost, leaps, and hangs on to the crossbar. He hangs there, with the dog clinging to his pants leg)

CURTAIN